D0875212

THE LONGEST SHOT

THE LONGEST SHOT

Lil E. Tee
and the Kentucky Derby

John Eisenberg

THE UNIVERSITY PRESS OF KENTUCKY

Copyright © 1996 by The University Press of Kentucky

Scholarly publisher for the Commonwealth,
serving Bellarmine College, Berea College, Centre
College of Kentucky, Eastern Kentucky University,
The Filson Club, Georgetown College, Kentucky
Historical Society, Kentucky State University,
Morehead State University, Murray State University,
Northern Kentucky University, Transylvania University,
University of Kentucky, University of Louisville,
and Western Kentucky University.

Editorial and Sales Offices: The University Press of Kentucky
663 South Limestone Street, Lexington, Kentucky 40508-4008

Library of Congress Cataloging-in-Publication Data

Eisenberg, John, 1956-
    The longest shot : Lil E. Tee and the Kentucky Derby / John
Eisenberg
      p.   cm.
    Includes index.
    ISBN 0-8131-1956-1 (cloth : alk. paper)
    1. Lil E. Tee (Race horse) 2. Race horses—Pennsylvania—
Biography. 3. Kentucky Derby, Louisville, Ky. I. Title.
SF355.L55E57   1996
798.4-dc20   95-41243

Manufactured in the United States of America

To Mary Wynne,
for her love and support,
and for her peerless zookeeping.

Contents

Illustrations follow page 84

ACKNOWLEDGMENTS

Most of the material in this book was compiled in interviews with close to one hundred subjects. Only conversations recounted word for word are included. Any mistakes are mine.

A complete list of those interviewed: Fred Aime, Dr. David Allen, John Ed Anthony, Judy Batcha, Tom Bohannan, David Braddy, Don Brauer, Kim Brazzel, Dr. George Burch, Dr. Joseph Burch, Jane Burrow, Dr. Doug Byars, Charles Cella, Roy Cohen, Carol Day, Pat Day, Sheila Day, Mary Deppa, Dr. Rick Doran, Mary Lynn Dudley, Kip Elser, Ron Felix, Brent Fernung, John Fernung, Bobby Frankel, Dr. Wilbur Giles, Jimmy Gill, Mike Gotchey, Bob Gregorka, Don Grisham, Bob Gulick, Max Hall, Mike Hargrave, Dr. Edward "Pug" Hart, Dr. Alex Harthill, Joe Hirsch, Susan Holmes, Bruce Hundley, Barry Irwin, Al Jevremovic, Stanley Joselson, Harry King, Harold Kitchen, Dan Lasater, Larry Littman, D. Wayne Lukas, William MacKinnon, Ryan Mahan, Lauren Marks, Christine Martin, Ron McAnally, Mark McDermott, Shug McGaughey, Bill McGreevy, Jim McGreevy, Tom McGreevy, Jim McKay, Steve Morguelan, Randy Moss, Steve Nagler, Gary Norwood, Dr. Robert O'Neil, Leslie Paramore, Mike Paramore, Cal Partee, Cal Partee Jr., Tim Patterson, Allen Paulson, Craig Pearl, Bill Perry, Jim Plemmons, Bob Ray, Jim Read, Jennie Rees, Bill Rice, Shelley Riley, Hilmer Schmidt, Fred Seitz, Wally Shute, Jeff Siegel, Gene St. Leon, Augustus "Ernie" Summers, Mike Trivigno, David Vivian, Ric Waldman, Jack Werk, Phil Werkmeister, Gary West, Julian "Buck" Wheat, Dr. Nat White, Lurline Whiting, Lyle Whiting, Lynn Whiting, Nellie Whiting, Chuck Wieneke, Joan Wieneke, Gary Wilfert, Arnold Winick.

Thanks in particular to Lynn Whiting for his time, memory, and patience, and to Larry Littman for being a good sport.

Thanks to Leonard Epstein for reading a version of the manuscript and making suggestions; thanks to Seymour Eisenberg for reading a version and being my safety net on all things medical; thanks to Dale Austin for reading a version and being my racing guru; and thanks to Jean Eisenberg for reading every version.

Thanks to Damon Thayer, Larry Littman, Chick Lang Jr., the Kentucky Derby Museum, Karl Schmitt and Tony Terry at Churchill Downs, the Ocala Breeders' Sales Company, Old Frankfort Stud, the Jockey Club, the Keeneland library, Jim Bolus, and Charles Cella for providing research and background material.

Thanks to the Maryland Horse Breeders Association for providing office space to someone who never asked for it, and for unlimited use of their fine library. Back issues of the *Blood-Horse* magazine and the *Thoroughbred Times* were invaluable, as were sales catalogs from Keeneland and OBS.

Thanks to Jack Gibbons and Marty Kaiser for giving me a little more time to write in 1993.

This book was written on the run, on a laptop computer, in airports and on airplanes, in hotel rooms and press rooms at major sporting events, and at home during vacations and on my days off from work. Thanks most of all to Mary Wynne, Anna, and Wick for understanding.

Pedigree of Lil E. Tee

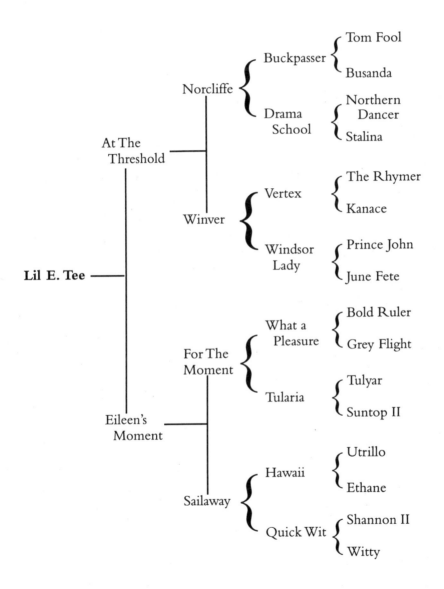

INTRODUCTION

Something strange had happened out there on the track. You knew by the sound of the crowd. The din that had accompanied the stretch run, the rattling roar of one hundred thirty thousand voices, tailed off into a high, hollow shriek as the horses crossed the finish line. There was little exultation. It was not the sound that usually greeted a Kentucky Derby winner. It was the sound of confusion. The winner was who? What was that name? What kind of a Derby winner was that? What kind of a name was Lil E. Tee? How did you spell that? What happened to Arazi? Was there some mistake? A mix-up? This race was supposed to be Arazi's coronation as the next Secretariat, right?

Something strange had indeed happened. A dark bay colt with an inelegant name and a dime store pedigree had won the one hundred eighteenth Kentucky Derby at Churchill Downs in Louisville, Kentucky, on the first Saturday in May of 1992. He was a classic portrait of obscurity, a shadowy figure about which little was known, racing against more accomplished, well-known contenders. Few racetrackers had given him a chance. Few bettors had put their money on him. He was a 17-to-1 shot on the tote board at Churchill, and as high as 58-to-1 at simulcasting outlets across North America. If Pat Day had not been his jockey, he would have been lumped with the no-hopers in the mutuel field.

He was a prayer of a play. A prayer, answered.

Who was he?

Lynn Whiting had no idea. Oh, he thought he did. A guileful trainer of thoroughbreds for almost twenty-five years, one of the best in the business, he had mothered Lil E. Tee relentlessly in the seven months that the colt had been in his barn. He had figured there was nothing about Lil E. Tee he did not know. But he would soon know that was

1

wrong. In the coming days, as he celebrated the defining victory of his career, he would listen, flabbergasted, as members of the racing press came to him with stories they had uncovered about the new Derby winner, stories about the horse being sold for a pittance as a yearling, turned down by an auction company, bought by a blacksmith, sliced open in an equine clinic. "How could this possibly be?" Whiting would wonder. Such a horse bore no resemblance to his strapping Derby winner.

Who was Lil E. Tee? The people at ABC Sports knew no more than Whiting as the horse crossed the finish line. Even though a team of producers, researchers, and announcers had spent hundreds of hours preparing to televise the race, the network had no well of Lil E. Tee background to uncap, no insight gleaned from barn chatter, no isolated instant replays breaking down the colt's trip around the racetrack—in sum, nothing to tell the nation about the winner other than basic information: his owner, trainer, jockey, and record.

Had any of the other seventeen horses in the field won, ABC was prepared to illuminate the legend of the new Derby winner. The network had done its homework, as always. But the tentacles of this research monster had somehow missed Lil E. Tee. It was almost as if he were an equine Greta Garbo, fiercely protecting his privacy.

Lil E. Tee was a Derby winner from nowhere: nowhere, in this case, defined as the great mass of ordinariness that is 98 percent of the thoroughbred breed. He was a member of the bourgeoisie, his blood offering no more than a fool's hope for success beyond his mediocre realm. His sire was a failure at stud. His dam had flopped miserably on the racetrack. The blueprint for his racing career had him at Delaware Park, Penn National Race Course, or elsewhere in the minor leagues, where he would race in obscurity.

But something had gone very, very right.

In most cases, bloodlines say all there is to say about a horse; pedigrees separate racing's haves and have-nots. But occasionally common blood produces horses of uncommon ability. They are known in the industry as "freaks," short for genetic freaks. They mock conventional breeding practices and common racing wisdom. They embody the sport's mighty capriciousness.

Lil E. Tee was the freak's freak. ABC broadcaster Jim McKay would call his Derby victory "a real-life fairy tale" on the telecast of the Preakness Stakes two weeks later. It was the story of a jockey who found God in a hotel room and salvation on a longshot; a father who rode horses at county fairs in Nebraska during the Depression and began a love affair with racing that carried his son to the Derby winner's circle more than a half-century later; a rich old man who had just about given up the idea of getting his hands on the Derby trophy, the one thing his money could not buy. Mostly, it was a story about a horse with a heart as large as any ever measured, a stunningly resilient commoner who rose up to win his country's most important race, assisted by the shrewd horsemanship of his handlers and the requisite dose of luck.

But in the dizzy moments after Lil E. Tee crossed the finish line at Churchill Downs, when the bright lights of victory suddenly shone on his glistening hide, only a few citizens of the racing nation were aware of the text of his longshot story.

Not his trainer, owner, or jockey. Not the media.

A blacksmith in Ocala, Florida. An veterinary surgeon in Ringoes, New Jersey. A veterinarian who owned a farm in New Freedom, Pennsylvania.

They knew about Lil E. Tee.

A trainer at Calder Race Course. A pinhooker in Camden, South Carolina. A horse owner in Miami whose office wall was lined with winner's circle pictures from Penn National, Finger Lakes, and Delaware Park.

They knew about Lil E. Tee.

A farm manager in Pennington, New Jersey. A pinhooker in Ocala, and his wife, an exercise rider. A businessman in Springfield, Illinois.

They knew about Lil E. Tee.

A collection of obscure horsemen who dealt mostly in average horses and had previously regarded the Derby as an unreachable province: they were the only ones who knew of the transience, illness, and sheer disdain that had marked the horse's life. They were the only ones who knew how dirty the rags had been before these riches.

They were the only ones, at the moment of victory, who understood how little sense it all made.

How truly improbable this dream was.

1

"I was not expecting much."

The alarm sounded at four in the morning in the house on the grounds of Pin Oak Lane Farm, breaking the stillness of the chilly country night. A sudden clanging in the darkness would jangle anyone else's nerves, but not those of Dr. William Solomon, the lanky veterinarian who owned the four hundred-acre horse farm set in gently rolling hills and tall poplar groves on the Pennsylvania-Maryland border, forty miles north of Baltimore.

The ringing heralded the beginning of a new life in the foaling barn that stood across a driveway from Solomon's front door. The alarm was connected to a magnetic transmitter that Solomon sutured into the birth canals of mares on the verge of delivering their foals. When the foal pushed through the canal, the magnet separated from the transmitter and set off the alarm in Solomon's house. It was necessary because Pin Oak Lane had two foaling barns, one by Solomon's house in Pennsylvania and one down the road in Maryland. If a mare went into labor when the foaling attendant was at the Maryland barn, the alarm told Solomon that someone needed to hustle to the Pennsylvania barn and deliver the foal. The alarm was a common sound in the spring, the heart of breeding season.

This time, in the early hours of March 29, 1989, Solomon could hear from his bedroom that Duane Grove, the night foaling attendant, was in the barn delivering the foal. Solomon could relax. Grove was an experienced hand. Solomon often went outside to see the new foals Grove had delivered, but only because he already was awake, not because Grove's work needed checking.

Occasionally Grove would hasten the process and buzz Solomon on the intercom shortly after the delivery, suggesting that Solomon come down. That usually meant all was not well with the foal, or did not appear to be.

This time, Grove buzzed Solomon almost immediately after the delivery. There might be a problem, he said on the intercom. Solomon rose and dressed, shrugging into a coat to fight the winter chill lingering into the first days of spring. He went downstairs, out the door, and across the driveway to the foaling barn. The big mare that had delivered was huddled with her foal in the stall closest to the house, cast hazily in the dim light. It was cold enough inside the barn to see the wisps of their hurried breath.

The foal was a thoroughbred colt, a dark bay with a ring of white on his right rear ankle. He appeared weak and somewhat disoriented. A healthy foal would rise tentatively on shaky legs, fall softly to the straw once or twice, then rise and reach for his dam's teat. This one remained on the ground.

Solomon studied the foal for several minutes and decided to follow the usual routine. He injected the foal with thirty ounces of colostrum, the milk that a mother's body produces immediately after birth to enable her to begin feeding naturally. Colostrum was laden with antibodies, the disease-fighting proteins the foal needed to ward off infection while his own immune system developed in his first hours of life. Solomon administered this extra dose to every foal as a form of biological insurance, in case the mare was unable to produce colostrum and pass it on to the newborn.

Solomon returned to his house after finishing with the foal, intending to check back in several hours. It was almost five o'clock now. Pin Oak Lane would soon be yawning and stretching, slowly coming alive. It was a busy, bucolic commercial horse farm at which standardbreds and thoroughbreds were sired, foaled, boarded, and trained. Many farms in south-central Pennsylvania had standardbred clients; standardbreds were prominent in the area thanks to Hanover Shoe Farms, the nation's largest commercial standardbred breeding farm, located in nearby Hanover. It had produced a string of champion trotters and pacers, turning Pennsylvania into one of the dominant states in standardbred breeding.

Solomon had grown up twenty miles from Hanover Shoe Farms. His first job after vet school was at Hanover Shoe Farms. From there he went to Castleton Farm in Lexington, Kentucky, then returned to Pennsylvania in 1973 to open a veterinary practice based at Pin Oak Lane. Over the next decade he built a thriving business using standardbred clients and reinvested the profits in the farm. He bought four additional tracts of land to more than double the farm's size, took on boarders, became a commercial standardbred breeder, and opened a training track. In the early 1980s he included thoroughbreds in the operation, became a commercial thoroughbred breeder, and joined the hierarchy of the Pennsylvania Horse Breeders Association.

Of the one hundred foals delivered every year at Pin Oak Lane, three-fourths were standardbreds. Their pedigrees often were competitive nationally, as was true with many Pennsylvania standardbreds. It was not unthinkable that a champion standardbred could come from Pin Oak Lane. Napoletano, a standardbred foaled and raised at the farm and sold by Solomon as a yearling, had become a star pacer in Europe just the year before.

It was far more unlikely that one of the twenty-five or so thoroughbreds foaled annually at Pin Oak Lane would become a star. The crop was only one-third as large as the standardbred crop, and the average pedigree was not nearly as competitive nationally. This was particularly true of those delivered in the Pennsylvania barn. Pennsylvania breeding and racing was inferior to that in Maryland. A breeder who chose to have a horse foaled in Pennsylvania instead of Maryland rarely was operating with great expectations, at least not realistic ones. Such was certainly the case with the new foal in Solomon's barn. "I was not expecting much," the breeder, Larry Littman, said later.

When Solomon returned to the foaling barn for an update at nine o'clock, the news was distressing: Littman's foal had remained weak and disoriented and had not nursed until four hours after delivery. This was dangerous. First nursings usually occurred within an hour of birth. A delay in the presence of colostrum in the bloodstream could mean the foal was lacking antibodies. If he went forty-eight hours without antibodies, he would be vulnerable to viruses causing diarrhea, pneumonia, and a fatal blood infection.

Solomon waited two hours to allow the dam's milk to seep into the foal's bloodstream, then took a blood sample and ran it through a spectrometer to check for antibodies. Sure enough, the blood tested almost off the bottom of the scale. The foal had almost no capacity to ward off infection.

Thinking it was possible he had not waited long enough after the first nursing to allow the colostrum to enhance the foal's blood, Solomon waited until after lunch, took another blood sample, and tested it. Same results. Normal, healthy blood registered between eight hundred and fifteen hundred on an arbitrary scale, the number reflecting the amount of light shining through the blood in the spectrometer. Five hundred or lower signaled trouble. This foal's blood had twice registered around one hundred.

After the second test Solomon went to work. He administered a dose of hyperimmune plasma, blood soaked with antibodies, which had been collected from mature horses inoculated with vaccines. The hope was that the immunity-rich blood would give the foal the protection it needed. That evening Solomon reviewed the dam's paperwork. Her name was Eileen's Moment. She had spent three weeks at Pin Oak Lane after wintering at Bonita Farm in Maryland. She was the first mare owned by Littman to deliver at Pin Oak Lane.

Solomon went to bed hoping he would not need to phone Littman with the sad news that the foal had not survived. As much as it was understood in the horse business that sometimes things did not work out, even if you took every precaution and tried every antidote, a foal's death was still a shame. Always a shame.

The foal was not even a day old and already of uncertain lot. Hyperimmune plasma was the only treatment for his condition. If it failed to work, the foal would lack the antibodies necessary to live a healthy life. He would be in trouble. Big trouble. Basically, he would have AIDS.

FORTY-EIGHT thousand one hundred ninety-six thoroughbred foals were delivered in North America in 1989. Approximately half would make it to the races. One thousand or so would win stakes races. Four hundred six, slightly less than 1 percent of the original crop, would show enough potential to encourage their owners to nominate them to the Kentucky Derby as three-year-olds in 1992. Eighteen would run in the race on the first Saturday in May. One would win.

Statistically, each foal faced the same enormously long odds of becoming the one Derby winner among the mass of newborn horseflesh stretching from Alaska to Florida. Yet it was wrong to suggest that every foal had the same chance of winning this equine lottery. There were varying degrees of probability. It was as if the Derby winner's circle was the peak of a triangle filled with foals: a few were closer to the peak, many more squashed at the bottom.

For instance, a long-range handicapper seeking the Derby winner three years hence would have been wise to concentrate on the eight thousand-plus foals delivered in Kentucky in 1989. History advanced this lesson powerfully: eighty-eight of the one hundred fifteen Derby winners had come from the princely breeding fields of the bluegrass state. No other state had produced more than four Derby winners. Thirty-seven states had never produced one.

As well, there was reason to concentrate on the progeny of the expensive stallions that ruled the breeding and racing industries. They cost more for a reason: they faithfully produced more stakes-caliber horses and Derby contenders.

Seattle Slew, the legendary Triple Crown winner standing at Three Chimneys Farm in Kentucky for a $250,000 stud fee, had sired four Derby horses and one winner, Swale, in seven years at stud. He sired fifty-five foals delivered in 1989, of which seven would be Derby nominees three years later. Six of those seven would win stakes races. One would be named Horse of the Year.

Alydar, standing for a $230,000 fee at Calumet Farm, had sired one Derby winner, Alysheba, and the 1989 favorite, Easy Goer, in six years at stud. He sired seventy-seven foals delivered in 1989, of which seven would be 1992 Derby nominees, four stakes winners, and two Derby contenders.

Blushing Groom, a top English miler in the 1970s, now standing for a $160,000 fee at Gainesway Farm in Kentucky, sired forty-five foals delivered in 1989. Two would sell for more than $1 million as yearlings. Another would demonstrate such powers of acceleration as a two-year-old that an Arab sheikh would be moved to pay more than $5 million just for the right to own half.

Born into such company as a future competitor, the new foal in the Pennsylvania barn at Pin Oak Lane Farm stood at a confluence of absurdly long odds. Here, truly, was a foal at the bottom of the triangle of Derby contenders.

As a horse bred in Pennsylvania, he was automatically excluded from the list of legitimate contenders. A Pennsylvania-bred had never won the Derby. The state simply was not in the business of producing classic three-year-olds. Out of some fifteen thousand Pennsylvania-breds delivered since 1966, only three had run in the Derby. Agitate had finished third in 1974, Parfaitement sixteenth in 1983, and Rhoman Rule ninth in 1985. A Pennsylvania breeder trying to make headlines with a three-year-old thoroughbred was better off buying a state lottery ticket than breeding a horse.

Other parts of Pennsylvania's thoroughbred history were not quite so bleak. A century earlier, a Pennsylvania-bred named Iroquois had become the first horse bred outside of England to win the Epsom Derby. More recently, the state had produced Eclipse Award winners such as Ambassador of Luck, Martie's Anger, and Flatterer. The esteemed sire Danzig was a Pennsylvania-bred, as was a gelding named Yankee Affair, winner of $2.8 million between 1984 and 1989.

Still, Pennsylvania ranked far below Kentucky in the horse industry's order. And if geography alone were not enough to dismiss the new foal in Solomon's barn as a Derby contender, his pedigree was a clunker, too. His dam, Eileen's Moment, had finished far out of the running in each of her six career starts. His sire, At The Threshold, was an accomplished racehorse that finished third in the 1984 Kentucky Derby, but had shown no ability to sire stakes-caliber horses. By the end of 1989, At The Threshold would have only one stakes winner among sixty-two sons and daughters at the races.

Being foaled in a minor thoroughbred state, with distinctly common blood, would not limit what the new foal in Bill Solomon's barn could accomplish. But Kentucky Derby hopes were just balderdash for horses born into such modest circumstances. Suggesting that At The Threshold and Eileen's Moment could produce a horse capable of bucking such odds and winning the Derby was not unlike suggesting that the horse could win the race galloping backward around the outside rail. The idea was preposterous.

LUCK is the current that runs racing. As much as pedigrees establish class, and the instincts and industriousness of trainers and jockeys help decide races, there is only one commandment: thou shalt be lucky, or else.

The wise old trainer Charlie Whittingham once said that thoroughbreds bruised as easily as strawberries. Indeed, they are a chosen but delicate breed, twelve-hundred-pound athletes balanced on matchstick legs. So much can go wrong, and often does. Almost half of the newborn foals in North America never make it to the races, their careers aborted by injury, illness, death, or lack of promise. A foal needs good luck to avoid these many endangerments, then more good luck to amount to anything more than fodder at the races.

Even the career of a champion, a horse of rare ability, is a precarious event. What if the breeder had chosen a different set of parents? What if the horse had wound up in the hands of a different owner who used a trainer with different methods? What if the horse had stepped on a nail three days before a big race instead of three days after?

The course of every horse's life takes it through a succession of such intersections offering turns in the wrong direction, toward the injury and obscurity that befalls so many thoroughbreds. The new foal in Solomon's Pennsylvania barn arrived at such an intersection immediately, in the first hours of life. Already, he was a bruised strawberry. Already, he needed a dose of good luck. And he got it.

When Solomon awoke on the day after he had injected the foal with hyperimmune plasma, the news was good. The foal's condition had improved considerably. Duane Grove had taken a blood sample in the middle of the night and tested it. It had scored six hundred on the spectrometer, above the danger line.

Solomon tested another blood sample later in the day. The results were the same: above five hundred. The hyperimmune plasma had worked. The foal was safe.

Eileen's Moment and the foal soon moved out of the foaling barn and up a hill to the broodmare paddock. A secretary at Pin Oak Lane phoned Larry Littman with the news of the foaling and the scare. A few days later, word came back from Littman's farm manager that Eileen's Moment would leave for Kentucky, where she would be bred to Big Spruce. Naturally, the foal would accompany her.

The horses left Pin Oak Lane when the foal was a week old. Littman and Solomon never spoke. They would not meet, in fact, until three years later in Hershey, Pennsylvania, at the annual Iroqouis Awards Banquet given by the Pennsylvania Horse Breeders Association, at which Littman would be given a hero's reception for having bred this troubled son of At The Threshold.

2

"The fee was cheap."

He was not a patriarchal horse farmer, not a landed baron with a handlebar mustache, not a scion of wealth raised on a manicured lawn. Larry Littman was a high school dropout, a machinist's son who played ball in the streets, a rowhouse kid raised amid the urban clutter of northeast Philadelphia, far from Kentucky's pristine bluegrass country. That he would wind up on the roll call of thoroughbred racing history was as much of a longshot as the horse that would put him there in 1992.

He was a child of the Depression and World War II, part of what became a particularly pragmatic generation of Americans. He began working when he·was twelve years old, peeling garlic in a delicatessen. Later, he worked as a busboy and a caddie and sold newspapers and magazines. He dropped out of high school and joined the army because he did not believe that the lessons of the classroom would help him support a family one day. He spent seven months fighting in the Korean War and returned to a job in his father's machine shop in Philadelphia. Soon he was running the floor, as the head of manufacturing. His friend Bob Silver was the head of engineering.

One of the items produced at the shop was a thermocoupler used to ascertain the temperature of molten metals. It was a small device that covered the end of a long rod dipped into the metal; at the tip was a carbon graphite plug covering a tiny twist of platinum wire that recorded temperatures up to almost three thousand degrees. After two dips the device had to be replaced. Figuring it could be improved upon, Littman and Silver tinkered around in the shop and developed a disposable thermocoupler composed of numerous layers of cardboard. It was lighter, cheaper, and faster. They approached Littman's father about manufacturing it in the shop, but he was not interested. Littman and Silver decided to start their own company in a rented garage. Littman's father chipped in 25 percent of the seed money.

Business boomed immediately. Disposable thermocouplers cut costs and sped production for steel companies. It was a hot product.

Two years later Silver died from leukemia, leaving Littman in charge. In the next two decades, his company, Electro-Nite, grew to encompass three hundred employees worldwide and plants in Europe, Asia, Africa, and South America. Littman moved to the suburbs and raised two sons with his wife, Roslyn. He took up golf and, though not a natural athlete, practiced so intensely that he lowered his handicap to five. The story was illustrative. Littman was a self-made success.

In 1984 he found a buyer for Electro-Nite, cashed out a multimillion-dollar fortune, and retired at age fifty-three. He moved to Florida with Roslyn, took up sport fishing, and played golf. But the laconic drumbeat of retirement left him feeling restless. He was addicted to work, to the invigorating rush of dealmaking and numbers-crunching. Finally, after a month, Roslyn told him to go do something, dear, anything, just stop moping around the house. He decided to start a racing stable.

For years he had gone to the track as a casual bettor with his father, in the process developing a deep fondness for the game. Now that he had all this money and time, why not bet on his own horses? D.H. Lawrence had written that a man was a lord if he had a horse. Littman, the former garlic peeler, did not mind becoming a lord.

If the urge to buy racehorses had not struck him, if he had just settled quietly into his retirement, another horse would have won the Kentucky Derby eight years later. Such fateful turns are typical in racing; decisions made with no consideration of the sport can become integral to a race years later. Littman's decision to start a stable did not seem the kind that would resonate in racing history. But it was.

His first decision was to base his outfit in Philadelphia. He planned to keep an office there, commute from Florida, and do some investing and consulting work. That he keep his stable there made sense. It was still home. Picking a trainer was easy. Dennis "Goose" Heimer was the top trainer at Philadelphia Park. A rumpled college graduate who read the *New York Times* and played the stock market, Goose had forty horses in his barn and a keen sense for placing them appropriately at tracks from Maryland to New York. A steady flow of stakes winners were testimony to his ability.

Now all Littman needed was horses. Goose advised him to aim

high, explaining that it cost as much to keep a Secretariat in the barn as it did a $2,500 claimer. Littman set aside $400,000 to get started. Goose suggested they begin buying at the July sale of selected yearlings at Keeneland Race Course in Lexington, Kentucky. Goose studied the sale catalog, in which each yearling's pedigree was detailed, and picked out a half-dozen possibilities.

"You mean I'm going to get six for $400,000?" Littman asked.

"Not exactly," Goose said dryly.

The Keeneland July sale was the most expensive in the world. A team of pedigree experts and veterinarians spent months screening fashionable, impeccably bred yearlings, eliminating four of every five candidates to arrive at a class of around three hundred. Those making the cut were sold at a two-day auction attended by an international set of high-rolling buyers.

The sale had ambled along for years as one of the most important in the country along with the September sale at Keeneland and the August sale at Saratoga. But that changed when foreign investors turned the July sale into their personal battleground in the early 1980s. The average sale price had increased from $53,000 in 1974 to $520,000 in 1983, due mostly to the competition between four brothers from the ruling family of the Persian Gulf emirate of Dubai and Robert Sangster, owner of a British bookmaking operation specializing in soccer pools. Canadian investors had also played a part, buying the first million-dollar yearling in 1976.

Sangster and a group of investors had purchased a steady supply of yearlings for close to a decade when the sheikhs arrived in 1980 with a seemingly bottomless supply of petrol dollars. In 1982 Sangster paid $4.25 million for a grandson of Northern Dancer, and Sheikh Mohammed bin Rashid al Maktoum bought nineteen yearlings for $12.8 million. In 1983 Sheikh Mohammed bought a Northern Dancer colt for an astounding $10.2 million. Aggressive American buyers such as Allen Paulson, the chairman of Gulfstream Aerospace, joined in the bidding, often buying yearlings for more than $1 million.

The July sale had become a high-society affair marked by private jets, limousines, and sprawling parties. The seats in the sales pavilion were reserved only for those buyers with the largest bank accounts.

"I guess I won't get six for $400,000, huh?" Littman said after Goose told him the story.

"Probably not," Goose said.

They flew to Lexington several days before the sale and inspected the stock with other prospective buyers. Goose gave Littman a beginner's lesson in pedigree and conformation. They sat in the pavilion in the evenings and watched the spectacular bidding. The sheikhs combined to buy thirty-five yearlings at an average price of $1.3 million. Shiekh Mohammed spent $8.25 million for one Northern Dancer colt. Sangster and his associates bought twenty-three yearlings at an average price of $1.5 million. Paulson bought twenty-two for $7.725 million. The average sale price was $598,000. The market was rising to an astonishing height.

Into the frenzy stepped Littman. On the second night of the sale, relying strictly on Goose's opinion, he bought a colt for $110,000. The next day he bought another for $135,000. (The sale's third day featured slightly less fashionable yearlings that had been turned down by the Keeneland selectors, but still were among the best of that year's crop.)

Near the end of the third-day session, Goose said to Littman. "Well, you got two. That's not bad." Goose went to arrange to have the colts shipped to New Jersey, where Littman would board them at Josco Farm, owned by Littman's friend Stanley Joselson.

"When I get back we can go catch the plane," Goose said.

"Fine," Littman said. "I'll wait here and read the newspaper."

Goose left. Littman unfolded his paper to read, but kept his eyes on the sales ring. A colt sired by Halo was brought in. Halo's progeny had brought almost a $200,000 average at the select sale. The bidding for this colt began much lower and slowly rose to $35,000. Littman offered a bid. The colt could have had a kangaroo's pouch for all Littman knew about conformation, but Littman figured he was a smart businessman who knew a deal, and this colt had to be a deal.

The bidding passed $40,000, $45,000, $50,000. Littman stayed in. But when his $55,000 bid was topped by one of $57,000, he suddenly felt relief. What was he doing buying a horse without Goose? The auctioneer asked for more bids. Littman remained motionless. The colt was sold for $57,000. "Thank goodness," Littman thought. "What was I thinking?"

But then there was commotion on the stand. The auctioneer returned to the microphone and explained that the $57,000 bid had been withdrawn. He asked if the $55,000 bid was still good. Littman hesitated briefly and raised his hand: yes, it was.

Upon returning, Goose noticed the new purchase slip in Littman's hand. "What did you do?" Goose asked. "I thought you were reading the paper."

Littman shrugged. "I bought a horse," he said.

"What's it look like?" Goose asked.

"How the hell do I know?" Littman said.

They went to the barn to see the Halo colt. "You bought this?" Goose said slowly.

"I bought it," Littman said.

"Well," Goose said, "it's crooked as hell."

The colt's knees were bent forward instead of forming a sleek, straight line, no doubt the reason the colt had failed to make the select sale. But there was no turning back. The crooked-legged colt joined his more expensive stablemates at Josco Farm.

The careers of Littman's first three purchases offered a vivid lesson in racing's unpredictability. The $135,000 colt, which Littman named Lil's Best, earned $31,000 in allowance races, hit the board in nine of twelve starts, then stepped in a hole during a race at Garden State and had to be destroyed. The $110,000 colt, named Lil Bill L., earned less than $50,000 despite racing until he was five; he wound up running in claiming races at Penn National. The cheapest of the three, the crooked-legged colt Littman had bought blindly, developed into a stakes-winning sprinter named Lil Tyler. (The L-I-L in the names was Littman's initials. The name of his new stable? Lil Stable, of course.)

Lil Tyler's imperfect knees had no effect on his racing ability. As one vet said, "He walks funny, but he sure can run." As a juvenile, Lil Tyler won an allowance race and the Devil's Bag Stakes in Maryland. To begin his three-year-old year he won the Goss L. Stryker Stakes, Star de Naskra Stakes, and a division of the General George Stakes, all in Maryland. In April he was the betting favorite in the Derby Trial at Churchill Downs, and although he finished thirteenth and won only once more in his career, he retired with four stakes wins and $217,000 in earnings.

Two elemental lessons were evident in the successes and failures of Lil Tyler, Lil's Best, and Lil Bill L. One was that money did not buy success. The other was that luck was every bit as important as knowledge. "The luck factor in this business is powerful," Littman said later. "Whether you're buying or breeding or whatever, if you do everything right, use all the systems and numbers and guidelines, it just means you need to be 75 percent lucky instead of 95 percent. No matter how smart you are, luck is what you need above all else."

Both lessons would visit Littman again in stunning fashion eight years later, on the first Saturday in May 1992.

EILEEN'S Moment was a two-year-old filly blessed with possibilities, or so it seemed. She was a long-backed bay, attractive, physically sound, earnest in her morning workouts. Her grandsire was What a Pleasure, sire of Kentucky Derby winner Foolish Pleasure. Her great-grandsire was the legendary Bold Ruler. Not a bad package, in all. There was just one problem. As they say around the racetrack, she could not outrun a fat man running uphill.

In her first start, a maiden race at Calder Race Course in Miami in September of her two-year-old year, 1984, she broke slowly and finished eighth. Ten days later, she ran last in a field of eleven maidens. Then she ran seventh in a $25,000 claiming race. Making her fourth start in a month nine days later in a $30,000 claiming race at Calder, she ran fourth in the early going but quickly faded and lumbered across the finish line again in seventh. When it turned out she had bucked her shins, her trainer, William MacKinnon, took her out of training and pointed her toward 1985.

One morning in early November, another trainer, Ron Felix, stopped by MacKinnon's barn at Calder. "Is that filly for sale?" Felix asked.

"Every horse in the barn is for sale," said MacKinnon, who trained privately for Irvin Feiner, a breeder who owned a farm in Ocala.

"I know someone who might want her," Felix said.

"Fine," MacKinnon said.

That someone was Goose Heimer, now filling out the remainder of Littman's new stable. Felix and Goose had been friends since their days as grooms in the late 1960s. They talked often. Several months earlier Felix had touted Eileen's Moment to Goose on the basis of her looks and pedigree. Now Goose was interested. He knew she had run poorly, but she was young enough that she still could develop into a useful runner. Even if she did not, she might have residual value as a broodmare.

Goose wanted her mostly because he figured Littman would enjoy having a horse to follow in person in Florida. He called Littman to discuss the arrangements. Felix would train the horse for Goose and campaign her in Florida. Sure enough, Littman was enthusiastic. He did not care that he had never even seen the filly. Goose's recommendation was sufficient.

A bill of sale was drawn up. Felix served as the agent for Littman, MacKinnon as the agent for Irvin Feiner. There were two mistakes on the bill. Littman's name was misspelled Lipman. Eileen's Moment's dam was misidentified as Sailaway Monet, instead of her correct name, Sailaway. No matter. The bill was signed by the agents and notarized eight days before Christmas. Littman then made his one and only contribution to the transaction: he wrote a check for $28,000 and gave it to Goose.

Felix moved Eileen's Moment into his barn at Calder and kept her out of action for another three months, giving her shins time to heal. In early March 1985, she returned to the track in a maiden race at Gulfstream Park in Hallandale, Florida. Littman came out hoping she would make a better runner as a three-year-old. She ran ninth.

At the end of March she made her sixth career start in a $20,000 claiming race at Hialeah Park in Miami. She ran seventh. Her career now consisted of six starts, with three sevenths, one eighth, one ninth, one eleventh, and career earnings of $570. Even though Littman had owned her for only two starts, he knew it was time to admit she had no place on the racetrack. Not now. Not ever.

"She ran in slow motion," Littman said later. "You have heard of those competitive horses that can't stand to have anyone running in front of them? Eileen couldn't stand to have anyone behind her."

Goose suggested trying her as a broodmare. Littman was becoming interested in pedigrees and thinking of breeding a small crop of horses. Eileen's Moment was shipped upstate to Southland Farm in Ocala. Littman had become friendly with Southland's co-owner, John Fernung, a breeder for whom Goose also trained. Fernung and his younger brother and farm manager, Brent, had begun advising Littman on bloodstock matters.

By the time Eileen's Moment reached Southland it was too late to breed her that year. She would have to wait until 1986.

LITTMAN returned to Keeneland in July 1985 and spent $167,000 to buy three yearling colts on the third day. The select sale was as outlandish as ever. Robert Sangster and an associate purchased a halfbrother to Seattle Slew for a record $13.1 million. The average sale price was $537,000. Littman was amazed at the amounts of money coursing through the veins of the breeding industry. He had begun his stable as a sporting venture, but, watching these yearlings sell for such high prices, he was drawn to the business of breeding. It looked so easy: you bought a quality mare, paid for a service by a top stallion, took the yearling to Keeneland, and sold it for millions. He knew it was not nearly that easy, but the lure of the big score was irresistible.

"Where else could I make something for $50,000 with the hope of selling it for $10 million?" he said later. "I guess that was a naive thought for a supposedly astute businessman, but I was fascinated."

Meanwhile, his racing outfit was taking off. Lil Stable's horses won eight races and $110,000 in 1985, and sixteen races and $265,000 in 1986. Lil Tyler was the centerpiece, but there were others. A colt Littman bought at Keeneland and named Lil Fappi broke his maiden by six lengths and won several small stakes and more than $100,000. But as much as winning was a boost to Littman's ego, he found himself becoming bored.

"Standing in the winner's circle made you feel good, but it wasn't me," he explained. "I had always gotten a thrill out of building something, and in this case I wasn't building anything because I couldn't train the horses. The success of a horse is basically in the trainer's hands. I couldn't do that, so it wasn't hands-on for me. I'd go to the barn a couple times a week, talk to Goose, see what he was doing. But it wasn't me doing it. Breeding was different. That was something I could say I did. It was hands-on."

The mysterious, complicated business of matching pedigrees intrigued Littman. His thermocoupler device had relied on precision, gauging high temperatures with little margin of error, and the seemingly precise nature of breeding, with its guiding spate of numbers and theories, appealed to him. Trying to predict how blood would run was the greatest gamble in a sport of gambling, and Littman began to see it as more challenging than cheering for horses he had bought at sales. He also saw the potential for making millions.

In spring 1986 Littman made a major decision: Lil Stable would become primarily a breeding operation. Yes, Littman still would buy a few sale colts and operate a racing stable, but most of his investment would now go to broodmares and stud fees. He set aside $2 million to get started and established high goals. His intent was to breed horses that could sell at Keeneland or Saratoga: stakes-caliber horses. Littman knew it would take time, patience, and plenty of money. He knew it would be difficult to crack the Kentucky breeding society. But just as he had turned a small machine shop in northeast Philadelphia into an international company worth millions, he set out to make Lil Stable a force in thorough-bred breeding.

TAKING John Fernung's advice, Littman bred Eileen's Moment to a stallion named Tri Jet in spring 1986. The reasoning was sound. Tri Jet, standing in Ocala for $25,000, and Eileen's Moment's dam, Sailaway, had produced a stakes-winning filly named Thirty Zip that had won thirteen races and more than a half-million dollars. Why not mix the same bloodlines again?

A REPRESENTATIVE of Pennfield Biomechanics, a new company that specialized in analyzing horses' physical structure and running action, came to Goose's barn and offered to work for free. The company was trying to build a client base. Littman had them study several mares. One was Eileen's Moment.

Pennfield's report pointed out that her stride was not properly synchronized, a flaw that had no doubt contributed to her failure on the racetrack. But the overall tone of the report was positive: "[Eileen's Moment] has the potential to outproduce herself significantly when mated with stallions who complement her good qualities. It appears she could make a somewhat better than average broodmare...[although] she is likely to show inconsistency, she would appear to be worth taking a chance with."

Attached to the report were charts predicting the biomechanical efficiency of potential foals produced by Eileen's Moment and several cheap sires. Littman had given Pennfield the names of the sires as potential breeding partners for Eileen's Moment. Clearly, he did not have big plans for her.

LITTMAN had the strong will and self-confidence common to successful businessmen. Once he decided to become a major breeder, he moved boldly. Over the next two years he spent $1.5 million to buy twenty mares and fillies.

At the 1986 Keeneland July sale he bought a yearling filly for $335,000, then returned to Keeneland for the November breeding stock sale and bought three mares for $410,000. In 1987 he bought two yearling fillies at Keeneland, one at Saratoga, and eight broodmares at various other sales. "We were buying a hell of a lot of horses," Littman said later. His spending spree was so furious that he accidentally bought one horse he had not planned to buy; he bid on the wrong one of two by the same sire auctioned in succession. He also bought two cheaper fillies out of claiming races and turned them into broodmares. Each purchase was important: a breeder was only as good as his mares.

Littman and Goose became familiar faces on the sale circuit. Littman developed strong opinions about pedigrees. Before a sale he studied the catalogue intently, narrowing his choices to ten or fifteen, helped at times by Jack Werk, a breeding analyst who championed the use of genetic "nicking"—assessing the racing history of the cross of the mare's and sire's bloodlines—as a predictor for a foal's racing ability. Littman gave his "paper" picks to Goose, who flew to the sale early and cut the list to three or four on the basis of conformation. Littman then flew in for the sale and handled the bidding. It was not unusual for him to overpay. "When he wanted a horse, he just bought it," said Brent Fernung, who was among those advising Littman. "He had really strong opinions. He was turning down million-dollar horses on pedigree."

Needing to breed seventeen mares in the spring of 1988, Littman reserved seasons to such highly regarded stallions as Topsider, which had an $85,000 stud fee; Alleged, which stood for $80,000; and Danzig Connection and Miswaki, which stood for $40,000 apiece. In all, he spent more than $350,000 on stud fees for what would become his foal crop of 1989. He then spent hours studying bloodlines and applying various breeding theories to his stock, searching for the best possible combinations. He checked the Dosage Index of the potential foals—Dosage was a ratio quantifying speed inherited through bloodlines to endurance based on four generations of the horse's pedigree—and other basics such as the grade of the genetic "nick" (which ranged from A to F) and the sire's production history. "Then I put all the numbers in a pot and made up my mind," Littman said later. He was having fun.

"Larry was extremely enthusiastic, knew what was going on, and convinced me that he applied quite a bit of science to it," said Kip Elser, a pinhooker who later sold Littman's two-year-olds.

"Larry had his own theories of how to do it, and he stuck to them," said his friend and fellow breeder, Stanley Joselson. "No one could change his mind. Not Goose, not anyone. He's a very strong-willed person."

Littman was not about to breed Eileen's Moment to one of the expensive sires he had contracted. She had potential, but she was still unproven. So far Littman had bred her to Tri Jet and, again at John Fernung's urging, to Premiership, a $5,000 stallion standing at Southland Farm. She had delivered a filly by Tri Jet in the spring of 1987.

Littman mulled what to do next with her through the year leading up to the breeding season of 1988. He asked Jack Werk to suggest compatible studs. If she was being bred to produce a horse for the sales market, Werk wrote in a report, try a $10,000 stud named Cutlass, a son of the great Damascus. If she was being bred to produce a racehorse, Werk wrote, try Aracoid, a Grade I winner, primarily a turf horse, standing for $7,500.

Then one day John Fernung suggested At The Threshold, one of the half-dozen studs standing at Southland Farm. As a three-year-old in 1984, At The Threshold had won the Jim Beam Stakes, Arlington Classic Stakes, American Derby, and Ohio Derby, and had finished third in the Kentucky Derby. In his fourth year at stud, he was still an unknown quantity. His first crop had included six sale yearlings selling for a $21,000 average, hardly the stuff of greatness. But three others had just sold for a $67,000 average at a two-year-old sale, and that was not bad.

At The Threshold's stud fee was $6,500. "I'll give you the season for $5,000," Fernung said.

Littman liked the idea. The stud fee was cheaper than those Werk had suggested, but Littman saw no reason to invest too much in Eileen's Moment when he had so many other mares with better pedigrees and produce records. Breeding Eileen's Moment to At The Threshold would be cheap and easy. She was already boarded at Southland Farm. She would not have to leave the farm.

Before committing, Littman, as always, weighed his numbers. There was reason for optimism. The Dosage of the potential foal was 3.0, surprisingly low; anything below 4.0 was considered of quality and high potential. At The Threshold's father, a former Canadian Horse of the Year named Norcliffe, and Eileen's Moment's dam, Sailaway, had produced a colt named Cutter Sam that had won almost $250,000. Norcliffe was by Buckpasser, grandsire of 1985 Kentucky Derby winner Spend a Buck.

Littman decided to take a shot. Eileen's Moment and At The Threshold were assigned a date in the breeding shed. Littman's decision was based almost entirely on factors unrelated to conventional breeding practices. "I did my homework and checked everything out like always," he said later, "but the main reason I bred them was that the fee was cheap and the stallion was nearby and available. I didn't consider anything nearly as much as that."

It was the perfect beginning to an improbable dream: a marriage of convenience, utterly devoid of pretense or grand design. A cheapie.

BY the start of 1989, the breeding industry was in a slump. The average price of a Keeneland July yearling had declined 39 percent since 1984. The average price of a North American sale yearling had dropped 25 percent. The freefall had begun with a 1986 tax code change prohibiting many owners from writing off losses, and was propelled by a recession in the national economy and the realization by buyers that the prices paid earlier in the decade were wildly inflated. Few horses made back that kind of initial investment.

Littman had built up his breeding operation at a time when the price of horseflesh was steadily dropping. The high-market prices he paid were quickly outdated. "My timing," he said later, "was exemplary for a fool's."

By the beginning of 1989, he had spent most of his $2 million in start-up costs and still had not bred a major sale yearling. But he was undaunted. Believing that the industry slump could not last much longer, he continued to expand his operation. He stood Lil Tyler at stud in California and made plans to stand Lil Fappi in New Jersey. Goose talked him into renting a horse farm in New Jersey, giving the operation a home base.

Lil Stable was growing quickly. Seeking to make it more economical, Littman decided to sell his mares that, in his opinion, did not cross well with Lil Fappi or Lil Tyler. He was going to breed more to his stallions now; if you stood a stallion, you had to support it. Eileen's Moment was one of those mares marked for sale. Her sire and Lil Fappi's dam were by the same sire. Littman was adamantly opposed to such close inbreeding.

Eileen's Moment was entered in the winter sale of mixed horses at the Ocala Breeders' Sales Company. She took her place in the ring at the front of the auditorium on January 23, 1989. That she was in foal to At The Threshold was noted at the bottom of her page in the sales catalog. Littman set a reserve price of $20,000. If the bidding did not reach that high, he would keep the horse.

Before opening the bidding, the auctioneer, Vernon Martin, gave a brief sales pitch. He mentioned that Eileen's Moment's dam, Sailaway, had produced Thirty Zip and Cutter Sam. "This is a good family here,"

Martin said. At the end of his pitch he said that the mare was in foal to At The Threshold.

The bidding began quickly, rising in thousand-dollar bumps to $8,000 before slowing to $500 bumps that came more slowly. It almost stopped at $11,500. "Is that all we have?" Martin asked.

But the bidding regained speed, passing $13,000, $15,000, $17,000. The goal at OBS was to get a horse in the ring every two minutes, but this took longer. "They really worked at it," Bob Gulick, OBS director of sales, said later.

At $18,000, Martin again asked if that was all. Another bid raised the total to $18,500. But that was it. The auditorium fell silent. "Any more?" Martin asked for the third time. Not this time. "Sale," Martin announced. The bidding had fallen $1,500 short of Littman's reserve price.

But for that small amount, another owner would have wound up in possession of the foal in Eileen's Moment's belly, the foal that would one day mock the foundation of theories, numbers, and practices on which the entire breeding industry rests. What would have happened if Eileen's Moment had sold that day? Who knows? Maybe the foal would have remained in the obscurity for which it was intended. Maybe not. It is a moot point. At the end of the bidding, Littman still owned Eileen's Moment.

JOHN Fernung sold his share of Southland Farm to his partner and opened another farm in Ocala. He called it Sylvan Crest Stud. Had Littman and Fernung remained friendly, Eileen's Moment probably would have returned there from the sales ring and delivered her foal by At The Threshold. The foal would have been a Florida-bred, as were her first two foals. But Littman and Fernung had an argument and parted ways, and Littman moved his breeding stock out of Florida.

Eileen's Moment was shipped to Bonita Farm in Maryland, with instructions to send her to Pennsylvania for foaling. Her third foal would be a Pennsylvania-bred. Littman considered leaving her in Maryland, where the quality of racing and breeding was higher, but he had already bred a handful of horses there and needed to vary his stock. Besides, Eileen's Moment's upcoming foal seemed a perfect fit for Pennsylvania, which, like many states, had a state-supported breeders' fund program that paid bonuses to breeders and owners of horses that won at Pennsylvania tracks, often in races restricted to state-breds. Breeding a cheap horse in a mediocre racing state with such a program was a way to give the horse value. It gave the horse a way to make money.

Of the seventeen horses scheduled for his foal crop of 1989, Littman penciled in three for foaling in Kentucky, five for New Jersey, two for Maryland, three for Pennsylvania, and four for California. The Kentucky-breds were those of the highest stock, followed by the Maryland-breds and Jersey-breds. The California-breds were Lil Tyler's offspring. Of those sired by stallions with measurable records, the Pennsylvania-breds were the lowliest. One was sired by Danzig Connection, a Belmont winner, but out of a young mare that, despite expensive breeding, had shown even less racing talent than Eileen's Moment. Another was sired by a stallion with a thousand-dollar fee. Eileen's Moment's At The Threshold foal fit right in.

3

"He was just a horse."

The horse farm that Littman leased was a thirty-six-acre spread in Pennington, New Jersey, in the rolling countryside between Philadelphia and Trenton. Stanley Joselson's Josco Farm was right across the street. Littman's farm had not had tenants for a year. Tall weeds had sprouted in the sheds and along the fence line. The barn roof leaked. Not a single piece of equipment could be found anywhere on the grounds. But there were a modern house, a swimming pool, and three large fields in back, a feed tower, a barn, and a small field and six paddocks in front. The place was a mess, but it had possibilities.

The rent was $3,000 a month. Littman and Goose agreed to a deal. Littman would pay the rent. Goose and his girlfriend, Mary Deppa, would live in the house and run the farm for free. Mary would provide the bulk of the labor. Goose and Mary moved in on April Fool's Day and spent two months getting the place in shape for Littman's horses. They cleaned, mowed, weeded, filled two dumpsters with trash, and began renovating the apartment attached to the barn. A shingle went up by the front gate: Lil Stable.

In June, Littman's stock began arriving from Maryland, Kentucky, and other farms in New Jersey. It was a rowdy clan of more than forty broodmares, yearlings, and foals. Mary brought along her yearling show horse, Timmy. The fields of Lil Stable went from empty to full within weeks.

Among the first to arrive were Eileen's Moment and her big, awkward foal. They had spent sixty days at Windmill Farm in Kentucky while Eileen's Moment was successfully bred to Big Spruce. The foal had been wormed once and shown no effects of the immune deficiency that had caused such concern at his birth. He spent his days outside, in the spring sunshine.

Mary nicknamed the foal AT&T, for At The Threshold. The sight of him in the field validated the low expectations of his breeding. He did not compare visually well with the high-priced foals in the new crop, the colts sired by Alleged, Topsider, and Danzig Connection, and a filly sired by Miswaki. He ran with his neck arched high in the air, as if he were straining to see how tall he could stand. He had so much extra running action that his knees seemed on the verge of banging against his chin. "He just didn't look good in the field at all," Littman said later.

The mares and foals lived in the back fields, which sloped down from the house to a grove of trees and a pond at the back of the property. They spent nights and most days outside, coming in only in the mornings to be fed, wormed, and given occasional foot treatments and vaccinations. They spent the afternoons sleeping and sunning. Sometimes they wandered into the sheds, leaned against the back windows, and let the sun beat down on their faces. In the evenings they paired off and competed, rearing up and batting each other with their forelegs, or getting down on their knees and nipping at each other. Sometimes they raced or chased each other. AT&T became fast friends with Timmy. They were the biggest of the foals. They played at the bottom of the field.

"It was a nice, carefree existence, lots of fresh air and exercise, a nice way for them to grow up," Mary said later. "All they had to do basically was mind their manners when we asked them, which wasn't that often."

Goose left at dawn for the racetrack and came home late, but Mary was not alone. Goose's fourteen-year-old daughter, Marya, was spending the summer at the farm. Marya was fond of horses and show competitions, drawing her close to her father's girlfriend. They awoke before dawn and turned horses out of the barn, raked the stalls, and brought the foals and mares in for breakfast. The foals began to play tough as they got older. AT&T was among the feistiest, often rearing and nipping and trying to bolt.

One afternoon Mary and Marya heard an awful braying in the field and ran to see what was wrong. They found AT&T in an agitated state at the bottom of the field, but Mary found no cuts on him, and he did not seemed injured. It was impossible to tell what had upset him. He calmed down when taken to his mother. Mary shrugged. Whatever.

Several days later this happened again. AT&T began bellowing and refused to stop until Mary took him to Eileen's Moment. Mary smiled. She had solved the mystery. AT&T was hungry. Even though his mother was only thirty yards away in the same field, and all he had to do was walk over to her, he preferred to stand and yell.

"Eileen would look at him and kind of roll her eyes, like, 'God, he's so stupid,' " Mary said later. AT&T's loud fits soon became commonplace. One day Mary and Marya were leaning on the fence, watching him sound off again.

"Well, there he goes," Mary said.

"Calling for mommy," Marya said. "Phoning home."

Mary nodded. "AT&T, phoning home," she said.

Marya laughed. "But E.T. phones home," she said.

They both laughed now, thinking the same thought: E.T. was the perfect nickname for this horse. Several years earlier there had been a movie about an enormously popular ugly alien creature named E.T.— short for extraterrestrial—that was left behind on Earth and went around talking about getting a chance to "phone home." AT&T was an equine E.T. in many ways. Unattractive. Goofy. Mary and Marya began calling the horse E.T. It was a perfect fit as a nickname. Listening to the horse scream for his mother in the afternoons, it was not difficult to envision him coming from outer space.

MARY Deppa was thirty-one years old and just over five feet tall, with shoulder-length dark hair, a smart, wry manner, and a smile that made you smile back. She had been Goose's girlfriend for three years, since meeting him one day at Philadelphia Park in 1986; Goose and his wife were estranged. Raised in a small house outside New Orleans, Mary had worked with horses since she was fifteen. She was competent and tough. Early in their relationship Goose had sent her to Hialeah and Monmouth Park to oversee small strings of horses he sent there. She was more than up to the task. Littman had grown to know her through Goose and never doubted that she could handle running the farm.

Toward the end of the summer she oversaw the weaning of the foals, a new experience for her. She sent the mares in shifts to Josco Farm. Everything went smoothly. E.T. even made a friend. "We had an orphan filly with a big, ugly nursemare," Mary said later, "and we weaned her and E.T. at the same time. She went right to him and stuck by him like glue."

Mary was pleased that she had handled the new task. She was feeling at home on the farm. In the mornings she could see the sun rise over a hill. In the evenings she and Goose ate dinner on the porch overlooking the back fields. They watched the horses play in the gathering dusk, and sometimes just sat and listened when it was too dark to see.

There was only one lingering problem: Goose was always tired. He had complained before about feeling lethargic, for which no one blamed him—he worked long hours and was under pressure to win— but he had always snapped out of it before. This time he just could not seem to get over it. Mary asked him to go see a doctor, but he refused. He never went to a doctor. If he needed medicine, he just asked a vet.

"The only thing stupid about Goose was that he didn't know how to take care of himself," Littman said later, "He never had his blood-pressure checked. He never ate anything but meat. His diet was awful."

He needed to be careful. His father and uncle had died of heart attacks in their forties. Goose was forty-two. At different times he told Mary he thought he might have lyme disease, bursitis, and pneumonia. He took several medications a vet had given him. Mary and Marya begged him to go to a doctor.

"We tried crying, but it didn't work," Mary said later. "We tried getting angry, but that didn't work either."

In September, Goose and Littman flew to the fall yearling sale at Keeneland. Littman sold a Riverman filly for $100,000 and a Lyphard's Wish colt for $92,000, both of which he had purchased in utero. He also sold a disappointing Topsider colt, which he had bred, for $8,500.

Goose was tired at Keeneland, but once he came home he did not miss a day at the track. One day in late September he saddled a horse at Philadelphia Park for Stanley Joselson, who came down to the paddock before the race. "You don't look so good," Joselson said. "Go see a doctor."

"Ah," Goose said, waving his hand, "it's just a little pneumonia." Back at the farm that evening he was particularly hungry. Mary fixed a big dinner. He ate every bite and went to bed early. An hour later, his heart stopped.

Mary discovered him in bed and called an ambulance. The paramedics rushed him to the hospital—too late. Goose was dead of a heart attack at forty-two—precisely the same age at which his father had suffered the same fate.

His death staggered Lil Stable. Even though the racing side of the operation had dwindled with Littman's increased emphasis on breeding, Goose had remained Littman's primary bloodstock adviser. "He was more than just my trainer," Littman said later. "He was my friend and adviser. I trusted him implicitly. And I missed him terribly."

Said Kip Elser, "We were paralyzed when Goose died. Larry still had quality people advising him. Mary, Goose's assistants, a few others. Everyone was qualified. But we all missed that guy at the top."

No one missed him more than Mary. She was broken-hearted. She cried every day as autumn dissolved into winter. The farm turned bleak: trees bare, flower boxes empty, songbirds silent. The gray setting fit Mary's somber mood. She lost herself in the business of running the farm. "No one else was going to take care of those horses," she said later.

Then, as if Goose's death had cursed Lil Stable, there was a run of bad luck. Eileen's Moment aborted her foal by Big Spruce. An old mare died of colic. One of Mary's dogs fell into the frozen pond, and Mary had to go in waist-high to pull it out. One of the weanlings developed allergy problems and died the next year of a defective immune system. Early the next year there was an outbreak of Potomac horse fever. Eight horses became ill and two died, including Mary's favorite mare, Lil Mary.

"Everyone started calling me 'Killer Mary,'" Mary said later. "I would ask the vets, 'What could I have done?' They would say, 'Nothing, it isn't your fault, bad things happen with horses.' But I had never been around sick ones before. It was a little spooky."

Six weeks after Goose's death, Littman entered the Alleged weanling in the Keeneland breeding stock sale. His $70,000 reserve price was not met. The horse had a Keeneland pedigree but was pot-bellied and toed-out.

LITTMAN separated his young horses into three groups. The most fashionable and well-bred would be sold as yearlings, where they would command the highest prices. Those not as blue-blooded or attractive, yet still salable, would be sold as two-year-olds. Those not worthy of sale would race for Lil Stable. Sometimes the ugly ones turned out to be runners.

From the moment At The Threshold and Eileen's Moment were given a date in the breeding shed in 1988, their foal was projected as a two-year-old sale horse. Although sales of two-year-olds in training were thriving in the depressed racing economy because buyers were seeking more proven commodities—horses that had shown they could run—the sales still were harbors for cheaper bloodstock. On the average, a two-year-old sold for roughly half as much as a yearling. E.T. had to sell as a two-year-old, of course. Even if he had turned out to be beautiful, he did not have the breeding to sell as a yearling. And he certainly had not turned out beautiful.

When Eileen's Moment's Tri Jet filly and Premiership colt sold as two-year-olds (for a surprisingly high $44,000 average), the course of E.T.'s future seemingly was set. When Fred Seitz, a bloodstock agent and farm owner from Kentucky, came to Lil Stable in the spring of 1990 seeking yearlings to include in his consignment at the Keeneland fall yearling sale, he did not even bother to assess E.T. E.T. was not a Keeneland-caliber yearling. Clearly, the colt was going to sell as a two-year-old.

Littman picked out nine yearlings for Seitz to review: those with pedigrees that gave them a chance of selling at Keeneland. Seitz and Littman stood outside the barn while Mary brought them out. Seitz assigned each a grade ranging from three to seven, the higher the better.

The Danzig Connection colt was Seitz's favorite. "Large, attractive, slightly fine-boned ... a very nice horse," Seitz wrote in his notes. He gave the horse a grade of six. Seitz also was fond of the Topsider colt, which was out of a mare by Secretariat. "Smooth, attractive, good shoulder, well-balanced, exceptional mover," Seitz wrote. The grade was five-plus to six.

Those two were the stars of the class, Seitz felt. Of the rest, he was most fond of a filly sired by Vigors, a five-plus. The Alleged colt and Miswaki filly were a disappointing four-plus, slightly below average. Seitz decided to take three for his consignment: the Danzig Connection and Topsider colts, and the Miswaki filly.

Several weeks later, another bloodstock agent came to the farm. Ric Waldman was the manager of Windfields Farm, where Northern Dancer stood at stud, and also operated a consulting business. Regarded as a shrewd judge of broodmares, he inspected thousands of horses a year. Waldman and Littman had met in Florida and become friends. Waldman lived in Lexington, but often had business at Windfields, in Chesapeake City, Maryland. One day he drove the extra hour north to Lil Stable to assess his friend's yearling crop. Unlike Seitz, he was not seeking horses for a consignment. He was just trying to help Littman. He looked at the entire yearling crop and suggested the sales at which each horse belonged.

"I didn't think it was a real strong crop," Waldman said later. "The Danzig Connection colt was above average. Nothing else was particularly notable. The Topsider colt was OK, but not very big. The Miswaki filly was decent. There wasn't anything that totally turned me on, though."

Waldman was the first bloodstock professional to judge E.T. The colt was led out of the barn and turned around.

"I wrote in my notes that he was plain and [structurally] correct," Waldman said later, "but certainly nothing special. His breeding suggested that if he was going to bring anything at all, it wouldn't be at a yearling sale. It would have to be once he was in training [as a two-year-old]. Maybe he would train better than his pedigree."

Of course, there was no reason to believe E.T. would show any talent once he was broken and put in training. "He was just a horse," Mary said later. "We had lots of better ones. We thought he was better than a few, but not many. He was real big and not a good mover. When you look at yearlings, you look for ones put together smoothly, moving low to the ground. That wasn't him. He was so big and gawky, with all that extra knee action and his head in the air. Of all the yearlings, you'd have never picked him out as one that would turn into a good racehorse."

WHEN it was time to name E.T. officially, Littman listed three choices on a name-claiming form and sent it in to the Jockey Club.

A name was available if it was not too similar to a name that had been used in the last ten years. Littman's first choice was At the Moment, a combination of E.T.'s sire's and dam's names. The Jockey Club turned the name down. A colt foaled just the year before had that name.

Littman's second choice was E. Tee. Again, the Jockey Club said no. In the last decade horses had been named E.T. Call Home, E.T. Come Home, E.T. Go Home, E.T. Phone Home, E.T. Run Home, E.T. Home, and E.T.'s Gone Home.

Littman's third choice was Lil E. Tee. The Jockey Club approved it, despite the similarity to the other extraterrestrial names.

Lil E. Tee it was.

SOME two months after Ric Waldman assessed E.T. as "certainly nothing special," the stars of the national yearling crop were auctioned at Keeneland's July sale. They were everything E.T. was not: well-bred, fashionable, and desirable. The yearling selling for the highest price was a Seattle Slew colt out of Weekend Surprise, the dam of Preakness winner Summer Squall. The colt sold for $2.9 million apiece. Colts by Alydar,

Mr. Prospector, Danzig, and two by Blushing Groom also sold for more than $1 million. Late on the second day another Blushing Groom colt entered the ring, but he was small and failed to draw the $300,000 reserve price set by owner Allen Paulson.

The sales-topping Seattle Slew colt would develop into a champion named A.P. Indy. And the Blushing Groom colt that did not meet Paulson's reserve price would emerge as one of racing's hottest superstars in years. His name? Arazi.

E.T. was behaving strangely when Mary found him in the back field one day in May. He jerked his head around, sank to his knees, rolled on the ground, and got back up. Mary called her vet, Dr. Tim Patterson, an assistant at the Mid-Atlantic Equine Medical Center in nearby Ringoes, New Jersey. Patterson came to the farm and examined E.T. The colt had a slightly accelerated heart rate but otherwise seemed fine. Patterson gave him a dose of Banamine, a painkiller and mild relaxant. E.T. was fine in an hour.

Two weeks passed without incident. Then Mary found E.T. thrashing in the field again. She called Patterson, who returned to the farm, examined the colt, and again prescribed Banamine. Again, E.T. quickly recovered.

Patterson guessed that E.T. was having occasional trouble digesting a particular food. It was difficult to know for sure. Colic was vague that way. It is a benign problem in human babies: they cry for six months, then stop as suddenly as they start, for no apparent reason and without medical scars. Equine colic is the same in that it is a term for a broad range of intestinal ailments, but different in that it can be far more serious, even fatal. It can result from gas, a twisted intestine, a parasite that causes spasm in the stomach wall, or a food particle blocking the large intestine. Eighty percent of the cases are resolved with routine treatment. Often the problem is just gas. Since the Banamine worked, ET's problem was probably just that.

When a third episode occurred a week later, the situation became more worrisome. The Banamine worked again, but neither Patterson nor Mary understood what was happening. It might just be gas, but it also might be a more serious illness such as colitis, or even ulcers. That the episodes came so far apart implied that the problem was not serious, but what was it?

A fourth episode occurred three days later. This time Mary just called Patterson and told him she was giving E.T. a dose of Banamine. It worked again, although this time E.T. thrashed for longer before calming down. He was getting worse. "Something's not right," Patterson told Mary.

Several nights later Mary crept outside at ten o'clock, pointed a flashlight at E.T. and saw him beginning to thrash again. Another episode was coming. She considered calling Patterson, but decided against it and just administered the Banamine herself. The next afternoon E.T. suffered his worst episode yet. It was not just gas, that was clear. The colt was in serious pain. This time Patterson found danger signs: a distended small intestine and rapid breathing bordering on hyperventilation. Patterson and Mary agreed that it was time to take the colt to the clinic. They loaded him in Mary's van and she drove him over.

At the clinic ET was in a fighting mood. He snapped at technicians, who resorted to putting him in ankle stocks to control him. "He was a jerk, made things extremely difficult," said Dr. Rick Doran, the surgeon at the clinic.

E.T. had a distended bowel and a high heart rate. A gulp of water flushed back out of his mouth, a possible sign of a twisted intestine. But he responded to treatment and was fine the next morning after a night at the clinic.

"Come get him, he's fine," Doran told Mary on the phone.

"I know he's not fine," she said. "He's going to colic again as soon as I get him home."

"But he's really OK," Doran said. "There isn't much we can do."

Back at the farm, E.T. ate his supper and played in the field. Mary, who was afraid to leave the farm when a horse was even mildly ill, felt confident enough to drive to a horse show in Virginia the next day. She returned that evening to the startling sight of three men trying to shove ET into the back of a van. He was in trouble again.

Paul Ruiz, the groom living in the barn apartment, had found E.T. on the ground and called Patterson. The vet drove to the farm, examined E.T., and ordered the colt sent back to the clinic immediately. But E.T. was so agitated that Ruiz and Patterson were unable to load him in the van. They called the trainer at Josco Farm across the street. The three men finally succeeded in loading E.T. just as Mary arrived.

Mary waited at the farm to hear from Doran. She hoped E.T. would not need surgery, but it was obviously a possibility. It did not make sense economically, of course. E.T. had already cost Littman at least $10,000 between the stud fee, vet bills, board bills, and feed. Colic surgery could mean another $5,000. Whether E.T. could sell for $15,000, especially after surgery, was debatable. Not that such a concern would weigh in the decision to operate. To not go in, if it was necessary, was inhumane. "I knew it wasn't financially sound to spend more on a horse we figured was not going to be a racehorse," Littman said later, "but you can't let a horse die."

Doran called late that night. E.T. was tranquilized after yet another episode at the clinic, his second of the day.

"What do you want me to do?" Doran asked.

"If you have to go in, go in," Mary said.

"If something changes you'll hear from me," Doran said. He called at 9:30 the next morning. E.T. was beginning to thrash.

"We're going in," Doran told Mary. She got in her car and headed for the clinic.

IN the pre-op room E.T. was led into a large, square cell covered by thick pads. Given an anesthetic, he was asleep in fifteen minutes. Doran's assistants went back into the cell and attached a hobble to each ankle. The hobbles were attached to a gurney that lifted E.T. into the air upside down, with his legs sticking up and his back hanging just above the floor. Connected to a set of runners on the ceiling, the gurney carried E.T. through a set of double doors into the operating room, where he was laid on his back on a table and attached to heart and blood pressure monitors.

Had it been twenty years earlier, E.T.'s future would have been in doubt. Until then, colic surgery was traumatic for horses; approximately three of every four subjected to surgery either died or were debilitated. Many clinics did not have heart and blood pressure monitors. Surgeons sutured by hand, a tedious process that left the abdomen open for longer and increased the risk of infection. Many horses died from shock or developed intestinal adhesions. "The prognosis was always guarded," Doran explained later.

But just as major advancements had been made in human medicine in twenty years, colic surgery had become more modern and effective. Instead of suturing by hand, surgeons used a stapling gun and stainless steel staples, diminishing the operating time and chance of infection. More sophisticated anesthetic products and techniques sped the process and prevented shock. Positioning horses upside down improved access to the intestine. Heart and blood pressure monitors provided more control.

Survival and recovery rates depended on the type of colic, but all were much higher by now. Some horses still were debilitated by adhesions or chronic conditions such as an inflamed abdominal cavity, but generally what had once been a doomsday was just a routine setback. Horses commonly returned to the races after colic surgery. One of Doran's "patients" was back at the track three weeks after the operation.

Of course, the odds of a recovery depended on the seriousness of the colic. Most trainers agreed that a horse was more likely to recover if no intestine was removed.

Upon opening up E.T., Doran left the operating room, ran upstairs to his office, and grabbed his camera.

"What are you doing? Is it that bad?" Mary cried.

Doran laughed and told Mary not to worry; he just wanted to take a picture of the unusual condition he had found inside E.T.: the ileum, the end of the small intestine, was being suctioned into the large intestine, cutting off the flow of food and water and leading to painful obstructions. The Banamine helped the small intestine return to its normal position and pass food and water. The episodes had become more frequent because the ileum had become scarred and swollen and was sticking inside the large intestine.

Doran pulled the small intestine out of the large intestine and tacked a row of staples across the scarred end. He then stapled the end onto the large intestine and sliced open a new end of the small intestine, several inches behind the ileum. He cut a new opening on the large intestine and connected it to the new ileum. "Basically," Doran said later, "I rerouted his plumbing."

The operation lasted ninety minutes. E.T. awoke in the padded cell and was returned to his stall. Mary helped put on the leg bandages and went home.

For several days E.T. ran a fever and continued to paw the ground and thrash. One night he became tangled in his intravenous line. "He was kind of a twit," according to Doran.

Mary came for a visit and explained to the clinic's assistants and technicians that E.T. was the poor, unfortunate son of Lil Stable, the sickly, awkward extraterrestrial. The clinic employees laughed.

"But you'll all say you knew him when," Mary said, smiling. Everyone laughed again.

Doran mulled going back in for a second operation, but E.T. finally improved. Three days after the operation a student assistant at the clinic wrote on the colt's chart during rounds that E.T. still was pawing the ground, "but it doesn't seem like it's from pain as much as from being pissed off." His fever persisted for two more days, then disappeared. He was discharged two days later, a week after the operation.

At Lil Stable he remained in the barn for a month, his exercise limited to walking. Remarkably, he was as gentle as an old house cat, though not yet broken. He had lost 150 pounds, and though he soon began eating normally, the increased nutrition did not translate into pounds. His manure was runny and he was thin when Mary turned him back out into the field after Labor Day.

Soon he was sent to be broken at what was formerly Josco Farm, now under new ownership and called Batcha Farm. The trainer who handled the breaking told Mary he was impressed with E.T., claiming that the colt had a nice, strong running style.

"We kind of looked at the guy funny, thinking, like, there wasn't much to like," Mary said later.

LITTMAN'S Danzig Connection colt, Topsider colt, and Miswaki filly entered the ring at Keeneland's September yearling sale. They had left Lil Stable in July and prepped for the sale at Fred Seitz's farm in Kentucky. All three failed to draw the reserve prices Littman had set.

Two months later Littman returned to Keeneland for the breeding stock sale. He sold three mares and two weanlings for $400,000, taking a loss on all five horses. The price of horseflesh was continuing to drop. The market was all but collapsing. Littman was selling for losses of as much as 50 percent because the horses probably would have even less value the next year.

Between the two Keeneland sales, Kip Elser came to Lil Stable to inspect the yearling crop for prospective two-year-old sale horses. Elser was a farm owner from Camden, South Carolina, who made a living as a pinhooker, buying yearlings, selling them as two-year-olds and profiting on the turnaround. Occasionally, he sold horses for clients, as was the case with Littman, who had met him through Goose. Elser sold all of Littman's two-year-olds, mostly in Florida.

The yearlings were being broken across the street on the training track at Batcha Farm. Littman, Mary, and Elser went to see them. Elser selected three for his consignment: the colts by Topsider, Danzig Connection, and Alleged. He turned E.T. down.

Littman was surprised. Elser had sold Eileen's Moment's Tri Jet filly and Premiership colt as two-year-olds at a sale at Calder, and Littman had expected E.T. to sell there also, despite the colt's looks and sickliness. But Elser could not see it happening.

"I saw a big, awkward colt that had been through colic surgery, which had knocked him back a fair bit," Elser said later. "He was a ways behind the others developmentally. Things were not going well for Larry. He wasn't winning at the races and wasn't selling much. We were trying to save him some money and not run up expenses on horses that we didn't feel real good about. If [E.T.] hadn't had colic surgery, it probably would have been different. He would have come down to South Carolina and we would have at least tried to get him ready for the sale. But I just didn't think I could get this horse ready in the hundred or so days until the sale. I didn't think he would come around in time to bring back the additional money we had to put into him."

Disappointed that his plan for E.T. had been scotched, Littman tried another approach. He entered E.T. in the March sale of selected two-year-olds at the Ocala Breeders' Sales Company. The average price at the sale was $30,000. If E.T. commanded that much, Littman would at least turn a small profit.

Littman asked Brent Fernung to serve as his consignor at the OBS sale. Fernung had started his own outfit in Ocala, Journeyman Bloodstock, after the breakup of Southland Farm. Fernung agreed to sell E.T. for Littman.

Littman arranged to ship E.T. to Fernung in Ocala. The van came in mid-December and took E.T. away.

4

"The look of eagles"

Average horses can easily become lost in the great shuffle of horseflesh in Ocala. Built on a foundation of rich limestone soil and caressed by a warm, sunny climate, Ocala and the surrounding countryside of Marion County are home to some four hundred horse farms where three thousand foals are delivered every year. Almost four thousand horses are sold every year by the Ocala Breeders' Sales Company (OBS). Horses are always coming and going to and from sales, competing for the favor of the hundreds of horsemen in the area. The competition is relentless and tough. Losers far outnumber winners.

From the moment he arrived, without ceremony, on a cool December night in 1990, E.T. was on the verge of disappearing into the masses.

A van dropped him off near midnight at Indian Hill Farm. Chuck Wieneke, a pinhooker who rented stall space at the farm, led him into the barn and looked him over in the dim light.

"Good gracious," Wieneke said. The colt had long hair. His ribs showed in his thin chest. His front legs seemed to come from the same socket.

"I think he was originally picked up at New Bolton," said the van driver, referring to the New Bolton Center, a veterinary facility located in Kennett Square, Pennsylvania, and operated by the University of Pennsylvania Veterinary Medical School. The driver's information was incorrect, but Wieneke did not doubt it. E.T. had the look of a horse that had been sick.

Wieneke had met the colt as a favor to John Fernung, for whom he was pinhooking several horses at Indian Hill Farm. Brent Fernung, John's brother, was supposed to sell E.T. at the March sale of selected

38

two-year-olds at OBS. Brent was going to be surprised, thought Wieneke, who doubted the OBS selectors would accept a horse in such poor condition.

Wieneke put up E.T. and drove home. His wife, Joan, asked him how the horse looked.

"Well," Wieneke said, "he looks like he's fixing to die."

JOAN Wieneke took one look at E.T. the next morning and nicknamed him Harry. It was the perfect name, she thought, for a horse so gawky and hairy. Hairy, Harry.

"If he isn't a Harry, I don't know what one is," Joan said.

Brent Fernung came out for a look. He was as surprised as Wieneke had been the night before. "The horse is high-withered anyway, so without any meat on him he looked like a camel with a hump," Fernung said later.

In the three-and-a-half months since he underwent surgery, E.T. had regained few of the 150 pounds he had lost. His gaunt frame and long hair made him an awful sight. Joan, who was her husband's exercise rider, took "Harry" out for a gallop. The colt ran with his head held high, resembling a submarine with its periscope raised. His convoluted knee action made it appear that he was jumping up and down more than running.

Fernung was dismayed, but not surprised. He had seen many At The Threshold horses. "They tended to be big, correct, and muscled, just couldn't run," Fernung said later. E.T. fit the description perfectly— except that he could run a bit, according to Joan.

"He just about took off on me," she said after the gallop. "I know he doesn't look good, but this is one strong horse."

Fernung called Bob Gulick, director of sales at OBS, with the news that E.T. had arrived. The colt's pedigree had already been approved by the OBS selectors, but he still had to pass a physical inspection before being accepted into the sale. The sale's entry deadline had passed, but Gulick agreed to come to Indian Hill the next day to inspect E.T.

"When I got there the colt was out in a field by himself," Gulick said later, "and he looked like the wrath of God. He was thin and narrow, very much out of shape and out of condition. He looked droopy and thin, and without good flesh and muscle tone he looked saggy. The top line sagged. He was also very narrow in the chest, depressed . . . just did not have much going for him."

Gulick filled out a grading card. OBS grades ranged from one to one hundred. Below sixty was deemed unsuitable for sale. E.T. scored a fifty-nine. He would not be officially turned down until the OBS selectors made their final decision at a later meeting, but Fernung was sure of E.T.'s fate. Furnung called another selector on the OBS board, Lauren Marks.

"Any shot, Lauren?" Fernung asked.

"I don't think so," Marks said.

"Will it do any good if I told you I can have him looking a lot better by the sale?" Fernung asked.

"I don't think so," Marks said. "Brent, the horse was borderline on pedigree to begin with." She later added, "There wasn't a lot of disagreement from Brent. He didn't push as hard as he has on some other horses, or as hard as some people push on other horses."

Fernung called Littman with the news that OBS had turned down E.T. They discussed their options. E.T. could return to New Jersey and either be put in training to race for Lil Stable or be entered in a smaller sale at Timonium, Maryland. Littman said no: he did not want E.T. back. What was the use? E.T. would not sell for a high enough price at Timonium to warrant going to the trouble and expense of shipping him back. And Littman was not sure E.T. had the talent to become a racehorse.

Another option was to let Fernung keep E.T. and train him, get him into better shape, and put him in the April two-year-old sale at OBS, a huge, nonselect sale at which the average price was $10,000.

"If you do that, what will he be worth by the sale?" Littman asked.

"Oh, somewhere around the average, like $12,000," Fernung said.

"What will it cost me to get him there?" Littman asked.

"You know, the going rate," Fernung said. "About a thousand a month. For five months. So, like five grand."

Littman had already invested $15,000 in E.T. Why should he spend more if E.T. was only going to sell for $12,000? Littman would not make back the extra money needed to get E.T. into shape for the sale.

"I'd just be throwing good money after bad," Littman said. There was only one option left. "Can you sell him to someone now?"

"What do you want for him?" Fernung asked.

"Whatever you can get," Littman said.

"OK," Fernung said, "I'll look around and let you know."

It was not unusual for a breeder to take a horse with little potential and sell it privately for a small price—basically give the horse away, as a way of cutting overhead. E.T. was a perfect candidate. He was just a horse—cheaply bred, sickly; a horse on which Littman was going to lose money.

"Anyone who knows the breeding business would have done what I did," Littman said later. Mary supported Littman's decision to dump E.T. She had always supported the horse, but now even she was no longer sure how much he would command at sale.

"I had liked the horse," Mary said later. "I had still thought he was better than the Premiership [colt out of Eileen's Moment], which was nothing special and sold for $40,000. I had thought he was still salable as a two-year-old for $20,000 or $30,000. But when four good people tell you to get rid of a horse, you begin to doubt yourself. Fred [Seitz] and Ric [Waldman] didn't hate him so much as they just didn't like him. Kip [Elser] liked him even less. Brent [Fernung] hated him. It just seemed like things were getting worse."

Fernung drove to Indian Hill the next day. "Don't bother training the horse," he told Wieneke. "The man wants to sell. There's no use him paying a training bill."

Wieneke cocked his head. "You mean the horse can be bought?" he asked.

"Sure can."

"How much?"

"Oh, like $3,000," Fernung said.

"I'll take him," Wieneke said. Fernung was surprised, but pleased that the sale might go so easily. He did not want to have to hustle for such a small commission.

"Let me confirm the price," Fernung said. "Give me a few days." As he turned to leave, Fernung looked at E.T., paused, and turned back to Wieneke.

"What do you want with that horse, Chuck?" Fernung asked. "He's just a piece of hide."

CHUCK Wieneke was one of twelve thousand residents of Marion County who earned a horse-related living. He was a second-generation horseman, the son of a Virginian who had raised and raced horses and built a farm outside Ocala. Wieneke had moved from Manassas, Virginia, to Ocala when he was sixteen. He was forty-three years old now, with a moustache, straight black hair, a clipped Virginia accent, and a throaty smoker's rasp. He wore a belt buckle with his name on it. He lived with Joan and their young son at Green Key Farm, a small, well-kept acreage with a stable. His brother, Gordon, lived next door.

Through the years he had run another farm, managed some broodmares, and taken two unsuccessful stabs at starting a racing stable, once at Hialeah and once at the new Birmingham Race Course in Birmingham, Alabama. Sometimes the living was better than others. When he ran out of money in Birmingham in 1986, he suddenly saw the future in certain terms. "Let's stick with what we know," he told Joan. "Let's go home and pinhook."

He bought young, cheap horses, fed and trained them, then sold the improved product for a profit. There was money in it if you knew what you were doing, and most people who knew Wieneke agreed that he did. He usually bought horses for $5,000 or less and sold them for close to $20,000. He was just one of hundreds of pinhookers scraping out a living in Marion County, but he had a knack.

"He can get a bad horse looking as good as anyone's in a sale," said Mike Paramore, a blacksmith with whom Wieneke had co-owned and sold several horses. "Chuck would cook for them if it would make a difference."

"Chuck feeds his horses well, has nice paddocks at his farm, breaks them right, breaks them slowly, just takes good care of them," said one of Wieneke's best clients, Al Jevremovic, a businessman and horse owner from Miami. "Seeing what he can do with a $500 horse, you have to wonder how many good horses go by the wayside because of neglect."

His life was a nonstop rush of sixteen-hour days. Money was tight. His divorce from his first wife had almost bankrupted him, as had his training failures at Hialeah and Birmingham. Sometimes he had to borrow against the value of some stock Joan had inherited to buy a horse he really wanted. "He's got some wheeler-dealer in him, that's for sure," Paramore said later.

His friends kidded him about trading in cheap horseflesh, but he tended to pick horses that could be turned around and sold for a profit. "I try to envision what they would look like after a month in my care," he said later. "A lot of times they don't look good when they're for sale. You have to be able to visualize it. A lot of it is luck. A lot is being in the right place at the right time. But you have to have that eye. If you're gonna pinhook, you better be able to spot some things. I buy some of the worst-looking horses you ever saw. People laugh at me. But there's usually something in there that I think makes it worth the risk."

Upon returning from Birmingham in 1986 he spent $500 on a crooked weanling at a mixed sale at OBS. No one else was bidding. Joan was furious. "What are you bringing that sorry-looking thing home for?" she said.

"You watch," Wieneke said. They named the horse Wonkie's Best. Wieneke sold him as a two-year-old for $15,000 to Jevremovic, who planned to run him at Gulfstream Park.

"The only thing I want," Wieneke told Jevremovic, "is a copy of the picture the first time he wins."

Jevremovic smiled. "You think he's gonna win one, huh?"

"He's a racehorse," Wieneke said. "There's nothing down there in Miami that can outrun him." Jevremovic laughed.

Wonkie's Best won his first start by twelve lengths. Then he won an allowance race. Jevremovic sold him for $150,000. The horse went to New York, worked on a sloppy track one morning, stepped in a hole, broke his leg, and had to be destroyed. Wieneke was devastated. But Wonkie was the beginning of a profitable pipeline to Jevremovic, to whom Wieneke sold a half-dozen horses in the next three years. Each won at least one race and was sold for a profit. Jevremovic was a loyal customer. He listened when Wieneke called touting a horse.

From the moment he saw E.T. gallop for the first time, Wieneke had Jevremovic in mind. Something about the horse reminded him of Wonkie's Best. E.T. did look awful, but that large frame and long stride offered room for improvement. E.T. was Wieneke's kind of horse. In fact, Wieneke was so excited by E.T.'s potential that his obsession with the Tampa Bay Derby was rekindled. Wieneke had always dreamed about winning the Grade III stake for three-year-olds, run at Tampa Bay Downs in the spring. It was a modest goal, but Wieneke was serious about it.

"As soon as I saw E.T., I wanted to get Al as my partner in [owning] him," Wieneke said later, "and when we got to the April sale, maybe Al would say 'Aw, let's just keep him and run him.' Maybe he was my Tampa Bay Derby horse."

Wieneke called Jevremovic that night. "I've got an opportunity to buy a real nice colt up here for $3,000. He looks like he's gonna die right now, but I swear he's gonna win the Tampa Bay Derby."

Jevremovic laughed. "Chuck," he said, "you're not making sense.

You tell me he's a nice colt. Then you tell me he looks like death."

Wieneke tried to explain. "The horse is in bad shape right now, but when I'm done with him he's gonna bring $25,000 or $30,000 in the April sale."

Jevremovic paused. "Do you need the money, Chuck?" he asked, "because if that's it, I would be happy to give it you."

"No," Wieneke said, "it's not the money. I love this horse. In fact, if you want to win the Tampa Bay Derby, come up here and take a look at him and we can go partners."

Jevremovic laughed softly and turned down the offer. "I don't buy sale horses, Chuck, just racehorses," he said. "But if the horse is so terrific, I'll probably end up buying him in the April sale anyway. Just let me know how it's going."

Wieneke was disappointed; so much for the Tampa Bay Derby. Now he had to find another way to buy E.T. He did not have the cash. He had already bought eight yearlings that year, several times resorting to borrowing money against the value of Joan's stock to fund purchases. Joan said they had enough yearlings when he told her he wanted to buy E.T.

"But I want this one bad," Wieneke said. "This is my kind of horse."

Joan looked at him evenly. "You better find a partner then, Chuck," she said. "We just don't have the money."

Wieneke had pinhooked several horses with partners. They split the purchase price and bills, then split the return on the sale. Sometimes the other partner put up the purchase price and Wieneke put up his training services. Wieneke preferred the latter arrangement because he did not have to put up any money. Wieneke approached his brother, Gordon, who was in the barn at Indian Hill one morning.

"I'm gonna give you a chance to make some money, Gordon," Wieneke said. "You want to go partners on this one?"

Gordon looked at E.T. "Not on that horse," he said. "No way."

As Joan said later, "You have to understand. E.T. was practically slobbering when he first got here."

According to Wieneke, "Everyone was laughing at me. But they were just laughing at the shape the horse was in. They weren't taking the time to see what the horse could become."

Two days passed without word from Fernung. Wieneke began to worry that he might not get the horse. He had seen in the *Daily Racing Form* that Lil Herman, the two-year-old Premiership colt out of Eileen's

Moment, had won a race in Maryland. That meant that Eileen's Moment's first two offspring were winners at the track. E.T. was the third offspring. Wieneke worried that Littman would see that and back out of the sale. He called Fernung.

"Did you see about Lil Herman?" Wieneke asked.

"Yeah," Fernung said. "It might change the price or kill the sale or something, I don't know. Let me talk to Littman."

Wieneke fretted even more after that, particularly after he researched E.T.'s pedigree and found Cutter Sam and Thirty Zip, winners of more than $800,000 combined, in E.T.'s pedigree. "Littman's gonna back out, I'm sure," he told Joan. Wieneke wanted E.T. so badly that he was not deterred even after his veterinarian, Mike Gotchey, found a small ridge on E.T.'s belly during a pre-purchase exam.

"Has this horse had colic surgery?" Gotchey asked. Wieneke had no idea. No one had mentioned it. There was no scarring or evidence of suturing. Wieneke recalled that the van driver had said something about picking up the horse at New Bolton.

"It may have happened," Gotchey told Wieneke, "but if so, the surgeon did a hell of a job."

Wieneke shrugged. "I'm not gonna let it worry me," he told Joan. "If he had surgery, he looks like he's come along fine."

Another day passed. Wieneke decided just to get the $3,000 and give it to Fernung. It was Thursday, and Wieneke did not trust what might happen over the weekend. The next morning he told Joan to go into town and borrow the money.

"We've got too much work to do," she said. Around noon he brought it up again.

"Come on, Chuck," Joan said.

That afternoon, Mike Paramore, Wieneke's blacksmith, came to Indian Hill to put new shoes on E.T. Paramore was forty years old, with a broad chest, thick arms, and a soft way with touchy horses. He had worked in Ocala for twenty years. He noticed while shoeing E.T. that Wieneke was chain-smoking and pacing. Wieneke finally approached him as he was finishing up.

"Can you loan me $3,000?" Wieneke asked. "I can't get to the bank."

"Sure," Paramore said. "What do you need it for?"

Wieneke nodded at E.T. "I'm hoping to buy him."

Paramore went outside to his truck and wrote a check for $3,000.

"What do you want me to make it out to, Chuck, you or cash?" he asked.

Wieneke thought for a moment. "Just make it out to Journeyman Bloodstock," he said. That was the name of Brent Fernung's outfit.

Paramore handed over the check. Wieneke looked at him. "You want in for half, Mike?" he asked. Paramore sifted the idea for a moment.

"Sure," he said. He knew nothing about the horse, but if anyone knew about Wieneke's ability to turn around a bad-looking horse, Paramore did. Wieneke and Paramore had sold $200,000 worth of horses over the years.

"Right now I'm not even sure I've got the horse," Wieneke warned Paramore.

Paramore nodded. "If you get it, we can work it anyway you want," he said.

"Let me talk to Joan over the weekend," Wieneke said. "We might want all of the horse. I can pay you back Monday, if so."

Paramore nodded and drove off. Wieneke called Fernung to say he had the money. On Monday morning, Fernung came to Indian Hill, took the check, and gave Wieneke the ownership papers. Suddenly, the deal was done. A $3,000 check had bought a piece of racing history.

BRENT Fernung told Littman he could sell E.T. for $2,000, a thousand dollars less than the price to which Wieneke had agreed. When Littman said the price was fine, Fernung kept the extra thousand. The standard commission for arranging a sale was 10 percent. Fernung pocketed an extra $700.

"I felt that Larry and Mary knew the horse wouldn't be accepted for the sale when they sent him to me," Fernung said later. "I resented the idea that they just dumped him on me. Larry knew what he was doing. He was dumping the horse on me, saying, 'He'll find someone.' I felt like they were lying to me and I was mad that they had sent me a horse I couldn't sell. At one point I flat out asked them, 'Has this horse had colic surgery?' Mike Gotchey had found that ridge on his belly. But they said no. So I just told Larry I could get him $2,000 and I made me a grand."

Littman later disputed this version of the story. "It's very hard for me to believe Brent didn't know about the surgery," he said. "I can't believe he didn't. I'm not saying he did or didn't. It's hard for me to

believe he didn't. Because we were very friendly at that time, Brent and
I. His brother owed me money and hadn't paid me, but Brent and I
were very friendly."

According to Fernung he had told Littman there was "extra money,"
meaning the price was higher than $2,000, but that $2,000 would be
Littman's cut after the commission. Littman later denied Fernung told
him that.

"If he says he deserved a 33 percent commission because the horse
was so lousy, I can say that any honorable businessman, before he did
that, would call the owner and say, 'Look, I put a lot of crap into this for
$100 and I deserve more than that,' " Littman said later. "I probably would
have said OK. But you don't charge someone 33 percent without telling
them in this business, not if you want to keep a reputation."

Fernung said later, "I was a middle man, an independent broker in
the operation. If I'd been selling the horse for public auction for Larry, I
would have been working for him, but at that point I felt like I had a
man willing to sell a horse for X amount, a man willing to buy a horse
for X amount, and I just found a spot where I could make a little money,
too. Larry called me later when he found out and raised hell about that
thousand. But you know, that's life. I wasn't very happy about the horse
when I got him."

Paramore's $3,000 check went to Fernung, who sent Littman a
check for $2,000. Wieneke chose to "go partners" with Paramore.
Wieneke put up his training services instead of returning half of the
purchase price to Paramore.

"The horse is going to bring $25,000 in the April sale," Wieneke said.

"I hope so," Paramore said.

The next week Wieneke bumped into Hilmer Schmidt, the owner
of Indian Hill Farm. Schmidt had seen E.T. in the field. "That's sure a
big horse out there," Schmidt said.

"I bought him for $3,000," Wieneke said. "You want him for ten?"

Schmidt laughed. "Man," he said, "I'm not gonna let you make
$7,000 on me overnight."

WHEN E.T. was battling a lung infection as a four-year-old, his veterinarian, Dr. Alex Harthill, sought another opinion from Dr. Doug Byars,
director of the Hagyard-Davidson-McGee veterinary clinic in Lexington. Byars hooked E.T. to an ultrasound machine and measured the size
of his heart and lungs. They were enormous.

"Out of the hundreds of horses I have measured, the only heart I've seen as big was Affirmed's," Byars said later. E.T.'s heart was approximately 12.3 centimeters across the width of the left chamber when the heart was dilated. The average for an athletic horse in training, Byars said, is around 11.3, and around 11 otherwise. While it has never been determined that there was a correlation between heart/lung size and racing talent, Byars and Harthill looked at the ultrasound pictures and shook their heads. The hell with science.

"The horse had one huge motor in there," Byars said later.

E.T. was a freak. A genetic freak. The pedestrian blood of his sire and dam had produced a monstrous racing machine. But there was no way of knowing until E.T. was put in training, until it became clear that the colt's average looks and pedigree simply did not matter. The blood-stock agents who had disdained him were not mistaken. They just assessed him before his anatomical advantages became apparent.

Ric Waldman assessed him as a yearling only for sale potential, not racing potential. Waldman's appropriately indifferent opinion was based solely on E.T.'s looks and pedigree. He never saw the horse run.

Kip Elser assessed E.T. strictly as a financial proposition, not as a racing entity. The colt was not worth taking to a sale in Florida, Elser felt, because he would not sell for enough to warrant running up Littman's bills by taking him from Lil Stable. Whether E.T. could run was irrelevant.

Brent Fernung, more than the others, made a mistake, although it was understandable. He was standing by Chuck Wieneke when Joan Wieneke galloped E.T. that first morning at Indian Hill Farm. He heard Joan mention that she was surprised that such an ungainly colt could generate such power. But Fernung did not care. He was blinded by E.T.'s condition, which, in Fernung's defense, was indeed blinding.

A consensus was forming. Littman did not want E.T. Fernung did not want E.T. OBS did not want E.T. The horse was just about out of options, perilously close to the discard pile. But Joan's comment was the start of another consensus that built in the coming months, the consensus of just about every jockey and exercise rider who rode E.T. It had started with the trainer who broke E.T. at Batcha Farm. He was impressed. So was Joan Wieneke.

If Chuck Wieneke had not seen the colt gallop and not started dreaming about winning the Tampa Bay Derby, this second consensus might have stopped at that point. Without Wieneke's interest, E.T.'s racing career might never have begun. But Wieneke did want him. Wieneke chose not to pass on E.T. as he had on many similarly mediocre horses. Wieneke's intentions were modest—he was just wanted a cheap horse to pinhook—but they succeeded in giving E.T.'s freakish athletic tools the chance they needed to develop. They allowed racing history to take its course.

THE first thing Wieneke did was give E.T. a haircut. "That made a huge difference," Paramore said later. "He looked rough with all that long hair, but once he was clipped he looked a lot better."

E.T. was fed king oats, sweet feed, and barkers mixed with corn oil to return the luster to his coat. He went on a vitamin program and took one dose of Equipoise, a powerful equine steroid named after a famous horse from the 1930s.

"It gets [a horse] to feeling unreal, really gets the appetite going," Wieneke said later about Equipoise. "It brings them alive. I don't like to use it unless I have to. Not that it does them any harm. I've had a lot of good horses use it. You just don't want to do unnatural things."

There was an immediate and palpable change. E.T. began filling out and recovering his shine. "From day one you could tell he'd do good," Paramore remarked. "He had a little of that 'go' juice to begin with."

Wieneke moved slowly with him on the track. "He was supposedly broken when he got here, but we nearly had to start from scratch as far as turning and handling."

Joan took him out for two-mile gallops every morning on the training track at OBS, where Wieneke was basing his operation. Joan quickly came to dread the gallops. "He was strong from the beginning, but once he started putting on weight he really scared me," she said. "When he wanted to go, he just went. I was afraid I couldn't control him."

When E.T. developed a mild virus, Wieneke brought him home to Green Key Farm. Wieneke was going to be in Miami for two weeks at a sale; maybe Joan would get to know the colt better at home and not be so frightened.

"He was eating almost a bale of hay a day," Joan said later, "Chuck wanted him heavy, but this was ridiculous. Chuck would call from Miami and I'd say, 'What am I gonna do with this horse?'"

When Wieneke returned from Miami, E.T. was put in training at OBS. He was powerful but jumpy; strange noises sent him streaking down the track, all but dragging Joan. Wieneke tried putting cotton in his ears.

Three months after buying E.T., Wieneke could scoff at those who had laughed at him. "The horse just kept getting better and better all the time," Paramore said. "I brought my family around one Sunday afternoon. You couldn't help but notice how well he was doing."

IN early March, three Lil Stable two-year-olds entered the ring as part of Kip Elser's consignment at a sale in California. For the second time, the Danzig Connection colt, now named Lil Danzig, and the Alleged colt, named Allemaz, failed to draw Littman's reserve prices. Lil Peaches, a filly sired by Vigors, became the first of Littman's original crop of seventeen foals to sell at an auction. She brought $11,000. The Topsider colt, now named Topretariat, was supposed to have entered a select two-year-old sale in February but had injured an ankle at Elser's farm in South Carolina and was returned to Lil Stable. He was going to race for Lil Stable.

Littman was getting little return on the investment of more than $350,000 in stud fees that had produced his foal crop of 1989.

WIENEKE was in constant contact with Al Jevremovic while he worked on E.T. Wieneke was no fool. When you had a fish on the line, you pulled.

"I was like a third partner without putting up any money," Jevremovic said later. "Chuck loved this horse. He'd call and say, 'Al, the horse is doing this and that,' and I'd say, 'That's great, Chuck, that's great.' I knew a lot about the horse long before the April sale."

Toward the end of March, Wieneke decided to work E.T. one Saturday morning on the training track at OBS. A *Daily Racing Form* clocker would be there. The Form published workout times of young horses in training. A fast published work could enhance a horse's value. Wieneke told Joan to work E.T. a quarter-mile, but the colt heard a noise and took off early, at the three-eighths pole. The clocker timed him at :36^{1}/$_{5}$ for three-eighths of a mile.

"I was big-time surprised," Wieneke said later. "It was a great time." He called Jevremovic with the news.

"That's a real good time, Chuck," Jevremovic said. "It looks like you might have another Wonkie's Best on your hands."

"And the thing is, Joan didn't even let him run," Wieneke said. "She just let him go easy."

The April sale was three weeks away, and things were coming together. But then E.T. came down with another virus. Wieneke pumped him full of tetracycline. The stakes were high. According to OBS rules, E.T. had to breeze two furlongs or at least gallop on the training track the morning he was scheduled to be sold, giving buyers a chance to see him perform. If he appeared sickly or moved poorly, his price could drop and Wieneke's work would be wasted. In the weeks leading up to the sale, Wieneke could not decide if E.T. should breeze or gallop on the morning of the sale.

"What are you gonna do?" Paramore asked.

"I don't know," Wieneke said. "I just don't know."

THE April sale of two-year-olds in training at OBS bore little resemblance to a high-society Keeneland sale. It was the cheapest of the three two-year-old sales OBS held every year. There was a selected sale of Florida-breds in February. There was an open selected sale in March, the one for which E.T. had been turned down. The April sale was the safety net. OBS did no selecting. A horse did not have to pass an exam to enter. If the foal was registered with the Jockey Club and the owner had paid the $400 entry fee, the horse could entertain bidders.

Eleven hundred sixty horses were entered in 1991. The catalog was a colossal three inches thick. For four days, horse after horse was led into the ring before a sparse crowd salted around the OBS auditorium. The average sale price was $9,155, well below the national average for two-year-old sale horses. This was not the major leagues. E.T. was scheduled for the second day: April 23, 1991. That morning he spent time in the walking ring before heading over to the track. As he warmed up, the rider of another horse was injured in a fall. The track was cleared while an ambulance came and took away the rider. Then a thunderstorm hit and all workouts were called off.

Wieneke went to Bob Gulick's office. "My horse didn't get to work at all," he said. Gulick told him the sale announcer could use the three-week-old work published in the *Daily Racing Form* to help sell E.T.

Back at the barn Joan jogged E.T. on the shedrow during the storm. A crowd gathered to watch. "His head was bowed and he looked like a million bucks," Wieneke said later. "People thought he was a four-year-old."

"WOW," Bill McGreevy said to his brother Tom as E.T. sauntered in the walking ring that morning, before the thunderstorm hit. "Look at that expression. That's the look of eagles, isn't it?" It was an old race-track expression: the look of eagles. Knowing. Confident. Fierce. "You could just see it on Lil E. Tee's face that morning," Bill said later. "It was like, 'I can kick anyone's butt here.'"

Bill had seen enough. He nudged Tom and said, "That's the one I want."

Bill and Tom had spent the last five days at OBS studying the horses in the sale. Bill was finally buying a quality runner, a "real" racehorse, after a quarter-century of running cheap stock at Penn National, Delaware Park, and Timonium. The president of a company that distributed heavy construction machinery in Illinois and Missouri, he arranged a $50,000 line of credit with OBS and met Tom in Ocala.

Tom was a bloodstock agent, a well-regarded professional who could help Bill make the right choice. Tom and Bill were two of ten brothers and sisters in the McGreevy family. The eight boys had learned about horses on a neighbor's farm growing up in South Carolina, worked their way through college laying gas pipe, then sought their callings: airline pilot, real estate broker, financial consultant, horse trainer.

Tom had been a member of the horse and livestock judging teams at Penn State University in the early 1970s. Now, people paid him to buy horses for them. He had picked this sale as the ideal spot for Bill. A select sale was too expensive. Before coming to Ocala, Tom went through the catalog and picked out six or seven horses. The pressure was on. He had bought horses for buyers investing far more money than Bill ever would. But Bill was family, his oldest brother.

"If he was going to spend $25,000 for a horse after all those years," Tom said later, "I wanted to make the right decision."

Tom felt E.T. was the best horse in the sale: large, structurally correct, seemingly intelligent. A common pedigree was not that important, Tom felt, if the horse showed such superior characteristics. "I really like him," Tom told Bill. "I think he has the talent to be a stakes horse." Once Bill saw the look of eagles, he agreed that E.T. was the best of the horses Tom had picked out. Bill scribbled down a spending limit, the maximum he felt he should pay: $25,000.

HOW many shoes in all these years? Mike Paramore could not begin to estimate. He had been a blacksmith for twenty years, handling somewhere around a thousand horses a year, some needing four shoes, some two . . . ah, it was just a lot of shoes, that was how many.

An old blacksmith had once told him you only had so many horses in your back. Paramore had always remembered that. He was not necessarily approaching his limit at forty years old, but he was on his way. Twenty years of seven-day weeks, sunup to sundown. Twenty years of bending over and wrestling thousand-pound animals. How many shoes in twenty years? Who could say? The point was that it was a lot, enough hard work for three men, and there had to be payoffs. Rewards.

Sure, life was already good for a working-class kid from Ocala who had become a blacksmith after a hitch in the Army because it beat pumping gas. Paramore had a lake house, a wife and two young boys, and an income bordering on six figures. People were always surprised that a blacksmith could hammer out such a pleasant life, but Paramore was a rarity. Hundreds of blacksmiths had come and gone in Ocala in his time. Paramore had stuck with it. No one had given him a cent, and now look.

One reward was still missing, though; one was still unclaimed. He wanted a horse. A real horse. Not just another cheap turnaround to share for six months with Chuck Wieneke and sell for a profit. A big-time horse. A horse that belonged in New York. Paramore wanted to see his name in the program at Belmont or Aqueduct. That would mean he had made it. His own New York horse. His own little fairy tale. The time had come, too. Paramore finally had enough money in the bank to collect on his dream. He was going to buy a real horse, send it to Belmont, and fly up and watch it run. Rewards.

Paramore planned to bid on E.T. He always bid on the horses he owned with Wieneke—he was adept at the art of "running up" the sale price, bidding on his own horses to fan the notion that it was a horse in demand—but if it so happened that he got caught in the bidding and had to buy E.T., he would not complain. The colt had been in rough shape in December, but no longer. Wieneke had done a magnificent job. There was a lot to like about E.T. Maybe the colt could run in New York. Sure. Stranger things had happened.

JIMMY Gill set up shop in Ocala three days before the sale so that he could study the stock in relative peace. A big, red-faced Irishman from Philadelphia, Gill trained horses for himself and had clients for whom he bought and sold. People called him "The Deacon." At age fifty-five he split his years in half, spending the summers racing a small stable in Philadelphia and the winters looking for horses in Florida. He drove down and back every year, stopping at a North Carolina farm where his favorite horse, a sprinter named Send More Money, was retired.

E.T.'s barn was one of Gill's first stops. He had marked the page in the catalog because the colt was a Pennsylvania-bred. E.T. would be eligible for certain state-bred races back home. Once he saw E.T., he knew he would bid.

"He looked tough, no-nonsense, like he thought he could take on any challenge," Gill said later. Gill marked down $17,000-$19,000 in his book. That was his spending range. He was intending to buy the horse for himself, not a client. He would use his own money. He had to be careful.

AL Jevremovic and his trainer, Mike Trivigno, came up from Miami for the sale. Jevremovic was planning to bid on E.T. Chuck Wieneke had touted the horse to him for months. Once he saw the horse, he was pleased—so pleased he hung around Wieneke's barn all morning, as if he could annex E.T. by proximity.

Finally, he had Trivigno approach Wieneke two hours before the sale. "Chuck, we'll give you $20,000 for him right now," Trivigno said. Wieneke shook his head. No. He had sold plenty of horses for $20,000. He hoped E.T. might sell for more.

Paramore also found a buyer interested for $15,000. "Sorry," Wieneke said, "too low." Paramore shrugged. He was a co-owner, but he deferred to Wieneke on these matters.

"This horse is going to go back to my barn for $20,000," Wieneke told Trivigno, Paramore, and anyone else who asked. Trivigno relayed the news to Jevremovic.

"Well, we'll just have to bid," Jevremovic said.

Later Jevremovic struck up a conversation with a van driver from Pennsylvania.

"Looks like Lil E. Tee turned out OK, huh? After all that trouble?" the driver said.

"What are you talking about?" Jevremovic said.

"Our guy picked him up at New Bolton when we brought him down here," the driver said.

"You got the wrong horse," Jevremovic said.

"I got the right horse," the driver said.

"That's crazy, impossible," Jevremovic said.

"Nope," the driver said, smiling, "this horse flipped his stomach as a yearling."

Jevremovic shook his head. "I don't know anything about that," he said.

E.T. entered the ring in the late afternoon, following a colt named Ed's Whirl that sold for the princely sum of $5,000. On E.T.'s hip was written the number 417. He was big and proud, if a bit gawky.

At the podium were the announcer, John Henderson, and the auctioneer, Ryan Mahan. Henderson began his sales pitch. He mentioned Thirty Zip and Cutter Sam. He mentioned E.T.'s work at OBS and complimented the horse's size and appearance. He paused. It was time to start.

"DoIheartwentyfivetwentyfive?" began Mahan in rapid staccato.

The auctioneer dropped the price until someone jumped in at $3,000. Next came a bid of $4,000, followed quickly by a series of thousand-dollar bumps. Bill Rice, the manager of Triple E Farm in Ocala, was one of the bidders. So was Jimmy Jones, a horseman from Lexington. Paramore bid once. So did Jimmy Gill. They each nodded at a spotter, the spotter raised his hand, and Mahan recorded the bid: "Fivefivefive—doIhavesixsixsix—Ihavesixsixsix—doIhave sevensevenseven?"

The bidding passed $8,000, $10,000, $13,000, then slowed, the bumps suddenly coming in $500 increments. At $15,500, Bill McGreevy bid for the first time, bumping the price to $16,000. There was a brief pause. McGreevy's heart leapt. "Suddenly I thought that was it," he said later. "The guy was begging for $17,000."

It came. Paramore had "bumped," hoping to rebuild the bidding's momentum. Sure enough, the bidding picked back up. McGreevy bid $18,000, Gill $19,000, McGreevy $20,000. Bill Rice was out. So was Jimmy Jones. They did not think the colt was worth more than $20,000.

Paramore jumped back in at $21,000. McGreevy followed at $22,000. McGreevy was getting excited. He turned to his brother Tom. "I think we should go higher," he said. Tom nodded. The bidders all were seated within three rows on the left side of the auditorium. It was just the auction of an obscure horse at a minor sale, but Gill was caught up in the moment. He liked the horse. He liked the fact that other bidders liked the horse. He was a horseman, and a horseman was competitive about the horses that ran in his name. He had planned to spend no more than $19,000, but found himself nodding at his spotter.

"Igottwentythreetwentythree—doIhavetwentyfour twentyfour?"

There was a pause. No new bids. Gill's heart was hammering. Maybe, just maybe.

At the podium, Mahan dropped his auctioning voice, pausing the bidding. He leaned into the microphone and spoke to the crowd in a normal voice. "You're just wrong here, folks," he said. He recounted E.T.'s size and scope, the runners in the pedigree. It was basic salesmanship, part of Mahan's job. He sold thousands of horses a year around the country. It was the rare horse that caught his eye and stayed there. But he had noticed E.T. on the track that morning.

When the bidding reopened, Bill McGreevy quickly bid $24,000. Gill shook his head disappointedly. That was $5,000 above the limit he had set. He could not reconcile going any higher. He was out. There was a hush in the auditorium. Bill McGreevy waited for someone to chime in with a new bid. For a moment he thought the horse was his. Any second now, he expected Mahan to break into the most beautiful music to any bidder's ears: "Going once, going twice..."

But then there was a new bid: Twenty-five!

"Iheartwentyfivetwentyfivetwentyfive—doIheartwentysix twentysixtwentysix?"

The bid came from across the auditorium, in front of the podium, a spot from where there had been no bidding until now. McGreevy was stunned. It was a new bidder. McGreevy looked down at his catalog, at the limit he had scribbled on E.T.'s page: $25,000. Damn. If he bid again, he would surpass his limit. That was not the way he did business. He knew from the foreclosure and dispersal sales he regularly attended back home that a smart bidder was a disciplined bidder. He knew when someone was jumping in just as you were reaching your limit, you had to admit you were out of luck.

"I don't think I can go any higher," McGreevy told Tom. Tom nodded. It was Bill's money. Bill's call. They both liked the horse. But there were still seven hundred left in the sale. Bill did not flinch. He did not signal his spotter. He was out.

Ryan Mahan paused, then counted down. "Going once, going twice..." A final pause. "Sold!"

Al Jevremovic owned a new horse.

5

"He's going to win by a pole!"

In 1693 William Penn wrote that "men generally are more careful about the breeding of their horses . . . than the breeding of their children." There was probably still some truth to that statement in North America fifty years before E.T. was foaled. Racing was a closed society dominated by a small coterie of families such as the Wrights, Woodwards, Whitneys, and Vanderbilts. They owned the fashionable stallions and protected the thoroughbred breed from "common" blood. Horses showing little racing ability or signs of unsoundness simply were not allowed to reproduce. Colts sometimes were gelded. As a result, many of the four thousand foals delivered annually were "blue-blooded."

A revolution of sorts, beginning in the 1950s, forever changed racing and the genetic composition of the thoroughbred breed in North America. The sport increased in popularity after World War II, leading to year-round circuits in traditional racing states and new circuits in others. The increased demand for horses far exceeded what the closed society could produce. Simultaneously, many of the dynasty families lost their control over the sport when the patriarchs died. The closed society suddenly was opened wide, accepting new breeders, owners, and stallions. The sport of kings became a sport for serfs, too.

The size of the North American foal crop quintupled between 1950 and 1985, from nine thousand to more than fifty thousand. Naturally, the overall quality decreased. A huge equine underclass was spawned. It was inevitable that a horse would emerge from this underclass to win the Kentucky Derby. Through the '50s, the typical Derby winner was still a reflection of the sport as it was in those days, a silver-spoon homebred from Calumet Farm, Belair Stud, or one of the other top stables. But the new class of dead-end kids was growing, and it produced its first hero when Carry Back won the Kentucky Derby in 1961.

Carry Back was owned by a former racetracker named Jack Price. When the owner of a mare boarding at Price's farm in Ohio could not pay a $150 bill, he gave Price the mare, named Joppy. Price shipped Joppy and two mares to Florida but had them stop at Country Life Farm in Maryland and breed to an old sire named Saggy. Price struck a deal, buying three seasons to the $500 stud for $1,200. The other two mares produced horses that never won races. Joppy's foal was Carry Back.

Eight years after Carry Back's victory, a yearling with a crooked right foreleg was sold for $1,200 at Keeneland, shipped to Venezuela, and named Canonero II. Though he did not win a major stakes race in Venezuela as a three-year-old, his owners chose to run him in the Kentucky Derby. The trip from South America was calamitous. Twice the plane left Caracas, developed engine trouble, and returned for repairs. Upon finally making it to Miami, Canonero II spent four days in a quarantine facility, where he could not exercise. Then he made the eleven-hundred-mile trip to Louisville in a van. He arrived a few days before the race, galloped once or twice, and won the Derby.

Twelve years later, the son of a $5,000 sire named Buckaroo was bought privately for $12,500 as a yearling. Turned down for an OBS selected yearling sale due to poor conformation, he developed into a top runner and was loaded into the Derby starting gate with sons of such Keeneland-caliber stallions as Danzig, Graustark, and Mr. Prospector. Buckaroo's son, Spend a Buck, led all the way around the track and won by more than five lengths.

E.T. was foaled four years later. He probably would not have been allowed to exist when the closed society ruled racing. His sire, At The Threshold, might have become a stallion after running third in the Kentucky Derby, but his untalented dam, Eileen's Moment, probably would not have become a broodmare. Yet by the time he was foaled, it was understood that a Derby winner could come from the underclass. Such victories, though still rare and always surprising, were not regarded as impossible. Thus, though it was unthinkable that E.T. could become a Derby contender, much less a winner, there was this caveat to consider: the unthinkable had happened before.

AL Jevremovic fell in love with racing as a child in Belgrade, Yugoslavia, where racing was a Sunday social occasion. A doctor's son, he was enthralled by the sounds and smells and colors, the speed of the horses, the shouts of men. His family left Yugoslavia in 1944, spent six years in France, and came to the United States, where his father set up a medical practice in Ohio. Jevremovic served in the Korean War and started in the restaurant business upon his return. He never strayed far from the racetrack, trading a few cheap horses and hustling a jockey's book now and then.

At twenty-seven years old, he bought a coffee shop in Miami, sold it for a profit, and used the money to buy another place, which he also turned around and sold at a profit. In 1970 he took on a partner who turned around small hotels much as Jevremovic turned around restaurants. They wound up owning a string of small hotels on the East Coast. By the 1980s, Jevremovic was better able to indulge his longstanding love for racing. He bought horses that ran in allowance and claiming races at Penn National, Delaware Park, Finger Lakes, and other small tracks. When he moved to Fort Lauderdale in 1988, he covered his office walls with his many winner's circle pictures.

Over the years he bought and sold horses using the same principle with which he bought and sold hotels: never fall in love with a property. He usually paid between $10,000 and $25,000 for a horse, raised the horse's value with a victory or two, then sold the horse and used the money to buy another. He always sold, no matter how well a horse ran. He could not afford those of higher caliber, and racing cheap horses was a money-losing proposition.

"Carrying a horse at a smaller track is suicidal," he said later. "Even if you win, you can't make enough money to keep up with the costs of owning the horse. This sport is for the rich. The only way for a guy like me to stay involved is to sell for profit."

He had paid $45,000 for a horse the year before he bought E.T., but that was an extreme exception. He rarely spent more than $25,000, and usually less than $20,000. In the sale in which he bought E.T., he also bought five other horses, spending a total of $32,500, or an average of $6,500 per horse. E.T. cost considerably more, but the horse clearly had potential and Chuck Wieneke had always delivered before.

A solid, deliberate sixty-year-old, with gray hair, gold-rimmed glasses, a droopy gray mustache, and a rumbling voice still echoing of Eastern Europe, Jevremovic had sensed his opportunity when the bidding stalled at $24,000 and the auditorium fell silent. His plan, as always, had been to wait for the silence. That was how he operated. He rarely bid, avoiding getting involved in bidding wars. You tended to overpay when you got caught in those. Better to let the others fight it out, then surprise them at the end.

As Bill McGreevy, Jimmy Gill, and Mike Paramore drove up the price on E.T., Jevremovic sat in the middle of the front row of the auditorium, the worst possible vantage point. He did not bid, not even once to get his juices flowing. He was blind to the personality and psychology of the bidding and had no idea who was involved or how often they had bid. He just sensed that the moment was right at $24,000. The price was fair. E.T. was not worth much more or less. Up went his right hand. This was it, he told himself. Just this one bid. It already was more than he wanted to spend. Whoever topped him could have the horse.

The strategy worked. Bill McGreevy, the only other bidder left, was intimidated. Jevremovic bought E.T. with one bid. Tom McGreevy walked outside and ran across Mike Trivigno, Jevremovic's trainer. They knew each other from their days as rivals at Penn National.

"We just got that Pennsylvania-bred," Trivigno said.

McGreevy blinked. "I didn't know you guys were bidding," he said. "That was us. We were the underbidders."

Trivigno laughed. He shook his head. "One more bid and the horse was yours," Trivigno said.

"What do you mean?" McGreevy asked.

"The man said he wasn't going higher than $25,000," Trivigno said.

McGreevy congratulated Trivigno, went back inside, and gave his brother the bad news: they had fallen one bid short. Bill, already disappointed, felt even worse. He had wanted the horse. For a moment, he thought he had bought the horse. He did not remain upset for long, though. The next day he bought an Unreal Zeal filly, named Unquote, for $21,000. He returned to Illinois having forgotten the dark bay colt he had so narrowly lost.

Jevremovic was pleased to add E.T. to his stable, but he could not help laughing. This was not his finest hour as a businessman. He could have bought E.T. for $3,000 when Wieneke called in December offering to go partners but instead had spent $25,000 four months later.

"I'm sorry, Al," Wieneke said when Jevremovic met him at the barn after the sale.

"Why, Chuck?" Jevremovic said. "Why say such a thing?"

"Because you could have had the horse for $3,000," Wieneke said.

Jevremovic smiled. "It's OK, Chuck," he said. "I love the horse. I'm just glad I got him."

A post-purchase exam by a veterinarian was required to finalize the sale. Jevremovic had three days to give the horse back if there was a problem.

The vet came by the barn shortly after the bidding, spent twenty minutes examining E.T., and announced that the colt was "1 percent paralyzed." Wieneke and Jevremovic were stunned. A horse was "paralyzed" if its larynx did not operate properly, usually because of a degeneration of the nerve that supplied the muscles there. Horses with such a problem tended to make whistling or roaring sounds when exercising. For some it was irrelevant, for others problematic. The condition was relatively common, but neither Wieneke nor Jevremovic had heard of a horse being 1 percent paralyzed; they were either fully paralyzed or not at all.

"What are you telling us?" Wieneke asked.

"You could run into trouble some day," the vet said.

Wieneke turned to Jevremovic. "If this horse turns up paralyzed six months from now, you can come to my farm and pick out any two-year-old and it's yours for free," he said.

Jevremovic smiled. He was not worried. "I don't think it'll come to that, Chuck," he said. "I think the horse will be fine."

HAD Bill McGreevy bought E.T., the colt would have gone to McGreevy's brother, Jim, a thoroughbred trainer based at the Fair Hill Training Center in Maryland. E.T. probably would have begun his racing career at Delaware Park or Penn National. Had Jimmy Gill won the bidding, the colt probably would have started around Philadelphia. Because he was bought by Jevremovic, E.T. went downstate from Ocala to barn sixty-two on the backside at Calder Race Course, where Trivigno was stabled.

The plan was to give E.T. a couple of races at Calder in the summer and early fall, then ship him north for the Pennsylvania Futurity in early December. Jevremovic quickly discovered that the deadline for nominations to the Futurity had passed, however, and a $5,000 supplemental nomination fee made no sense for a $50,000 race. It was disappointing. But the original plan of getting E.T. to the races by July was unchanged. The colt would train through May and June, go to school in the starting gate, stretch out his works to five-eighths and three-quarters of a mile, then begin racing. There was never a problem finding a two-year-old race at Calder, which was a hotbed for two-year-olds.

At first, Trivigno was not so thrilled to have E.T. in the barn. He was "just a horse," Trivigno thought, nothing special. If someone other than Wieneke had been the seller, Trivigno would not have recommended buying him. He had that odd way of traveling, with his head held high. But Trivigno recognized that Wieneke had a knack, so maybe it was worth taking a shot.

Six days a week in the warm humid mornings at Calder, E.T. gradually built his endurance, jogging a mile and galloping a mile. On the seventh day he breezed, starting at three-eighths of a mile in May and building to five-eighths by early July. He worked out with Majic Fountain, another two-year-old Jevremovic had purchased from Wieneke. Majic Fountain often beat E.T. in their short sprints. Trivigno knew that should not happen—E.T. clearly was the better horse—but E.T.'s high-headedness prevented him from achieving the compact, economical style common to most top horses. Trivigno wondered if he would benefit from a shadow roll, a fleece-filled roll laid across the bridge of the nose. Horses tended to lower their heads to see over the obstruction. If E.T. lowered his head, his stride might level out.

"Everything bad about the way the horse moved was connected to his head being up in the air," Trivigno said later. "When the horse ran through the field as a yearling, he looked like he was climbing because his neck was stretched up in the air like a giraffe, and you can't run that way. That's why so many [bloodstock agents] didn't like him. They weren't wrong. But there are things a trainer can do to correct the problem."

A lifelong racetracker, Trivigno had grown up in New Jersey and worked in the Midwest and Northeast, and now was running a public stable in Florida. He had had success as the private trainer for Hillview Farm in the 1970s, but now most of his clients developed and sold younger horses. Trivigno knew what Jevremovic wanted him to accomplish with E.T.: get the colt to the races and win one or two. Jevremovic would sell at that point. Trivigno knew it. Even if E.T. was a star, Jevremovic would sell. He always sold.

While he contemplated putting a shadow roll on E.T., Trivigno had the colt schooled in the starting gate. E.T. was led back and forth through the gate to get accustomed to it, loaded into it with the doors closed, jogged out, and galloped out. E.T. was a willing student, neither skittish nor contrary. By July it was time for the last step of his ten-month journey from an unbroken colt at Batcha Farm in New Jersey to a race-ready thoroughbred at Calder: learning to break from the gate with other horses as the starting bell sounded. One morning E.T. was loaded into a stall with a young Panamanian rider, Tommy Brown, aboard. Brown was not a top rider, but Trivigno occasionally used him for races and often for morning workouts. Brown was planning to return to Panama at the end of the year, but before that Trivigno was going to use him for E.T.'s first race. When the bell sounded and the gate opened, Brown gave the reins a hard tug. Watching from the apron with Jevremovic, Trivigno frowned. "Rider's error," he recalled later. "Tommy was going to get the horse out of the gate without a problem, but he really sent him, pulled on the reins and sent the horse's head back and into the air."

The gate was in the chute behind the first turn. E.T. bolted out with his neck arched high and galloped frantically down the chute toward the point where it merged with the regular oval. "When he got to the [merger point] the horse was kind of confused at where he was," Trivigno said later.

Instead of easing down to the rail once he made the oval, E.T. made a sharp left turn and headed straight for the rail—and disaster. "His head was up so high that he couldn't see the rail," Trivigno said. "He was looking up at the sky."

The colt approached the rail and, panicking once he saw it in front of him, halted suddenly, just before he crashed. The force of the braking action sent Brown somersaulting out of the saddle and over E.T.'s head. The jockey crashed into the rail and fell to the ground, his legs bent awkwardly beneath him. He began to wail.

Activity immediately halted on the track. Trivigno and Jevremovic leaped over the outside rail and crossed the racing strip to get to Brown. Calder officials and a group of jockeys joined them. A call went out for paramedics, who arrived and, after spending fifteen minutes deciding how to move the injured jockey, loaded him into an ambulance and drove to the hospital.

"Why did I buy this horse?" Jevremovic moaned as the ambulance drove off.

"Aw, it's just something that happened, Al," Trivigno said.

E.T. was taken back to the barn, seemingly unharmed. "If he had not stopped short, he would have banged into the rail, hit it with his forearms, and probably rolled over the top like Tommy," Trivigno said later. "There's a concrete base under the rail. It could have been the end of him."

The word from the hospital was bad: Tommy Brown had broken both legs. He would be out at least six months. His career was in jeopardy. The only damage E.T. suffered was a slight tendon pull at the bottom of his left foreleg. He was given a month off from training.

E.T. wore a shadow roll when he resumed training in August. His head dropped, his stride leveled, and he began beating Majic Fountain in their morning duels. Either the roll or the month off had served him well.

"It wasn't by choice that we took our time, although we don't rush our babies," Trivigno said later. "But the accident changed everything. The horse probably would have won [a race] a lot sooner, and maybe [Jevremovic] would have decided to keep him. I've often wondered about that."

The colt was training sharply, working three-eighths in :35 and five-eighths in 1:01⅗. His reputation spread across the backside. Trivigno had several exercise riders to choose from every day. He began using Gene St. Leon, who had won an Eclipse Award as the nation's top apprentice in 1971 and gone on to win several thousand races, mostly in Florida. Now thirty-seven years old, he was coming back from a layoff and looking for mounts. Jevremovic ran into him one day and suggested he go by Trivigno's barn. Trivigno gave him a couple of mounts. Pretty soon he was on most of Trivigno's horses.

"St. Leon was a knowledgeable rider and certainly good in his day," Trivigno said later. "I was comfortable with him." St. Leon was happy for the steady stream of work, but particularly happy about riding E.T.

"I asked Mike if I could get on him," St. Leon explained. "All the boys in the shed wanted to. You couldn't help liking him. He was fun to get on, one of those horses you looked forward to getting on when you woke up. From the first time I got on him I thought he was special. He was very good on his feet, very in tune with his body. Always willing. Basically, I was slowing him down in his training, making sure he was doing the right things as far as switching leads more than asking for speed. Speed was never a problem. You could tell he had the gas to go."

St. Leon got the mount when Trivigno entered E.T. in a six-furlong maiden special race at Calder on September 28. The race quickly gained extra attention around the track. Several of the more promising two-year-olds on the grounds were entered. It would be more than just the fourth race on another weekday afternoon. Among those entered were colts named Bruce's Folly and Scream Machine, each of which had recorded fast training times and had run well in his first start. Sir Pinder, a grandson of Nijinsky II, was giving his owners big ideas. Grand Bay was trained by Cam Gambolati, the trainer of Spend a Buck; Gambolati was high on him, everyone said. There also was a gelding named Ima Big Leaguer, which had turned in several bullet works since arriving from the owner's farm in Ocala six weeks earlier; the horse's trainer, David Braddy, had said, "All I know is it's going to take a running S.O.B. to beat him."

Trivigno blew out E.T. four days before the race: a half-mile in :49 and change. After that, the colt walked a day, galloped for two, then walked again on the morning of the race.

Eight thousand fans gathered at Calder that afternoon and made Bruce's Folly a big favorite at 9-to-10, followed by E.T. at 4-to-1. Way Above and Ima Big Leaguer were at 9-1. Ten horses were entered. When the gate opened, Bruce's Folly broke outward, dropped to fifth and never contended. Way Above and Scream Machine moved in front, followed by Ima Big Leaguer and E.T. The horses sprinted up the backstretch and into the turn, covering the quarter-mile in :21³/₅, the half in a blazing :45¹/₅.

When Way Above and Scream Machine faded in the turn, Ima Big Leaguer zoomed by, followed by E.T. Once he had the lead, Ima Big Leaguer seemed intent on fulfilling the promise of those fast workouts he had recorded. He took a three-length lead. E.T. was second best, distantly, coming down the lane.

"You could tell it was his first day at the races," St. Leon said later. "He was like a kid going to school for the first time. His head was up in the air and he was looking around, taking in the sights. It wasn't that he was distracted so much as his mind wasn't totally on racing."

Ima Big Leaguer was pulling away at the wire. The winning margin was four-and-a-half lengths, and the time of 1:11²/₅ announced the arrival of a star. No two-year-old had run a faster six-furlong race at Calder that year.

"Caught a fast one," St. Leon said to Trivigno as he dismounted.

"Not too bad," Trivigno said.

"But we'll never lose to that horse again," St. Leon said.

"What do you mean?" Trivigno asked.

"We were just getting our feet wet," St. Leon said. "We've got a lot more horse than they do."

HALFWAY across the country, in Magnolia, Arkansas, the telephone rang in the one-story wood-framed offices of the Partee Flooring Mill. It was ten o'clock in the morning, two days after Ima Big Leaguer and E.T. had raced at Calder. Dr. Edward "Pug" Hart, the owner of Hart Farm, a breeding and training farm near Ocala, was phoning for Cal Partee, the eighty-two-year-old owner of the flooring mill.

Partee's secretary announced the call to her boss. Sloop-shouldered, with a gentle manner, a receding tuft of white hair, and a soft, almost unintelligible voice, Partee picked up the phone, smiling. "You got a two-year-old for me?" he asked with mock bluster. That was how he often greeted Hart, one of a group of friends and horsemen around the country who phoned from time to time to tell him about a horse he might want to buy.

"Well," Hart said, "I just might this time."

"I'm listening," Partee said.

"A colt," Hart said. "Ran huge at Calder the other day. Name is Ima Big Leaguer."

Hart had not seen the race. Tending two hundred head at Hart Farm left him no time for the races. But he read the *Daily Racing Form* every day, and his instincts still were sharp after more than twenty years as a veterinarian. Not that it took a genius to divine the existence of genuine talent in Ima Big Leaguer's race. It was quite a performance on Calder's slow racing strip. Hart knew he had to call Magnolia once he saw the time.

Cal Partee had made his fortune in lumber and oil, and loved to spend money on fast horses. He was among the dwindling population of old-fashioned racing sportsmen, in the game as much for love as for profit, and forever in search of a talented young runner. "Ever since I've known him," said Dan Lasater, one of the nation's top owners in the 1970s, "Cal has had a reputation of not being afraid to pay for what he thought was a quality racehorse."

A fixture at Oaklawn Park and Churchill Downs, Partee had owned horses for thirty-seven years, winning the Arkansas Derby, Illinois Derby, Jim Beam Stakes, Louisiana Derby, and numerous smaller stakes. Although he had downsized his stable after two hip replacements, back surgery, and a heart by-pass operation, he was still playing, still looking for a runner.

"I couldn't do anything more to make his day than to call him and tell him about a nice two-year-old he might be able to buy," said Lynn

Whiting, who had trained Partee's horses since 1978. Partee told Hart to give the horse's name to Whiting, who handled Partee's buying.

The day after Hart called him, Partee received another call from Ocala touting Ima Big Leaguer. Brent Fernung had met Partee while rubbing horses in Kentucky years earlier. Fernung knew Ima Big Leaguer's owner, Harold Kitchen, a breeder in Ocala. "Mr. Kitchen has a real good horse he might be willing to sell," Fernung told Partee.

Meanwhile, Whiting went to work after hearing from Pug Hart. He phoned Ima Big Leaguer's trainer, David Braddy, who was handling the sale for Kitchen, and ascertained that the horse's price was $200,000. Partee thought the price reasonable enough, but suggested that Hart call Kitchen—fellow Ocalans, they were friends—and get the scoop. Hart called Kitchen, who, while touting the horse's natural speed and potential, unloaded a surprise.

"Of course, he's a gelding," Kitchen said.

"Not a colt?" Hart asked, an alarm sounding in his head.

"He is not a colt," Kitchen said.

Hart knew instantly that the deal was off. Though able to handle losses in his racing stable, Partee tried to operate it intelligently, and he felt that investing in a gelding was unwise. Without the potential for residual value as a stallion, a horse had to make a profit on the racetrack. Few did. Sure enough, Partee quickly cooled on the idea of buying Ima Big Leaguer.

During this time Brent Fernung had been negotiating with Braddy on his own, as Partee's agent, offering $150,000, then $175,000. But Kitchen wanted $200,000. Once Partee waffled, Kitchen raised the price to $225,000 and offered Partee half; all along he had mostly wanted a partner, anyway. But Partee never took on a partner. Partee was not going to get his runner, at least not this one.

Then Whiting noticed a small detail on the chart of the race printed in the *Racing Times*. He called Partee.

"The horse that finished second to Ima Big Leaguer? Lil E. Tee?" Whiting said.

"Yeah?" Partee said.

"He's by At The Threshold," Whiting said. Partee still owned At The Threshold, now a sire.

"Is that right?" Partee asked.

EVERY track is an open-air bazaar, but Calder is a particularly active marketplace in the fall. The high caliber of the two-year-olds attracts bloodstock agents, pinhookers, brokers, breeders, and potential buyers and sellers, some scouting for themselves, others for trainers and owners around the country. The track is a virtual bulletin board of opinions. Which are the best two-year-olds? Which are for sale? At what price? Which owners will negotiate? Which are the best buys?

The prevailing opinion in the marketplace after Ima Big Leaguer's win was that he was Calder's best two-year-old. But that opinion was not unanimously held. Some observers were more impressed with E.T.'s larger frame and stride. "I felt E.T. was the better horse; I didn't like Ima Big Leaguer at all," said Roy Cohen, an owner who raced horses in Florida and Kentucky. "E.T. was real green, just a big, gawky horse, but you could see there was all sorts of room for improvement. He just looked like a horse that would go on."

Cohen had run a company that operated a ski resort in Vermont before retiring to Florida. He attended the races at Calder every day and kept extensive notes. He had a keen eye, and it was taken with E.T. He approached Jevremovic about buying the horse. Jevremovic agreed to let Cohen's veterinarian, Dr. Robert O'Neil, examine the colt. O'Neil examined and x-rayed E.T, and his report was a stunner: E.T. had sore shins and abnormal calcification in the feet. O'Neil recommended Cohen not buy the colt. He was concerned about E.T.'s physical soundness; the colt might not have a long racing career. Cohen went ahead and offered Jevremovic $75,000 for E.T. Certain that the horse was worth more, Jevremovic declined.

Several nights later Cohen received a call from Lynn Whiting, who, having failed to buy Ima Big Leaguer, was turning to Plan B.

"What do you know about Lil E. Tee?" Whiting asked. Whiting and Cohen had met through mutual friends. Whiting respected Cohen's opinion and occasionally used him as a talent scout in Florida.

"Lil E. Tee is a nice horse," Cohen said. "I like him better than Ima Big Leaguer. But he didn't vet out well at all."

Whiting asked Cohen to watch E.T. work out at Calder and file a scouting report. "Mr. Partee likes the idea of buying an At The Threshold colt," Whiting said. "I need to see if I'm going to have to come down there."

Cohen said he would happily perform the favor. He spent most of his mornings at Calder anyway. For two days he studied E.T. in the morning at Calder, watching the colt gallop and cool out. He liked what he saw.

"People liked the horse on the track," Cohen said later. "But the question was whether he was going to last."

JEVREMOVIC and Trivigno entered E.T. in a second race, eight days after the first.

"Sometimes I like to bring them back fast if they come out of a race good," Trivigno said later. "It puts them on their edge. E.T.'s first race wasn't much more than a workout anyway. He didn't put out too much coming down the lane."

Whiting saw that E.T.'s name was in the entries again and called Cohen in Florida. "Watch the race for me and tell me what you see."

"No problem," Cohen said.

E.T.'s second race was seven furlongs. The field was not nearly as strong as in his first race. "We were pretty sure we could win," Trivigno said later. So were the fans, who bet E.T. down to 4-to-5.

No one expected E.T. to win in the fashion he did, however. Breaking from the seventh hole, he immediately fought for the lead, running behind Scream Machine and a head in front of a longshot named It's Joseph. Racing together, they covered a quarter in :22⁴/₅, a half in :46.

"I was just sitting," St. Leon said later. "At the turn I chirped at him, and he switched leads, went through a hole, and took off."

Ten months earlier E.T. had been scrawny, hairy, and snubbed by bloodstock agents. But in the stretch run at Calder on October 6, 1991, in front of eight thousand fans on a warm, sunny afternoon, he offered vivid proof of his startling turnaround. Scream Machine and It's Joseph quickly fell away as E.T. took the lead and accelerated in the turn. Soon he was alone as he came down the lane, his lead expanding to three lengths, five, seven, then too many to count.

"He's going to win by a pole!" the track announcer shouted as E.T. thundered toward the finish line, all alone. He was so far in front at the end that the track cameraman became confused and focused on the horses racing for second. The *Daily Racing Form* race charter assessed the winning margin as eleven-and-a-half lengths. St. Leon thought that was conservative. "I remember looking back not too far after the wire, and he was a good eighth of a mile ahead," the jockey said. "He completely crucified the field."

The winning time of 1:24²/₅ was the fastest seven-furlong time of the Calder meeting for a two-year-old. "It's almost impossible for a horse to go that fast in his second start, especially at Calder," said Philip Werkmeister, a South Florida bloodstock agent.

After posing in the winner's circle, Jevremovic walked with St. Leon toward the jockeys' room.

"I think offers are gonna be coming," St. Leon said.

"I think you're right," Jevremovic said.

"I wish you wouldn't sell him too fast," St. Leon said. The jockey smelled wins—and money.

"If I had the money, I'd buy half myself," St. Leon said.

BRENT Fernung watched E.T. win on the big screen TV at OBS, which simulcast the races at Calder. He found a pay phone and called Lynn Whiting.

"We're on the wrong horse," he said, still thinking Partee wanted to buy Ima Big Leaguer. "The horse that ran second in that race is a much better horse. He just ran huge at Calder a minute ago."

Whiting paused. "Brent," he said, "we're already on him."

AS soon as E.T. was headed back to the barn, Trivigno hustled back to the paddock. E.T.'s training partner, Majic Fountain, was entered in the next race, a seven-furlong allowance for two-year-olds. The field was small, only five horses, but among them was Pistols and Roses, which would develop into the top young horse in Florida that winter.

Majic Fountain sprinted to an early lead along the rail, remained a head in front when Pistols and Roses challenged on the turn, and kept the lead down the stretch. The winning margin was a length. Jevremovic headed back to the winner's circle, ecstatic at the back-to-back victories. There was no doubting which horse was better, though. E.T.'s time was two and two-fifths seconds faster. In fact, E.T.'s time was one-fifth faster than the winning time in the Banyan Handicap, a $50,000-added race for older horses held later that afternoon.

Roy Cohen sought out Jevremovic in the stands after Majic Fountain's race. "He's a nice horse," Cohen said.

"Thank you, I think so," Jevremovic said. Both knew the one to which Cohen was referring.

"I just want to make sure that he is for sale," Cohen said. "I know someone who might be interested."

Jevremovic smiled. "Yes," he said, "the horse is for sale."

That night Cohen called Whiting with a scouting report. "He's a good horse, he can run," Cohen said, "and the guy is a seller."

JEVREMOVIC was indeed a seller. The success of his hotel business depended on selling, on knowing when a buyer was hooked or a property was ready for turning. The art of selling a horse borrowed heavily from those principles. You sold when the market was hot, after a big win, before the inevitable losses doused the embers of optimism.

As soon as E.T. crossed the finish line, Jevremovic knew the time was right. His conversation with Cohen in the grandstand only validated his opinion. A performance that impressive would have owners lining up to buy the horse. Sure, it was only one maiden race, but there were always owners seeking a horse with such proven talent. Jevremovic would listen happily to their pitches. He had never felt the sentimental yearning to own a classic horse, not if the horse could be sold for a high price. He was too pragmatic. It cost thousands of dollars to campaign a top horse.

Only one question still needed answering: what was the right price? Jevremovic had sold Wonkie's Best for $150,000, and E.T. was of a higher caliber. Ima Big Leaguer was selling for $225,000. The figure that popped into Jevremovic's head was $200,000—maybe too high for a maiden, but maybe not. As he drove home from Calder that evening, Jevremovic decided to set the price at $200,000 and not budge. He was a small-time owner, but he was a successful businessmen, and this was basically just another business transaction. Jevremovic smiled. This was going to be fun.

That night he called Werkmeister, the bloodstock agent who had sold Wonkie's Best and several other horses for Jevremovic. Werkmeister had a book of clients and could ascertain the level of interest within hours. "I wouldn't bother you with a horse that is just a horse," Jevremovic told him.

Werkmeister had not seen the race, but he knew E.T. was for real when he heard the winning time. He immediately called Bobby Frankel, the top California trainer who had bought Wonkie's Best and several other horses from Werkmeister. Werkmeister knew that one of the top owners in Frankel's stable was looking for a two-year-old.

Frankel listened to Werkmeister describe the horse and the race. "I'll take him," Frankel said. That was that. No haggling, no trouble, nothing. The buyer was there, the price was right. Of course, Frankel was not going to buy E.T. without investigating the horse's soundness and background. "I've got too much going on to take a trip there," Frankel told Werkmeister. "I can't come unless I'm sure we want him. Get some-one to check him out."

It was a common practice on a major out-of-town purchase: a local horseman would eyeball the horse for the potential buyer, performing a preliminary check of sorts. If the report was favorable, a veterinarian would perform a more extensive exam. If all went well, the buyer's trainer would fly in to close the deal, sometimes with the buyer along.

Werkmeister selected David Vivian as Frankel's Florida eyes. Vivian was a respected horseman whose opinion Frankel would trust. Vivian went to Calder the next morning. He watched E.T. gallop, come back to the barn, and cool out. He was not impressed. "He was a great big, awkward-going thing," Vivian said later. "I didn't like him."

Trivigno explained, "David didn't like the way the horse carried his head, way up in the air. Naturally, David was made to look like a fool in that situation, but he wasn't totally wrong. The horse did carry himself funny."

What really discouraged Vivian was a swollen area behind E.T.'s left front ankle, between the fetlock and back of the foot. It appeared to Vivian that E.T. was carrying the pressure of his weight in his pastern, resulting in soreness and swelling. "You could see the problem from ten yards away," Vivian said later. "You didn't have to be a scientist to see it."

Vivian had seen such an injury numerous times. Sometimes it proved irrelevant, sometimes not. This looked bad. And $200,000 was too much to gamble, he thought, particularly on a high-headed colt.

"I don't think the horse is sound," Vivian said when he called Werkmeister, "and I don't think the horse will stay sound."

Werkmeister called Bobby Frankel with the negative report. "We'll have to pass," Frankel said.

Werkmeister called Jevremovic with the news. It had been twenty-four hours since E.T.'s race. Werkmeister did indeed work fast. "Vivian didn't like the horse," Werkmeister said.

"I'm sorry he didn't," Jevremovic said. "He never saw the horse go."

Jevremovic was disappointed but also encouraged that his price had been met and still confident that others would show interest. Sure enough, Arnold Winick, a successful trainer for years in Chicago and Florida, called with an offer the next day. He had seen E.T.'s race. "He was a big, grand-looking horse," Winick said later, "and I thought he had great potential." The offer was $150,000. Jevremovic turned it down.

"Please don't offer me one-fifty," Jevremovic said. "You bring me a horse like Lil E. Tee that wins in 1:24 and 2, and I will pay one-fifty. So don't offer me one-fifty."

Winick said he was taking a trip to California, where his son, Randy, was a trainer, and would check with Jevremovic when he returned, in case the horse was still available. Jevremovic said that was fine.

Two more calls followed. One was from Don Brauer, a Florida bloodstock agent. The other was from Lynn Whiting, who inquired about the price and asked to have E.T. vetted out. Brauer was brokering for the Clover Racing Stable, a California-based syndicate operation headed by a former journalist, Barry Irwin, and a handicapper, Jeff Siegel. They formed groups of investors for whom they bought, sold, and campaigned horses, and in three years had hustled their way to national prominence. Brauer had sold close to a half-dozen horses to them. Ironically, he also had sold several to Whiting and Partee. But he was working for Clover now.

Brauer had originally touted Ima Big Leaguer to Irwin and Siegel and sent them a tape of the gelding's winning race. Irwin and Siegel made Harold Kitchen an offer without even seeing the tape. Kitchen turned them down, and they were relieved once they saw the tape. They, too, thought E.T. was the superior horse.

When E.T. won eight days later, Irwin told Brauer to investigate buying the horse on Clover's behalf. When Jevremovic told Brauer the price was $200,000, period, take it or leave it, Irwin and Siegel agreed to take it. "We really wanted the horse," Siegel said later.

They also did not have time to come to Florida unless they were sure they were going to buy the horse. They asked Jevremovic to sign a preliminary agreement giving them time to investigate E.T. and also the first option to buy for a week. The agreement stipulated that Clover would retain the option for a week as soon as, first, E.T. was vetted out; second, Irwin and Siegel saw a tape of E.T.'s second race and; and, third, they put down a nonrefundable $10,000 deposit by October 18.

Jevremovic signed a copy of the agreement. Clover had the advantage now. But then the vet Clover hired to examine the colt at Calder became the third horseman to advise against buying E.T.

"What he had on his shins was more than a bucked shin," Irwin explained. It wasn't a fracture, but somewhere between bucked shins and a fracture. There was a lot of profile on it. A buildup of calcium."

No one doubted that E.T. could run. But a lot of smart horsemen were wondering if he would run for long.

IN Kentucky, where he was based at Churchill Downs, Lynn Whiting was performing his own background check on E.T.—and already angling for the horse. Dr. George Burch, an old friend of Whiting's, who had performed prepurchase exams for Whiting for two decades, vetted out E.T. at Calder. Burch's report was more encouraging than those of the other vets.

"He's a big, good-looking, strong, powerful horse," Burch told Whiting on the phone. "He's got a few problems, he's a little dehydrated, and his hair coat isn't perfect. But he's my kind of horse, Lynnie. Rangy and full of scope. There's lots of room for improvement."

Burch had seen the same potential problems as the other vets. But vets have different experiences with injuries and hold varied views of their potential for harm. And, of course, x-rays taken at different angles can produce pictures that lead to different opinions.

"At the very least," Burch told Whiting, "I think you owe it to yourself to come down here and take a look." Whiting booked a seat on a flight to Florida for the coming Sunday, unaware that Clover would have the option to buy E.T. for five days after that.

Steve Morguelan, a fellow trainer and close friend of Whiting's, was also interested in E.T. An agent had sent him a tape of E.T.'s win. Impressed, Morguelan made plans to fly to Florida with a prospective buyer. Seeking more information about the horse, and knowing that Whiting usually had a grasp of the two-year-old market, Morguelan approached his friend.

"What do you know about a horse named Lil E. Tee?" Morguelan asked. "I think I'm going down to see him."

"Well," Whiting said, "as a matter of fact, I'm going down to look at him, too." They laughed. They did not want to compete for a horse. Whiting's plane reservations were a day earlier. Morguelan decided to back off, mostly in deference to Partee.

"Cancel the reservations," Morguelan told his prospective buyer. "Lynn and Mr. Partee are the logical buyers for the horse. Mr. Partee is a sportsman who has spent his money and raced for years. He had At The

Threshold. If they like the horse, they're going to buy it. And if they see a red flag, I probably would, too."

The next day Morguelan brought his tape of E.T.'s race to his barn and invited Whiting over to watch it. "If you don't like the horse, let me know," Morguelan said.

BRENT Fernung called Jevremovic about E.T., attempting to broker a deal on Partee's behalf, much as he had on Ima Big Leaguer. "I can do it, but the most I can get to you [after a commission] is one-fifty," Fernung said.

Jevremovic blew up. "Listen," he said, "don't call me. Don't bother me. He's not for sale for one-fifty. It's $200,000 to me, take it or leave it."

WHITING flew to Miami and came to Trivigno's barn at Calder the next morning. Gene St. Leon knew what Whiting's presence meant. "How much?" St. Leon asked.

"Two hundred, they say," Whiting said.

St. Leon clucked his tongue. "I wish I had a hundred," the jockey said. "I'd buy half right now."

Silently, deep in concentration, Whiting watched E.T. gallop and cool out, then came back the next day and watched again. Jevremovic was impressed. "Lynn did everything but sleep with the horse," Jevremovic said later. "He was incredibly thorough. Did it the right way. I told him that if I ever was going to spend a lot of money on a horse I'd love to send him."

Whiting was known for his thoroughness. He also understood, as did any top trainer, that the ability to buy the right horses is an essential skill. Champion horses are born, not trained. A top trainer knows how to develop and campaign a talented horse, but the talent must exist first. A horse of average ability could not improve just by practicing hard, as human athletes do. Racing does not work that way. Even the best trainers could not create the native talent common to all thoroughbred stars. Training is, thus, a defensive job in nature; the task is to protect and emphasize talent, not to create it. It is imperative that a trainer be able to spot potential and know when to gamble. Of course, every possible purchase is a gamble; horses always have injuries, ailments, and flaws that cause concern. Knowing when the odds are in your favor is the secret to buying the right horse.

E.T. was a particularly confounding case, even for a trainer as wise and experienced as Whiting. There was much about the horse to like, but also reason to wonder if he was worth the money. Basically, Whiting liked what he saw. His instincts told him to spend the $200,000. As Whiting said later, "He was a big, solid, two-year-old colt. He had a nice head, a lot of scope, good quarters, nice shoulders. There was a lot of horse, but he wasn't gross. Not a big, heavy kind of horse. I defined him in human terms as a basketball player. He was big but had some life to him."

Helping color Whiting's favorable opinion was the fact that he had trained At The Threshold; Partee still owned the horse at stud. E.T. did not closely resemble At The Threshold—"E.T. was bigger, had a nicer head, and was a lot more physical," Whiting said later—but At The Threshold was still a favorite of both men.

"If he had been by Dixieland Band or some other sire, we probably wouldn't have bought him," Whiting said later. "There were concerns." Almost a half-dozen, to be exact. The swelling on the foreleg. The abnormal calcification in the feet. The high-headed running style. A post-gallop runny nose, possibly a sign of an infection. And those sore shins.

"They were as rough a set of shins as I'd seen in a long time," Whiting said later. "He had a lot of what you'd call remodeling of the shin. A lot of calcium laid down. Under stress, the bone of a young horse can actually bend a bit. In this case if you ran your hand down the leg, you got an obvious response. But the horse jogged sound on the pavement. I watched him train. He could get over that racetrack."

Much to like, much to dislike. The conflicting opinions of the various vets swirled in Whiting's head. He wanted the colt. He believed he could minimize the impact of most of the problems. A shoeing change would ease the pressure in the pastern. The high-headedness might stem from a breathing problem, Whiting felt, that could be fought with antibiotics. A suspicious-looking navicular bone was relatively common, not necessarily a reason for concern. The shins were pretty typical two-year-old shins.

Still, the long list was intimidating. After he had been in Florida for two days, Whiting called Pug Hart, his friend in Ocala, and described the situation.

"It's a no-brainer, Lynnie," Hart said. "You've got to buy the horse."

"Why?" Whiting asked.

"Look," Hart said. "You go to those sales and spend $200,000 on yearlings that you don't know whether they can run worth a damn, and now here's a horse that broke his maiden by twelve lengths and runs faster than they run at Calder. It doesn't matter what the x-rays or vets say. The horse has run two high-quality races at Calder with sore shins, so I'd have to say he's probably a good horse, and good horses overcome vets and x-rays."

His friend's strong opinion made it easier for Whiting to follow his instincts. "What it came down to," Whiting said later, "was he just seemed to be the kind of horse you took a chance on. There wasn't anything you had to project with him. He had already established his abilities."

"Eight out of ten guys would have turned the horse down," trainer D. Wayne Lukas said later. "His pedigree, the fact that he was a K-mart special, that always turns people off who are looking for a classic horse. But Lynn probably saw more in the pedigree than anyone else would have. You tend to be partial to your own horses. When Lynn looked at Lil E. Tee he probably thought, 'Well, At The Threshold was a better horse than people thought,' so therefore it was a better risk in his eyes."

Said Whiting later, "I think we bought him to prove that At The Threshold was a good horse." Whiting called Partee and suggested buying the horse. "He's got some problems," Whiting said, "but if we can get by them, and I think we can, he's got the potential to be any kind of horse."

"Try $175,000," Partee said. "See if he'll deal." Whiting met with Jevremovic, tried to negotiate, and ran into a wall.

"He said there was something he didn't like, a line in the hoof or something, and tried one-seventy-five," Jevremovic said later. "I told him, 'Lynn, you don't want the horse because if he's not worth two hundred he's not worth one-seventy-five.' Well, he took his x-rays and paperwork and left."

Whiting called Partee. "We're getting nowhere at $175,000," he said. "The guy is not a dealer."

"OK," Partee said, "go to $200,000." Neither knew that Clover still had the first option to buy.

BARRY Irwin and Jeff Siegel wanted E.T. "We were out in California and we had seen the tape of his race," Siegel said later, "and we thought he had a nice way of going. There was a lot to like. We didn't necessarily think he would be a Derby horse. But he was a nice two-year-old who could maybe be a real nice three-year-old."

But their vet in Florida had not recommended making the purchase. Seeking another opinion, Irwin took the x-rays to a vet in California. "He didn't want me to buy the horse, either," Irwin explained. "He said, 'Listen, if you're going to bring me x-rays like this, don't even bring me x-rays because this horse has no shot.'" Irwin tried another vet. "Same response." This was going nowhere.

According to the agreement Jevremovic had signed, Clover had to transfer into Jevremovic's bank account a nonrefundable deposit of $10,000, which would extend Clover's rights on E.T. for another week. The deadline for depositing the money was 9 A.M., on Friday, October 18.

On Thursday, Irwin and Siegel decided not to buy the horse. "We just can't buy a horse that is questionable," Siegel said later. "We're not buying with our own money. We sell shares of horses to our clients. We couldn't buy a horse and represent him to our clients as sound, not when he possibly wasn't. That's not good. It was very disappointing."

ON Thursday afternoon, Whiting called Jevremovic with the news that Partee had given the go-ahead to buy the horse for $200,000. Jevremovic was out. His wife suggesting calling back the next morning.

The next morning was Clover's deadline. The money was not in Jevremovic's account at 9 a.m. He called Brauer, Clover's agent.

"Is the money coming?" he asked.

"I don't believe so," Brauer said.

"Well, I'm going to proceed," Jevremovic said.

"That's fine," Brauer said.

Whiting called back an hour later. "Mr. Partee will buy the horse for two hundred," he said.

"Lynn," Jevremovic said, "the horse is yours."

"That's great news," Whiting said, unaware that Clover's option had expired just an hour earlier. The paperwork was faxed and signed in a couple of hours. Whiting was anxious to get to Calder and get his hands on E.T. He was going to send the colt to Pug Hart's farm in Ocala for a week, then on to Churchill Downs, where Whiting raced in the fall. There was just one problem: the $200,000, which Partee was transferring by wire, was not yet in Jevremovic's account.

"I'd really like to get going," Whiting said.

"Let me see what I can do," Jevremovic said. He called the officer at his branch bank. "Call this bank in Magnolia, Arkansas, and see if Mr. Partee has sent the money," Jevremovic said. The bank officer called back ten minutes later.

"Mr. Jevremovic," she said, "Mr. Partee owns the bank."

MIKE Trivigno could not help feeling melancholy at the sight of E.T. leaving his barn. That was a good horse, he thought, one of the better young horses he had trained. He shook his head.

"What went on today?" his wife asked when he arrived home for dinner.

"Well," he said, "we probably sold the Kentucky Derby winner."

BRENT Fernung called Jevremovic.

"Hey," Fernung said, "we sold the horse."

"Excuse me?" Jevremovic said.

"We sold the horse," Fernung said.

"No," Jevremovic said. "I sold the horse."

"But I sent Partee a tape of the race," Fernung said. It was true, he had.

But Jevremovic stewed. "You called ten days ago and said take it or leave it, and I said leave it," he said. Click.

Fernung said later: "He thought I didn't have anything to do with the sale, but I did."

Partee gave Fernung a $2,000 commission.

E.T. stepped off the van at Hart Farm. "Holy Jesus," Pug Hart said.

This was the horse that had caused such a commotion?

"When he got here," Hart said later, "you had to wonder how a horse that big and awkward could run so fast. He was just a big, dumb-looking colt, as plain as could be. There was nothing special about him. He didn't have Easy Goer's back or any of the parts you figured went along with speed. He was just big and strong and looked sound. If you walked ten horses out in a field, you wouldn't have liked him any more than the other nine."

Hart had been around long enough to know that anything could happen, that sometimes the least logical horses were the fastest. Still, Hart could not believe that Lynn Whiting, his good friend, just about the smartest horseman he knew, had spent $200,000 on this colt.

6

"A dying breed"

Until he trained At The Threshold beginning in the fall of 1983, Lynn Whiting believed in miracles. His father had trained horses for forty years without taking one to the Kentucky Derby. Whiting had not come close to the Derby in his sixteen years of training. He had come to believe that a Derby contender had to be some sort of super horse, so rare and superior that a trainer just needed to stay out of the way. Finding such a horse, Whiting figured, was racing's version of a miracle.

At The Threshold taught him otherwise. The colt was a two-year-old that had won a maiden and two allowance races in eight starts when Partee bought him for $150,000 in November 1983. He finished his juvenile year by winning the Ashley T. Cole Stakes at Aqueduct, then began his three-year-old year with a victory in the Mountain Valley Stakes at Oaklawn Park. A dull third-place finish in the Southwest Stakes moved Whiting to tell Partee that this horse was not Derby caliber, but the colt proceeded to win the Jim Beam Stakes and finish fourth in the Arkansas Derby, and Whiting decided to run him in the Derby after all. He finished third.

"He was no superstar," Whiting said later, "but he was a consistent, professional horse that didn't make many mistakes, and he got to the Derby and came close."

Whiting stopped believing in miracles. "At The Threshold taught me that Derby horses aren't beamed down from another planet. They aren't up on the pedestals everyone wants to put them on. People are much too quick to come up with accolades for young horses. The good ones turn out to be just horses that can beat the other guys eight days out of ten. After At The Threshold I realized if you had a pretty nice horse and took care of him, and maybe if attrition took the top horses away, and maybe if someone else had bad luck, you had a chance to get there. It was not an impossible dream. No matter what anyone said, the top three-year-olds were not unbeatable."

When Partee bought E.T., he told Whiting he just hoped the colt was "a Saturday horse," one that could compete in stakes races, most of which are run on Saturdays. Whiting agreed. Neither mentioned taking the colt all the way to the Derby. With more than fifty years in racing between them, they knew it was too soon to indulge in Derby dreaming, all too aware that injuries, ailments, and bad luck often spoiled plans. Partee had nominated twenty-six horses for the Triple Crown since 1980, but only At The Threshold had run. Yet it was inevitable that the Derby was rattling around in the back of both men's minds. When Partee spent $200,000 for a two-year-old, as he had several times before, it was unspoken that he did so with a best case scenario in mind. The Derby was the goal. If the horse had talent, stayed healthy, and got lucky, he could be a Derby horse.

Of course, even though E.T. had already shown superior racing abilities at Calder, it still was a stretch to envision him making the Derby. His pedigree was a problem. At The Threshold had sired only one minor stakes winner in his first five crops. There was no evidence suggesting that E.T.'s father could sire a classic horse. But then, as At The Threshold had taught Whiting seven years earlier—and as the famed baseball logician Yogi Berra might have said—a classic horse did not necessarily have to be a classic horse.

WHEN E.T. raced for the first time in Partee's luminous silks of bright orange-red with large white polka dots, on November 1, 1991, racing's best and brightest were there to watch at Churchill Downs. The eighth Breeders' Cup was scheduled for the next day. The anticipation in the cool autumn air was almost palpable. E.T.'s race—a 1¹⁄₁₆-mile allowance for two-year-olds that had not won two races—was just a way to pass time. The real two-year-olds were running in the Breeders' Cup Juvenile the next day.

Partee flew up from Arkansas to watch E.T. race around two turns for the first time. The colt was weighted at 112 pounds, lowest in the field of six. For that reason, and also because Pat Day was his jockey, he was a 7-to-10 favorite. Bettors in the Midwest, particularly those at Churchill, tended to ride with Day regardless of the quality of his mount. Day had won more races at Churchill than any jockey in history.

For most of the race, run on a track rated sloppy, E.T. justified the bettors' support. He established a clear lead on the first turn and held it up the backside, pressed only mildly by an 8-to-1 shot named Correntino. Turning for home he was ahead by two lengths and in control as Correntino faded.

But then the 7-to-2 second choice, a Mr. Prospector colt named Choctaw Ridge, made a late run. Responding to a steady whipping from Patrick Valenzuela, Choctaw Ridge closed the lead to a head, a neck, then nosed in front past the eighth pole. Day urged E.T. to run, but the colt was just too big to change gears so quickly. It was too late. Choctaw Ridge held on to win by a neck.

Partee was immensely disappointed. "I thought he was going to be a good horse," he said when Whiting visited his box after the race, speaking in the past tense, as if the final judgment of E.T.'s talent already was in.

"He'll be fine, he'll be fine," Whiting insisted. But the race had left Whiting feeling uneasy, too. Why had E.T. failed in the stretch? Inexperience? Bordeom? Sore shins? A lack of competitiveness? Did he move too soon and run out of gas?

Whiting would have to find out.

OTHER trainers in Whiting's generation had won more races and made more headlines, but few had a better reputation among the racing cognoscenti, which regarded him as a meticulous caretaker and shrewd judge of talent. "There's no way to describe him other than a class act," said Gary Wilfert, racing director at Turfway Park, in Florence, Kentucky. "Lynn has no holes. Most people in this business do. But you'd be hard-pressed to find any with him, and that's an opinion you'd get from anyone around the country."

Whiting ran everything from cheap claimers to classic contenders, assessed them realistically, and possessed a remarkable knack for valuing them properly. Fifty-six percent of his starters had finished in the money since he began working for Partee in 1978. The national average was 30 percent. "I have total confidence in his ability to train a horse mentally and physically, and to know where to run the horse," Pat Day said. "If you ride for him, most of the time you're going to be competitive."

With Partee, Whiting had won the Jim Beam Stakes, Haskell Invitational Handicap, American Derby, Arlington Classic Stakes, and numerous other smaller stakes with such horses as At The Threshold, Big

Pistol, Clever Allemont, and J.T.'s Pet. In all, he had won more than $8 million in purses. "He is very, very good at his job," D. Wayne Lukas said.

The father of two teenage daughters, married for twenty-one years to a woman he met on a racetrack in New England, he enjoyed eating Cajun food and following sports on television, but he was in his true element only when immersed in the crafts of his profession: conditioning, spotting, buying, handicapping. Small and impassive, watchful and spare with words, he was an old-fashioned, hands-on trainer who approached his work obsessively, his unemotional mien masking his intensity and purposefulness. He rarely took a vacation.

"He is the real thing," Roy Cohen said. "He's very intense, always concentrating, never lets his hair down. Training is not an amateurish job. It's a lot harder than it looks. There are a lot of amateurs. You understand that when you measure them against a Lynn Whiting."

Dr. Gary Norwood, a veterinarian with whom Whiting had worked for two decades, said, "He is one of the two or three most astute horseman I've seen. He has a great feel for horses. He's totally on top of them. He pays attention to every habit they have, how they eat, how they travel on the track. He can see problems coming before anyone does."

At fifty-one years old, in his twenty-third year of operating a stable, he was so quiet that his wife and daughters kiddingly called him Mumbles and his barn help often had to guess what was on his mind. "When Lynn says something, you better catch it the first time around," said Craig Pearl, his assistant trainer. Yet he was friendly with reporters, popular with other trainers, even a bit of a practical joker. He had a dry wit and endless supply of country aphorisms he delivered in a soft twang. If you asked how he was doing, he might say, "Luck's the only reason I'm here." Recounting a gamble he had taken with a horse, he might say, "My fat was a little close to the fire there."

But his chicken-fried exterior did not fool the competition. "Lynn manages to bring off that laid-back, southwestern good ol' boy image, but he's smart like a fox," Lukas said. "You worry if he's in the race. He doesn't enter a horse just to see it in the post parade."

The only son of a man who trained horses for forty years, he had grown up on the racetrack, with barns as his playground and horseflesh the currency he valued. There was little chance of his pursuing the customary American boyhood dream of becoming a fireman or an outfielder. He was wheeled to the racetrack in a carriage on the ninth day of his life. His mother found him in a stall putting a muzzle on a horse when he was two. He was adept at bathing horses by seven, an experienced racetracker by his graduation from high school. He was the quintessential child of the American racetrack. As much as thoroughbreds were bred to race, he was bred to train them.

LYLE Whiting, Lynn's father, fell in love with horses during the Depression. He was a small, wiry teenager living on the sparse plains of Buffalo County, Nebraska. To make money, he sold animal hides and helped his father with the harvest on the farm where his family lived. One summer he took $35 of his savings to the county fair and brought home a mare, half bronco and half pacer. He harrowed a racetrack out of a wheat field and rode his horse around and around, day after day. When he stole a pair of his mother's underwear and cut it into leg bandages and a hood resembling blinkers for his horse, he was ready to race. "I challenged any country boy that come down the road," he said later, "and beat them all."

The next summer he won a relay race at the county fair. A man hired him to ride in a half-mile race and gave him $2 for winning. After that he rode at the fair every summer. One year he took his horse across the river to the neighboring county fair, lied to enter a race, and came home with the $25 first prize.

He left for the big city, Omaha, after high school, intent on learning to ride for a living. The family calling—farming—did not stir him. A man hired him to ride at fair meets across the great plains of Nebraska, Idaho, and Wyoming. He hitchhiked between fairs, occasionally digging his dinner out of a potato patch by the road, and raced on dusty half-mile prairie tracks. His first victory was in Clay Center, Nebraska, on a track without an inside rail. "As a matter of fact, I may have cut the corner a little," he said years later, still smiling at the memory.

When he won the riding title at the Nebraska state fair, he attracted the attention of Marion Van Berg, who took him to Seattle, Detroit, and St. Louis, then the next year to Phoenix and Tijuana, Mexico. It was 1937. Lyle was paid $2 to gallop a horse in the morning, $10 to ride in a race, and $25 to win. His parents had seen enough; they rented out their farm and came on the road with their son. Lyle's father bought a horse, built a trailer, and started training. The family traveled to racetracks throughout the west, from New Orleans to Spokane, Washington.

In Great Falls, Montana, Lyle courted Lurline Rutherford, the

Lil E. Tee with Pat Day aboard, in the post parade before the Kentucky Derby. Courtesy of Churchill Downs/Kinetic Corporation

Lil E. Tee inches ahead of Casual Lies in the final furlong of the Kentucky Derby. Courtesy of Churchill Downs/Kinetic Corporation

From left, Christine Martin, Pat Day, Bob Ray, and Craig Pearl celebrate with Lil E. Tee in the winner's circle at Churchill Downs. Courtesy of Churchill Downs/Kinetic Corporation

Pat Day and Cal Partee shake hands in the winner's circle at Churchill Downs. Courtesy of Churchill Downs/Kinetic Corporation

Pat Day aboard Lil E. Tee in the post parade before the Jim Beam Stakes. Photo by Patrick R. Lang

Lil E. Tee in the stretch run of the Jim Beam Stakes. Photo by Patrick R. Lang

Lyle Whiting in the paddock at Churchill Downs. Courtesy of Lyle and Lurline Whiting

A.Jevremovic's
Kindergarden Champ,2nd
Let It Besunny,3rd
7 Furlongs
1:24 2/5

Lil E.Tee

Calder Race Course

Gene St.Leon,up
M.Trivigno,Trainer
Oct.6,1991
Copyright
Jean Raftery

Lil E. Tee breaks his maiden "by a pole" at Calder Race Course on October 6, 1991. Photo by Jean Raftery

Larry Littman (in striped sweater) celebrates another victory for Lil Stable. Courtesy of Larry Littman

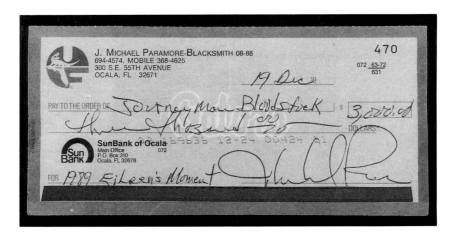

The check that bought a future Derby winner. Photo by Gene Sweeney

Lynn Whiting,
trainer of Lil E. Tee.
Photo by Barbara D. Livingston

W. Cal Partee,
owner of Lil E. Tee.
Photo by John Miller

Al Jevremovic.
Courtesy of Al Jevremovic

Chuck and Joan Wieneke at Green Key Farm. Courtesy of Chuck and Joan Wieneke

Lil E. Tee, age 6, at Old Frankfort Stud in Lexington. Photo by Lori Whiting

daughter of a railroad man. He brought her around to the racetrack and introduced her to his friends. Later in the meeting, he cut off a rider in a race. At the beginning of the next meeting, in Spokane, George Schilling, the presiding judge on the fair circuit, suspended Lyle for three days.

"Why three days?" Lyle asked.

"It's just enough time for you to get back to Great Falls and marry that pretty girl," Schilling said.

They had $500 and a used car on their wedding day. They followed the western racing circuits, bought a trailer home for $500, and became parents with Lynn's birth in 1939. "We saw everything on God's green earth," Lyle said later. "When you grow up in Nebraska and all you see is a cornfield, it's exciting. We were having fun and making some money."

Word of Lyle's talent spread. By 1941 he was riding in Chicago. During the next three years he rode against such top jockeys as Johnny Longden, Johnny Adams, George Woolf, and Sterling Young, on such top horses such as Occupation and First Fiddle. In 1942 and 1943 he won more than three hundred races and $350,000 in purses. Life was exciting and profitable, but Lyle grew weary of the physical stress. "I was big," he said later, "and tired of starving to death. I would go all day on a poached egg and a piece of toast."

In the spring of 1944 he caught a lucky break. He had been riding at Oaklawn for an insurance man from Massachusetts, W.E. Parker, who wanted a new trainer and offered the job to Lyle. It sounded good. Lyle would no longer have to make weight. He thought he could handle the job. He knew about conformation and handicapping. He decided to retire from riding.

When Parker returned to New England that summer, the Whitings went with him. Lyle went to work at Narragansett Park in Salem, New Hampshire. He arrived early every morning and stood by the paddock before every race, studying every horse. "I was the only trainer that stood by the paddock all day," he said later.

Parker's Mount Desert Stable was strong. Lyle's horses won ninety-four races and more than $250,000 in his first three years. He had found his calling. For the next forty years, in New England, Arkansas, Florida, and Kentucky, he got up early every morning and went to the track to train thoroughbreds. He got down on his knees at dawn and checked their legs. He walked with them to and from their workouts, listening to their breathing. He spent his afternoons at the paddock, studying each horse, particularly the claimers. He kept a small stable, between nine and twelve horses, to ensure that each received enough care and attention. "The horses came first, brother, they was going to eat before you," he said later.

"Lyle was a classic horseman," said Dr. Joe Burch, a veterinarian who worked with him for forty years. "No one knew more about the basic crafts of training. Conditioning. Breezing. Leg problems. Spotting them for what they were worth. He probably had as good an eye for young horses as anyone I ever knew. I'm not talking about academic education here. Just basic horse sense."

Things were not always easy, particularly in the early years. His earnings fell sharply when he split from Parker and opened a public stable in 1948. He won only a dozen races in 1952. His determination to keep a small stable put pressure on him. The daily rate he charged his owners was offset by his bills. To provide for his family—by now he had a second child, a daughter—he relied on the 10 percent of the purse money a trainer received. In other words, his horses had to win.

"Back then purses were real small, and second and third money wasn't too good, so you needed that first-place money," he said later. "That was how you ate. So you learned where to run your horses to get something back. You didn't waste starts. I always tried to run as cheap as I could. A lot of people can train a horse, but they get too high on them and run them where they can't win. I always knew where my horses belonged. I ran them about 25 percent less than what they were worth. And I was never off the board."

Many of his horses were claimers. "I lived on that game," he said later. "I knew every horse and whether he was worth claiming. If he could run and he was a claimer, I could tell you how many hairs he had in his tail, he was looked over so good. I made my share of mistakes, sure. But I knew value. I ran cheap, you might say. Lots of good ones I had didn't cost over $5,000."

Small, peppery, and opinionated, with a toothpick planted in the corner of his mouth, he was a racing purist, as satisfied making a smart claim in December as he was winning a springtime stake. He hired grooms who were serious, dutiful, and often became trainers themselves. He was adept at training a horse up to a big race using workouts instead of prep races.

"I wasn't a hustler or a promoter like these guys nowadays," he said later. "All I wanted was three grooms and nine horses. And they didn't have to be champions. Just good ones that could run. Oh, I liked a good horse as much as anyone. But I wouldn't have wanted the hassle of training a Kentucky Derby horse. I wouldn't have wanted that for nothing. I was too fussy. I wouldn't have wanted them bothered. I couldn't have stood to drag them out just to take pictures. I couldn't have stood that for anything. I never wanted it. Not one bit. I wasn't a big trainer and never had any desire to be."

The family split their year between New England and Arkansas, following the racing seasons. The kids had two sets of friends and attended two schools. Lyle managed to make ends meet. He bet every race, relying less on handicapping numbers than on what his eyes told him. Unlike most bettors, he came out ahead. "I was a pretty good handicapper," he said later.

His lot improved considerably in the late 1960s when he took a job training for B.A. Dario, the owner of Lincoln Downs, a racetrack in Rhode Island. Dario's stable featured young horses Dario had bred, the best of which was Great Mystery, a sprinter that won twenty races, including the Jerome Handicap, and set a track record at Keeneland covering six furlongs in 1:08²/₅. Lyle's success with Dario helped him attract other owners. His best years came late in his career. He won the Derby Trial Stakes in 1978 with Braze and Bold and in 1979 with Dreamy Prospect, earning almost $500,000 in purses in the two years.

His profession changed around him, but he never did. "Nowadays these guys drive their cars over to the grandstand or sit up in the grandstand and call down and say, 'Send so and so out,'" he said. "They never go near the horse, never go back to the barn. I don't get it. To me, the most important thing is watching him go off and watching him as he comes back. You can tell what kind of shape he is when he's coming off the track. I went back to the barn after every work."

According to Joe Burch, "What you've got today are so many hustlers and promoters. The percentage of real horsemen in the profession is declining. Trainers like Lyle Whiting are a dying breed."

A few were still around, of course. Lyle's only son, for instance.

IN the twin cities of his youth, Lynn Whiting lived within earshot of the racetrack. In Salem, New Hampshire, his parents parked their trailer home across the street from Narragansett Park. In Hot Springs, Arkansas, they lived two blocks from Oaklawn. Much as the city streets, suburbs, and country towns provided the fabric of other youngsters' lives in the '50s, the racetrack was Lynn Whiting's world. Day after day, year after year, horses and racing were all around him. Even as a small child, he was included in his father's operation. "I would send him to someone's barn to play," Lyle said later, "and tell him to look a certain horse over to see if it was sound."

His serious apprenticeship began in grade school. "When I was about ten my dad got a real kind three-year-old filly that didn't have a nerve in her body," Whiting said later. "I was too small to actually groom her, but I'd take a bench into the stall and sit down and brush her and care for her and learn to put bandages on. My dad had real good help. They'd go in the stall with me and teach me how to put on bandages. There were just numerous things you learned from being around horses and around people who were good, sound practitioners, no matter what their occupation was, exercise boy, veterinarian, whatever. I learned something from everybody." By his twelfth birthday he had a summer job in another trainer's barn. At thirteen, he became an owner/trainer.

"I had knocked around Hot Springs and had a little spending money, and maybe if my mother won the double she'd give me a little," Whiting said later. "I had a hundred bucks. My dad was going to buy a horse called King Taos for fifteen hundred. Well, that was just about all the money he could get his hands on. He was a hundred shy. So I gave him my hundred. I was supposed to have one-fifteenth of King Taos. We knocked around with that horse for a year or two. He won some money. I helped out. Walked him. Did menial tasks. The earnings were absorbed back into the business. I think I wound up with a piece of another horse called Deep Down. There was always a horse in the barn I had a few dollars in. It was just the incentive to keep your interest up. It's hard to keep a young boy interested in anything."

In high school, Whiting worked in his father's barn before and after school and all day in the summer. "He worked for me pretty steadily from eleventh grade on," Lyle said later. "School was easy for him. He never studied or nothing. He was kinda half-smart, so he could work all day."

As Lyle's shadow around the barn and paddock, the young boy slowly grasped the fundamentals of the job. "I guess I taught Lynnie a lot over the years, just by talking about what I was thinking, what I was seeing, what I liked about some horses and didn't like about others," Lyle said. "I taught him the basics."

As Whiting would later say, "My dad was a sharp man around the paddock. I just liked to stand there with him. You can't put a price on an education like that."

When Whiting was fourteen, one of Lyle's owners struck a deal with him. "We claimed a horse for $3,000, and he was mine to train. I cared for the horse, trained him, worked with him. We kept him in Dad's barn and raced him in Dad's name, but it was my horse. And you know what? We had a little success."

Whiting graduated from high school with more racing acumen than many professional trainers. His parents suggested he go to college, but he went to work full-time for Lyle. "What do I need to go to college for?" he asked. "I'm going to be a racetracker. I'm going to train horses."

In the early 1960s he was drafted into the army and spent two years in Germany with an artillery unit. His mother sent him *Daily Racing Forms*. Lyle was ecstatic when he returned. "I got to New York, called him and told him what plane I'd be on, and he went right to the barn and fired the help," Whiting said later. "I went to work the next day."

Whiting had $800. His parents suggested he buy a car. "I'd rather buy a horse," Whiting said. "What do I need a car for?" He returned to his job as Lyle's assistant, tending to a horse or two of his own, spending his days on the paddock fence. A year went by, then a second, third, and fourth. "I was kind of content to just sit there and help my dad," Whiting said later. "I had no real game plan. I guess everyone is afraid to leave the nest."

One autumn one of his friends in New England claimed a horse named Fortunatas, but the friend's trainer was leaving for Florida for the winter and there was no one to train the horse. Whiting took the problem to Lyle, expecting Lyle to help, as always. "Junior," Lyle said, "I'm going to Florida for the winter, too. It's time you went out on your own."

Whiting swallowed hard, took out his trainer's license, and hustled a stall. He was twenty-eight years old. Fortunatas ran third the first time out, then won by seven lengths. A $2,000 claim, the horse went on to win several $5,000 races. Owners began calling. Whiting had six horses in his barn by the next spring, fifteen by the end of the year, a solid stable of twenty-five claimers the following year. He shared the responsibility of running a stable with a friend and fellow racetracker named Wally Shute. Whiting handled the training and claiming. Shute handled the books and helped with the claiming. They took on a groom named Bill Perry, a longhaired kid who loved rock music.

Over the next few years they established a presence, albeit a small one, on the East Coast. They took horses to Maryland in the fall and winter and dabbled in New York and New Jersey. But their base was New England. They rented a trailer near Rockingham Park for $300 a month. They had no car. They lived at the track. "We were just having fun," Shute said later, "and by accident we started making a little bit of money."

In Whiting's first full year as a trainer, he finished in the money in 46 percent of his starts and earned $62,000 in purses in 1969. The next year, he won thirty-nine races and $139,000. The year after that, it was fifty-four wins and $178,000. His first stakes win came in 1971, when Beat The Traffic won the Old Line Handicap at Pimlico.

"Lynn didn't just walk out of a bar and start training," said Dr. Gary Norwood, who was working in New England at the time. "He had an education. He was ready when he went on his own. He was sharp."

Said Bill Perry, who later became a top trainer in New England, "He had a head start on some other guys just starting out. He knew quite a bit. We did well with some cheap claims. It was obvious Lynn was handy with a horse."

Not as handy as Lyle, at least not yet. Father and son often sent out competing horses in those days. Lyle, backed by Dario's stable, dominated his son. "You hate to beat your kid, but it happened," Lyle said later. "He beat me some, but I beat him a whole lot more. I run against him one time at Suffolk Downs on the turf, and I didn't know it, but they'd made a big bet on their horse and I beat him by a nose. I felt real bad about it."

As Whiting said later, "My dad had a bigger stick than I did."

Having his father around did offer some advantages: Whiting met his future wife, Muriel Nelson, when she went to work for Lyle as a groom. Everyone called her Nellie. Though he was twenty-five years younger than his father, Whiting struck many ractrackers as his father's twin.

"There was a lot of Lyle in Lynn," said Max Hall, a longtime jockeys' agent in New England. "They were those Midwestern types. They were gentlemen, very nice to deal with, very fair, pleasant, men of their word. It's been my experience that a lot of Midwestern trainers and riders come from the same mold. They don't say much. They're great with those one-word answers. Yep. Nope. Maybe. Could be. And you can't rush them. They move at a little slower gait than the average horseman. But they sure know what they're doing. Both of the Whitings ran totally professional barns. Everything was on time. If they said they wanted the rider there at seven o'clock, you were there at seven and the horse was ready. They didn't say much. But they didn't miss a thing. Took in a lot more with their eyes and ears than they ever let on. Both were very good horsemen, keen judges of horseflesh. They knew what they had. I was very impressed with Lynn as a youngster. Every day he'd be up by the walking ring with Billy Perry, watching every horse that ran, studying them for claiming purposes, marking down what kind of bandages, equipment, what kind of foot. A handful did it, but these guys went that extra mile."

The experience of working with claimers was invaluable. "It was the training ground," Whiting said later. "I liken it to a caterpillar turning into a butterfly. When you're knocking around with those cheap horses, you're the caterpillar. Claimers teach you the basic fundamentals. You're working on horses that are unsound. You see a multitude of problems: ankles, suspensories, tendons, bad feet, horses with hock trouble, stifle trouble. And one problem begets another, so you have to learn to deal with a lot of things. When you have mastered the claiming game and the care of the claiming horse, you're prepared for a good horse. I think every trainer needs to go through that. You can start at the top and work yourself down in this game, or start at the bottom and work up. This is a tough game. People that last in it are usually able to last because they do things right."

Whiting did things right. He made smart claims, ran his horses in the right places, and won a lot of races. He averaged fifty wins a year from 1972 to 1975. But he was increasingly anxious to train better horses. One year he talked one of his biggest owners into attending the Keeneland fall sale of yearlings. Gary Norwood came along and helped make the purchases. They bought several horses that turned into two-year-olds that sold for a profit. When Whiting went back to Keeneland the next year, Shute, Perry, and Norwood came along and bought horses of their own. Back home they threw their stock together and owned the horses jointly in the name of Cornerstone Stable.

The engine driving their operation quickly changed from claiming and racing to developing young horses for sale. They sought bargains at Keeneland every year, avoiding expensive pedigrees. The yearlings were broken at a farm in South Carolina and came north to race in New England. The partners ran up thousands of dollars of bills before their horses had a chance to make back the money on the racetrack and in sales. Turning a profit was tough. "We probably should have stuck with the claiming," Perry said later.

But the venture was neither an economic nor artistic failure. "Business wasn't bad," Whiting said later. A handful of Cornerstone's yearlings became quality horses. One yearling bought for $10,000 was sold for $200,000 after winning three races. A colt named Wardlaw, bought for $11,500 at Keeneland and sold to Dan Lasater for $30,000, won the Hawthorne Derby, ran second in the Illinois Derby, and earned $292,000 as a three-year-old.

By 1977 Whiting had been training for close to a decade. He was comfortable in his low-profile niche. But he was itchy to move on. New England racing was declining. Whiting's horsemanship suggested he was destined for bigger things. Cornerstone's emphasis on developing yearlings was not helping his career. He won just eleven races in 1977, down 80 percent in two years.

"It got to the point where I didn't have many horses to train," he said later. "As soon as a yearling proved his worth on the track, we'd turn him into cash. As a trainer you can die on the vine in a situation like that. You're not winning races, so you're not in front of the public, and it gets harder to find new people who want you to train for them, and the whole thing can kind of dwindle away if you're not careful."

Lyle encouraged him to come to the Midwest. Nellie, Whiting's wife, seconded the idea, even though she was a New Englander and it would mean leaving her family. But she was a racetracker and understood that her husband needed better owners and horses if he was going anywhere as a trainer. He was thirty-eight years old.

In the fall of 1977 Whiting sold his stock, claimed a horse for himself, and drove to Kentucky, where he took a job as the assistant to Bob Dunham, a New York-based trainer with a Kentucky division. Almost immediately his horse was claimed. When winter arrived he took Dunham's horses to New Orleans, rented a small second-floor apartment in a tough neighborhood near the track—"the apartment had cockroaches you could saddle and train"—and spent the winter at the claiming box. He was alone. Nellie, pregnant, was spending the winter at her mother's house in Florida. "I was just scuffling along with horses that weren't mine," Whiting explained.

He was looking for a private training job or, at least, several owners with whom he could start a new stable. At one point he almost took
a job with Clear Creek Stud, a Louisiana outfit. He called Nellie with
the news.

"Is this what you want?" she asked.

"Not really," he said.

"Well, then, don't take it," she said. He turned the job down and
returned to Kentucky that spring as Dunham's assistant. Then Dan Lasater
called.

Lasater was one of the leading owners in the country. Whiting had
sold him Wardlaw and run against several of his horses back east. Lasater
was impressed with Whiting. When Lasater's friend Cal Partee decided
to change trainers and called Lasater for suggestions, Lasater recommended
Whiting. "Do you want to go to work for Cal Partee?" Lasater asked
when he reached Whiting at Keeneland.

Whiting smiled. Who would not want to work for Partee? The
Arkansas lumberman always had runners; he had run a horse in the Kentucky Derby just the year before, and had fifteen horses in his barn right
now, including several promising two-year-olds. "Sounds like something
I'd be interested in," Whiting said, as understated as ever.

Lasater gave him Partee's phone number and told him to wait fifteen
minutes before calling, giving Lasater a chance to call first. Whiting and
Partee spoke, agreeing to meet the next day at the Executive Inn in Louisville. Anxious to make a good impression, Whiting went out and got a
haircut. With Lasater's recommendation, Whiting was all but assured of
the job. Partee asked just a few simple questions when they met.

"Do you smoke?"

"No."

"Drink?"

"I bought a bottle of bourbon in New Orleans over the winter
and I think I opened it once. I keep it around in case friends come
over."

"I have only one demand," Partee said. "I want you to be honest."

"That's never been a problem," Whiting said. They talked longer
and wound up going to dinner.

"Can you take the horses tomorrow morning?" Partee asked.

"I'm prepared to do that if it's necessary," Whiting said. The next
morning they went to barn eighteen on the backside at Churchill, where
Partee stabled his horses. Partee's longtime trainer, Harold "Baldy" Tinker,
was not there. Tinker's son, Mike, was in the tack room.

"Mike," Partee said, "this here is Lynn Whiting and he's gonna be taking over."

"I better call my dad and get him to come out," Mike said, and went to the barn office to make the call.

Whiting and Partee had a few minutes to kill. "You want to go see your dad?" Partee asked.

"Sure," Whiting said. "Sounds great." Lyle was stabled across the backside. Whiting and Partee drove to Lyle's barn and got out of the car.

Lyle spoke up before his son said a word. "Junior," he said, "what in the hell are you doing here?"

"I quit my job," Whiting said.

"What?" Lyle snapped. "How are you gonna eat?"

"Well, I'm going to go to work for Mr. Partee here."

Lyle said nothing. He just stared for a few moments, then turned and walked ten yards away, giving himself a moment to ingest the news. Then he turned around and came back. "Do you know what you've done?" Lyle asked sternly.

"No," Whiting said.

"Well," Lyle said, "you just went to work for the best son of a bitch in America."

THEY were brought together by fateful circumstances. Partee had not changed trainers in years. Whiting had never sought a job. The odds that they would scan the want ads simultaneously, much less find each other, were astronomical. But it was a perfect match, a joining of kindred philosophies.

Partee did not believe in interfering in his trainer's business. He asked only for competence and honesty and was always willing to pay for a quality horse. "A dream owner," Gary Norwood called him. Whiting was a perfect fit as the other half of a two-piece jigsaw puzzle. He was earnest, intuitive, and successful. Twenty-one percent of his starters had won in the nine years since he took out his license. The national average was 10 percent.

Whiting and Partee thrived from their first day together. Whiting was the leading trainer and Partee was the leading owner at the Churchill Downs fall meeting in 1978. At the spring meeting the next year, Partee was again the leading owner. Four more times in the next five years, Partee was the leading owner at one of the two Churchill meetings. Partee's earnings surpassed $300,000 in a year for the first time in 1980. Two years later, in a remarkable performance, ninety-one of the one hundred thirty-six starters Whiting sent out for Partee finished in the money. Of the many skills Whiting had learned from his father, none was more important than the ability to value horses. "It doesn't matter how good you train them if you don't know where to run them," Whiting said later.

Partee was thrilled. He was immensely fond of the unassuming Whiting, who kiddingly called Partee "Joe." Yet Partee yearned for more: when he began his stable in 1954 he had set out to win two races, the Arkansas Derby and Kentucky Derby. He had achieved the first goal in 1974 when J.R.'s Pet won the Arkansas Derby. The second goal was a far tougher proposition, but Partee was still determined to achieve it after almost four decades. Every year Whiting and Partee sought a Derby-caliber horse. Whiting investigated the horses and made recommendations. Partee put up the money.

In 1980 they spent $300,000 on a yearling that "wasn't worth a match," according to Whiting. A $200,000 purchase, Forbidden Pleasure, broke his maiden by nine lengths and went into the Southwest Stakes in March 1982 as a 1-to-2 favorite. "They were talking about him on the West Coast; he looked like he had all the tools," Whiting said later. But he bled in the Southwest and never fulfilled his promise. In 1984 they reached the Kentucky Derby with At The Threshold. They also had a late-blooming colt named Big Pistol that won five straight stakes and seven of ten races as a three-year-old, the Haskell among his victories. It was a huge year for the barn. Partee's horses won fifty-six races and $1.36 million in purses.

They thought they might have another Derby horse the next year: Clever Allemont, a $77,000 yearling purchase, won the Southwest and Rebel Stakes and went into the Arkansas Derby unbeaten. But he ran sixth there and suffered a quarter crack on his sesamoid bone. Two years later came J.T.'s Pet, a $35,000 yearling purchase that developed into a serious Derby contender, winning five in a row, including the Jim Beam Stakes. "J.T.'s Pet was the real thing; he could have gotten there," Whiting said later. A 2-to-5 favorite over Alysheba in his final Derby prep race, the Lexington Stakes, he ran fourth and turned up lame.

In 1988, a $40,000 purchase named Hey Pat broke his maiden by thirteen lengths and lost by a nose to Forty Niner in the Breeders' Futurity at Keeneland, but was never the same after running third in the Brown and Williamson Kentucky Jockey Club Stakes. "I think he chipped his knee there, although the x-rays couldn't find anything," Whiting said later.

Whiting celebrated his fiftieth birthday in 1989. He had become a startling recreation of Lyle as a horseman. He limited the size of his stable and got maximum production from his horses, saving their best performances for big races. He could train his horses up to a race using workouts instead of preps. He was a sharp handicapper. His caretaking was peerless. "My father was old-fashioned, and I am, too," Whiting said later. "Being hands-on with the horses, knowing them, is where you have your success."

He was different from Lyle in that he had won more big races in twenty years than Lyle had in forty, with the help of Partee's bakroll and a greater sense of ambition. "He passed me by a long time ago," Lyle said later. Yet he was similar to Lyle in that he was still something of a state secret, respected by racetrackers but obscure outside the sport. For all of his success, he had never scored the one big win to raise his national profile.

He did not want such a victory for the limelight it would bring; that was not what turned him on. He did not necessarily want it for the money, either, although he certainly would not turn down the money. He wanted it for the challenge. The challenge of training a big horse. The horse Lyle never had.

WHITING pushed through the front door of the track kitchen at Churchill Downs, bringing with him a gust of the chilly autumn dawn. He wore blue jeans, tennis shoes, a down jacket, and a baseball cap: clothes for a dirty job. He picked up orange juice, cereal, and milk in the cafeteria line and sat down to eat. It was November 12, 1991, not just another day for Whiting, although you could not tell by his customarily impassive face. This was the day he had chosen to run E.T. a second time in Partee's colors.

In the eleven days since the first race in which E.T. had lost in the stretch to Choctaw Ridge, Whiting had decided that Pat Day probably had contributed more to the loss than E.T. Day was Whiting's close friend, one of the best jockeys anywhere—Whiting wanted no one else on his top horses—but this time, Whiting thought, Day probably had extinguished E.T.'s fire prematurely. At least Whiting hoped that was the case.

The only way to find out was to give the colt another race. Whiting had considered running him in the Brown and Williamson Kentucky Jockey Club Stakes, a race for two-year-olds at the end of November, but decided E.T. was not mentally prepared to compete against stakes-caliber horses. Whiting also considered not running the colt at all a second time; E.T. was going to get December and January off while his sore shins were treated, so why not go ahead and start his vacation? Ultimately, Whiting decided that another race would be more useful as a barometer of E.T.'s ability than injurious to those shins. "We wanted to find out more about the horse," Whiting said later.

After gobbling down his breakfast, Whiting hunched up the collar of his jacket and walked through the cold to barn eighteen. He sent E.T. out for a half-mile gallop after dawn, presided over the works of the other horses in the barn, and spent time in his office taking care of paperwork, planning, and phone calls. At noon he went home for a shower and lunch. As he drove back to Churchill he was confident. The race was a flat mile. There was not much quality in the field. Whiting was more concerned about seeing E.T. finish well.

"Try to get him relaxed early," he told Day in the paddock. "Get him to the quarter pole, ask him to put his horse away and let him finish."

Races often do not proceed as trainers envision, but this time Whiting got precisely what he wanted. Breaking from the seventh hole, E.T. settled into fourth behind a tightly-bunched pack and moved easily along the backstretch. He was eager, though, and took off at the turn. Guided by Day, he passed one horse, another, a third, and moved into the lead on the turn. Day took out his whip and gave E.T. such a steady drumbeat of wake-up calls that the *Daily Racing Form* charter later wrote that E.T. had been "ridden hard," a rarity for Day. But the colt stayed awake and won by three lengths.

Day was not impressed. He felt that E.T. had put out a minimal effort, that the whipping had not elicited a significant response. Had anyone suggested to Day that E.T. would be his Derby mount the next spring, he would have laughed.

Whiting was more encouraged. He felt it was a reasonable performance considering E.T.'s sore shins, inexperience, and the short time between his races. The horse obviously had talent. When he made his run around the turn, the other horses just fell away. "I think we've got ourselves a Saturday horse," Whiting told Partee on the phone after the race.

"Well," Partee said, "I hope so."

7

"He knew
he was special."

Racing was a slumping industry by 1991. Track attendance, television ratings, foal crops, and auction prices had declined since the mid-1980s. Several tracks were considering closing. State supported lottery games and new gambling casinos were taking a bite out of the racing economy. Not since Spectacular Bid, a three-year-old in 1979, had there been a horse with the talent and charisma to transcend the sport's boundaries. Racing news, once the stuff of headlines, now was buried deep in most of the nation's sports pages.

These problems were far too numerous and complicated for one horse to correct, but a new headline-hogging superstar certainly would give the sport a boost. "We need a star desperately," D. Wayne Lukas said. "Sports today is dominated by personalities. Basketball has Michael Jordan, football has Joe Montana, baseball has Nolan Ryan. We need one of those."

And then suddenly one appeared—a horse with such talent that comparisons to Secretariat were, for once, not considered heretical. His name was Arazi. He was a two-year-old chestnut colt with a white blaze on his forehead and a stride so devastatingly quick that it left hardened racetrackers groping for adjectives.

His coming out party in North America came at Churchill Downs on November 2, 1991, in the Breeders' Cup Juvenile, in which he rallied from thirteenth in a fourteen-horse field to win by five lengths, zipping away from the others in the stretch as though they were jogging.

"He passed us like a sports car," said Pat Day, who finished sixth on a colt named Dance Floor.

"He might be the next Secretariat or Swaps," said Bruce Headley, the trainer of the runner-up, Bertrando.

"That's the next Kentucky Derby winner, right there," said Arazi's jockey, Patrick Valenzuela, after the colt angled to the inside approaching the turn, squeezed between horses, slipped past Bertrando, and pulled away. "It was like playing a video game when you're driving a little car. All I had to do was drive through [the pack]. I've never seen a horse do that."

The victory, Arazi's seventh straight, validated the volley of hyperbolic scouting reports that had reached America all summer and fall from France, where Arazi had won six of seven starts before coming to Louisville for the Juvenile. He was trained by a fifty-five-year-old Frenchman, Francois Boutin, one of Europe's top horsemen, and had a majestic set of co-owners, Allen Paulson and Sheikh Mohammed.

"I told you he was the best horse in the world," an ebullient Paulson told friends and reporters after the Juvenile.

Ralph Wilson Sr., owner of pro football's Buffalo Bills, had bred the colt in 1988, matching the sire Blushing Groom to a Northern Dancer mare named Danseur Fabuleux. When Wilson dispersed his stock in November 1989, Paulson bought the unnamed weanling for $350,000. One of the world's most avid thoroughbred owners, Paulson had spent tens of millions on bloodstock, owned farms in Kentucky and California, and raced on two continents. He often named his horses after air traffic control checkpoints. Arazi was a checkpoint in Arizona.

Failing to draw a $300,000 reserve price at the 1990 Keeneland July yearling sale, the colt was shipped to Boutin at the French equine center of Chantilly, in the wooded countryside north of Paris. After losing his first race in late May to a Mr. Prospector colt named Steinbeck, the colt won four in a row through the summer and in September ran away with the Prix de la Salamandre, a Group I race, the European equivalent of a Grade I stake. He stalked the top English two-year-olds and blew past them in the last two furlongs. At that point, Boutin, who had won the race eleven times, said that Arazi was the best two-year-old he had trained.

In early October the colt scored a three-length win in the Grand Criterium at Longchamp, in Paris, without his jockey needing to so much as raise the whip. "A brilliant performance," said Joe Hirsch, executive columnist for the *Daily Racing Form.* His winning streak stood at six, and he was the first horse since his sire to sweep all four of France's major races for juveniles. Sheikh Mohammed, who had sought the colt for months, finally talked Paulson into selling 50 percent for a staggering sum, reportedly between $5 million and $8 million.

Arazi's European juvenile championship was a certainty. But Paulson wanted the horse to run in the Breeders' Cup. Boutin was reluctant at first; he had little interest in American racing. But he finally relented. Arazi made the trip from France to Kentucky, and the joined forces of his hype and his impressive training at Churchill were such that bettors made him an even-money favorite. The hype, it turned out, was anything but groundless.

After the race Arazi was vanned to Paulson's farm in Kentucky. Surprisingly, bone chips were arthroscopically removed from each of the colt's front ankles several days later. Paulson and the doctors said the surgery was minor, mostly preventative; they were confident the colt would heal in time to train properly for the Kentucky Derby. Arazi returned to France to recuperate. Seven months away from the Derby, he was already clearly the favorite.

E. T.'S groom quit shortly after the colt arrived in Whiting's barn at Churchill Downs in mid-October. Whiting carefully sought a replacement. A competent groom was essential to a horse's happiness. "It's like when a kid goes to first grade," D. Wayne Lukas said. "The trainer is the teacher. But the groom is the mother."

Whiting had high standards for his grooms and assistants, as Lyle did. But hiring earnest, responsible help was not as simple now as in his father's earlier days. "The backside has really changed," said Craig Pearl, who had worked for five years as Whiting's exercise rider and assistant trainer, and had been on the racetrack for twenty-four of his forty-two years. "At one time people were here because they liked being around horses. Now, it's just a job like any other. It doesn't matter how they treat the horse. They don't care for the horse. I'm not saying everybody, but on the whole, you don't see much care for the horse anymore."

General conditions in the barns were abysmal. Alcohol and drug abuse was everywhere. Whiting was one of the few trainers determined to keep his standards high. He ran across as much bad help as anyone, but his tolerance was low. Among his grooms and assistants there was a tacit understanding: if you were late or sloppy or you did not care properly for the horses, you were gone. "Lynn comes from the old school, which is care and compassion for the horse," Pearl said. Whiting's help was young and old, black and white, male and female, but they shared a knowledge of horses and a seriousness about their work.

"I'm particular about who works in my barn," Whiting remarked later. "I don't like to take people in and teach them. I don't have time to take someone raw, work with them and bring them along. I prefer them to come to me efficient and adapt to my ways."

Craig Pearl had dropped out of high school, gone to work at the track, and never left. "I don't know nothing else," he said. He galloped horses for Lyle in the early 1970s at Rockingham Park and moved to Kentucky when New England racing declined. He was a solid rider and a faithful employee. Bob Ray, Whiting's other assistant, was thirty-nine years old but already a veteran of almost a quarter-century on the racetrack. He had worked for Whiting for four years, first as a groom and then as an assistant when he proved particularly competent.

"The backside is what I call home," Ray said. "Our family had some experience with horses when I was growing up in Arkansas. My uncle raced quarterhorses. One summer I came up to visit my brother in Louisville. His wife knew a trainer and got me a job walking hots. I was fifteen, making $100 a week, and that was great. It just seemed natural to me. It stills seems natural. It's kind of a gift. If you don't like it, there's no use trying to do it. It's hard work, demanding, dirty, long hours, lots of time, seven days a week. It's not a lifestyle for everybody."

Augustus "Ernie" Summers, the barn's night watchman, had worked for Whiting for eleven years. He was fifty-two years old, lived in a small spartan apartment at the end of the barn, and had worked on the racetrack since the Korean War. "Maryland, Detroit, New York, Chicago; you name it, I've worked there," he said. "It's not an office job. You have to love the horses. I don't even worry about the races. Derby, schmerby. As long as those horses are happy, that's what I want."

Soon after he began searching for a new groom, Whiting was introduced through another groom in the barn to Christine Martin, a forty-year-old divorcée with two decades of racetrack experience. She had started out working in her hometown of Omaha, Nebraska, and then had worked five years for trainer Buddy Delp. Slender and well-spoken, with short blond hair, she was an old-fashioned horse lover. She had no ambition to rise beyond the lowly status of groom. She also was not that interested in racing. Her purpose on the racetrack was to take care of horses.

Whiting ran his version of a background check. He spoke to a trainer for whom she had worked in Nebraska. The trainer recommended her. She seemed intelligent and neat. Whiting hired her. She and E.T. hit it off immediately. She learned that he responded to voices and spoke soothingly to him as she worked with him. Upon discovering that he had a sweet tooth, she began bringing to the barn cinnamon graham crackers, bought with her own money. She called him "Tee." Whiting gave her a raise after a week on the job.

"Chris and Tee got along great," Ernie Summers said later. "You can tell when a horse likes certain people. You can see it in their faces."

Christine remarked, "He was smart. He understood his routine. And even though he was a colt, he was never mean to me. He was just a joy. He carried himself in a certain way, like he knew he was special."

IN December, Whiting moved his horses from Churchill Downs to a barn on the backside at the Fair Grounds, in New Orleans. Whiting went for the mild weather and kind racing surface, which created a perfect situation for training. He ran his cheaper horses in the afternoon races to satisfy the racing secretary and get access to stalls, and gave his top horses the conditioning and veterinary treatments they needed to prepare for the upcoming year.

E.T. had sore shins and swelling in a tendon sheath on his right foreleg. These were routine problems, but they needed correcting if E.T. were to have any success as a three-year-old. Whiting's vet in New Orleans was his old friend and partner from the Cornerstone Stable, Gary Norwood. They went to work on E.T. Norwood removed the fluid with a needle and injected small doses of hyaluronic acid and steroid. The tendon sheath tightened. That was that.

The shins required considerably more attention. Thoroughbreds carry 65 percent of their weight on their forelegs, and a young horse's cannon bones often bend under the persistent pressure of training and racing. New bone often begins to form because the horse is young and developing. The unstable area is ripe for swelling and soreness. There were numerous theories regarding treatment. Whiting found that sore shins healed with rest and improved blood circulation in the area. The blood flow drew nutrients to the area, strengthening the "remodeled" bone.

Whiting attacked E.T.'s shins with a three-course program. The first course was rest; for a month E.T. was limited to jogging around the shedrow. The second and third courses were intended to stimulate circulation. There were two daily sessions with an electric apparatus called the boot, a pad that shot tiny laser beams through the shins. The shins also were given a daily coat of blistering paint, a mixture of iodine, menthol, and ether that caused inflammation and reduced pain. Whiting put the colt through two fifteen-day courses of paint.

E.T. resumed training in January. In his first workout he went three-eighths in :36 and galloped out a half in :50. He was pain free. A second work the following week was even more positive. Encouraged, Whiting plotted a racing campaign that would take E.T. all the way to the Kentucky Derby if luck and talent permitted. There were few options. Trainers on the coasts had numerous Derby prep races from which to choose, but those in the Midwest had only three Grade II stakes, three Grade III stakes, and a handful of ungraded stakes to consider.

Whiting's schedule for E.T. began with an allowance race in early February and the Southwest Stakes on March 7, both at Oaklawn Park. Next came the Jim Beam Stakes on March 28 at Turfway Park in Florence, Kentucky, then the Arkansas Derby back at Oaklawn on April 18. That made three major races in eight weeks, four in ten including the Kentucky Derby. It was a tough road, but the goal was to season E.T. without exhausting him, and Whiting was uncomfortable with any more or fewer races.

The schedule differed little from those Whiting had designed for At The Threshold, Clever Allemont, and J.T.'s Pet. He used the Southwest Stakes and Arkansas Derby because Oaklawn was his base in the late winter and early spring, and the Jim Beam, with its half-million-dollar purse, provided an opportunity to amass graded stakes earnings, which served as the tiebreaker if more than the maximum field of twenty horses were entered in the Kentucky Derby. It was a sensible schedule that left no room for injury or failure, but such was the lot of any Derby hopeful. As any trainer knew, just getting a horse to the Derby was a major accomplishment.

Whiting knew better than to get his hopes up now, but he could not help it. E.T. was a big, powerful horse that covered ground in a hurry, an intelligent, athletic horse that seemed capable of handling a tough three-year-old campaign. Normally conservative in his assessments of his horses, Whiting began boasting about E.T. to friends. At the end of January he moved his barn to Hot Springs for the opening of the Oaklawn meeting. Randy Moss, the turf writer for the *Dallas Morning*

News, came by the barn one morning. "C'mon, let me show you the next Kentucky Derby winner," Whiting said. Moss, who knew Whiting well, was shocked. Whiting never spoke that way, not even jokingly.

When Whiting told Partee that the horse was flourishing, Partee also became excited. In late January, shortly before the start of the Oaklawn meeting, Partee, on the mend from hip surgery, hobbled into the office of Charles Cella, owner of Oaklawn. Every year Partee dropped by to say hello to Cella, whose family had owned Oaklawn since the turn of the century.

"You got anything this year?" Cella asked.

Partee smiled. He was always honest in his appraisal of his own stock. If he had nothing, he said so. "Boss," Partee said, "I got me a winner this year."

THE deadline for early nominations for the 1992 Triple Crown was January 18. The owners of 389 three-year-olds made their horses eligible for the Kentucky Derby, Preakness, and Belmont by paying a $600 nomination fee. The nominees were, for the most part, the horses that had emerged as the best of the forty-eight thousand foals delivered three years earlier.

Arazi was the big name, but there also were four other Grade I winners: Bertrando, winner of the Norfolk Stakes and runner-up to Arazi in the Juvenile; A.P. Indy, winner of the Hollywood Futurity; Tri to Watch, winner of the Champagne Stakes; and Agincourt, winner of the Futurity Stakes. Considering his pedigree and his sickliness as a yearling, E.T. had accomplished quite a feat to be included in such company. Yet he was an outsider even among the top of his class. Only six of the nominees were Pennsylvania-breds. E.T. was the only nominee sired by At The Threshold. Danzig had eight, and Seattle Slew, Alydar, and Mr. Prospector had seven apiece. No matter how well he performed at the races, E.T. would always be a longshot.

THE Oaklawn meeting was one of Whiting's favorites. A day at the races was still a big event in Hot Springs. "There are baseball towns and football towns, but Hot Springs is a racing town," said Don Grisham, who covered Oaklawn and other tracks for thirty-five years for the *Daily Racing Form.*

For years Oaklawn was a small country track populated by vacationers who came to Hot Springs for the spa water. But in the late 1960s, after the federal government closed the illegal casinos in town, Oaklawn began adding stakes, gaining prestige and attracting better horses, particularly with its Racing Festival of the South, a collection of stakes run at the end of the meeting. By the '90s the caliber of racing was consistent and competitive, and the atmosphere was terrific: crowds of ten thousand on weekdays, thirty thousand on weekends, and more than sixty thousand for the Arkansas Derby. It was enough to make a horseman feel important again.

Whiting shared a barn with his friend Steve Morguelan and lived with Lyle and Lurline in their small house two blocks from the track. Lurline often rose with her son before dawn and cooked his breakfast. Lyle, though retired, still could be found by the paddock every day.

Pat Day, who had a house in Hot Springs, breezed E.T. one morning shortly after Whiting arrived. Day was impressed. This was not the same colt he had ridden in November. E.T. had benefited from the time off. "I like this colt a lot," Whiting told Day after the workout. "I'd sure like you to stay on him."

Day nodded, surprised to hear such optimism from his normally conservative friend. But Whiting was working Day as a politician would an undecided voter. He wanted Day on E.T. as often as possible. Day was adept at teaching horses to relax, obey the rider, and save their sprints for the final quarter-mile of a race. E.T. needed to learn those lessons. As a two-year-old he had raced hellishly, using daylight as an excuse to charge. He could get away with it at the shorter distances he had run as a juvenile, but a three-year-old that failed to conserve energy in a longer race was doomed to lose. The powerful, headstrong E.T. had to learn to "rate," the racing term for the tactic of waiting behind other horses and conserving speed until the jockey asked for a run. It was not going to be easy. E.T. manhandled Day during a workout in early February, all but dragging the jockey along.

As he trained for his allowance race, E.T. ran with his head high and consistently came off the track with nasal discharge. Both were characteristics Whiting had seen in horses not breathing properly. Whiting suspected that E.T. might have a mild infection, for which the colt received a regular dose of antibiotics. Whiting knew that Mike Trivigno had treated the high-headedness with a shadow roll, but Whiting did not believe that was the answer. He thought he could handle the problem medically.

Whiting picked out a six-furlong allowance race on February 9 for

E.T.'s first race of 1992. A longer distance would have given Day time to get E.T. behind horses and start teaching him to rate, but it was Whiting's experience that horses returning from layoffs often were too fresh and uncooperative the first time out, so Day probably would have trouble controlling E.T. anyway. Whiting settled on the shorter distance. The race was on a gray Sunday afternoon, with almost twenty-two thousand fans at the track. They bet E.T. down to 1-to-2, favoring Day, as usual. E.T. had not raced in eighty-nine days.

Breaking from the sixth hole, Day settled E.T. into fifth place, four lengths behind a pack of four horses. The leaders covered the first quarter in a fast :21⅘. Day tried to check E.T.'s acceleration up the backside, but the colt was just too strong. At the three-eighths pole E.T. was approaching the pack rapidly. "I was going to have to break his jaw to keep him in behind them," Day said later, "and I was going to jeopardize myself running up on them like that with nowhere to go. So I eased him out and he just went on and swooped past them all like they were standing still."

In front by a length at the top of the stretch, E.T. pulled away to win by four-and-a-half lengths. The winning time of 1:10⅕ was extremely fast.

The performance convinced Fred Aime, Day's agent, that E.T. was a legitimate talent. "The way he just went ahead and put away the horses was very impressive," Aime said later.

Whiting's friend Steve Morguelan felt the same. "It was just a real big performance," as Morguelan later described it.

The only drawback to the race was that it had failed as a teaching device. Day had not been able to control E.T. The colt had shot to the lead as brazenly as he had as a juvenile. "That's not what we needed," Day told Whiting as he dismounted. "He wasn't covered up [behind horses] for long."

Whiting agreed. But Whiting was excited about the performance, which validated his belief that E.T. had Derby potential. There was plenty of time to teach the colt to rate. What was important was that the talent was there. In the coming days Whiting would nudge Morguelan when E.T. was heading out to the track to gallop or breeze.

"C'mon," he would say, "let's go watch the big horse work."

Morguelan was enjoying watching the colt develop. Whiting's optimism intrigued him. The allowance race had excited him. He decided he wanted an interest in the horse, too. He contacted a friend in Las

Vegas who could get down a bet in a Derby future book. (Casinos take Derby bets months before the race.) Morguelan and Whiting each bet $100 on E.T. to win the Derby, at 100-to-1 odds. They knew it was a poor bet, that the chances of E.T. would even make it to the race, much less win, were 100-to-1. But what the hell.

ONE morning Whiting ran into John Ed Anthony on the backside at Oaklawn. Anthony, an Arkansas timberman, owned Loblolly Stable, one of the nation's top breeding/racing franchises. Forty-five Loblolly mares were bred every year, and the racing operation, based in New York, had produced a Belmont winner, Temperence Hill; an Arkansas Derby winner, Demons Begone; and Vanlandingham, a champion older horse.

Anthony and Whiting were rivals of a sort, but friendly. "You got anything this year?" Anthony asked.

"Well," Whiting said, hedging, "we got one that can run a little bit."

BY February, it had been three months since Arazi had raced. While the colt recovered from surgery in Chantilly, his coronation proceeded in the United States. He was voted the Eclipse Award as the best North American male two-year-old of 1991, even though the Juvenile had been his only race in North America. He was highweighted on the Experimental Free Handicap, an evaluation of two-year-olds made by a panel of racing secretaries; his assignment of 130 pounds was the highest in twenty-seven years. His future book odds dropped to an unprecedented 2-to-1. "It was insane, almost embarrassing; people were betting him no matter the circumstances," Bob Gregorka, racing director at the Sands Hotel and Casino, said later. To lay off some of the Arazi bets, Gregorka invented a gimmick bet in which the casino took Arazi and the bettor was given every other horse. It was an insane proposition three months before the Derby, but the coronation had come to that.

As Arazi's legend grew, the colt's American-based challengers slowly sorted themselves out. Bertrando, the speedy runner-up in the Juvenile, was back in training in California after a difficult two-year-old campaign. Pistols and Roses, a gray colt based in Florida, had won three straight stakes over the winter at Hialeah. Loblolly Stable's Pine Bluff had ended his two-year-old year with wins in the Remsen Stakes and Nashua Stakes at Aqueduct. Those three, Arazi, and A.P. Indy were the first five horses listed when the *Thoroughbred Times,* the *Blood-Horse* magazine, and the *Louisville Courier-Journal* began tracking the top Derby contenders with weekly polls in February, using the selections of various editors, turf writers, and experts.

A.P. Indy was a particularly intriguing colt. The dark brown colt had topped the 1990 Keeneland July sale when a Japanese industrialist, Tomonori Tsurumaki, bought him for $2.9 million. That he commanded such a price was no surprise. His sire was Seattle Slew. His dam was Weekend Surprise, a Secretariat mare that also had produced a Preakness winner, Summer Squall. A.P. Indy's blood was as blue as blue blood gets. Named for AutoPolis, an auto-racing track Tsurumaki owned in Japan, the colt had an unusual running style, with his head hung low. But it was effective. He had finished his juvenile year with a victory in the Hollywood Futurity, then opened his three-year-old campaign by winning the San Rafael Stakes at Santa Anita on February 29.

In the stretch of San Rafael, he trailed a 21-to-1 shot named Treekster by two lengths. His jockey, Eddie Delahoussaye, thought he was loafing. But he took off when Delahoussaye asked him to run. Lowering his head and digging in, he caught Treekster at the sixteenth pole and won by three-quarters of a length. The victory was his fourth in a row after a loss in his first race the previous summer.

Tsurumaki's trainer, Neil Drysdale, was an Englishman who had learned the trade as an assistant to Charlie Whittingham. He used a conservative approach similar to Whiting's; he had never taken a horse to the Kentucky Derby in eighteen years of training, saying he would not go unless he had a horse that could win. "We're trying not to get too excited too early," Drysdale said after the San Rafael. That was not easy: clearly, A.P. Indy was a Derby-caliber horse. His come-from-behind style showed his heart and class, and he certainly had the breeding. A week after the San Rafael, he jumped past Arazi to the top of the *Thoroughbred Times* poll of Derby contenders.

What were the chances of E.T. making such a poll? Nil. True, he had won three of five races and earned the respect of a handful of horsemen. But he had proven little; that became obvious when his record was compared to those of the horses listed in the polls. E.T. had run only in maiden and allowance races. He had not faced top competition. He had lost twice to inferior horses. Only once had he gone around two turns. He was still an unknown quantity.

That would change with his entry in the Southwest Stakes, an un-

graded race with a $100,000-added purse. Run at a distance of a mile, it
was the first test of the year for the best three-year-olds at Oaklawn. E.T.
would be challenged as never before. Three months earlier, Whiting had
not entered the colt in the Brown and Williamson Kentucky Jockey Club
Stakes because he had felt E.T. was not ready for stakes-caliber horses.
Now it was time to find out where E.T. stood. The Derby was eight
weeks away.

The favorite in the Southwest was Pine Bluff, an elegant bay colt
by Danzig, out of one of John Ed Anthony's top mares, Rowdy Angel.
"Pine Bluff was an outstanding individual from the moment he was born,
the pick of the litter at every point along the way," Anthony said later.
The colt had broken his maiden at Saratoga, finished third in the Belmont
Futurity and Champagne Stakes, and bombed in the Breeders' Cup Juvenile. When Anthony's trainer, Tom Bohannan, let him run on the lead
instead of being rated, he responded by winning the Remsen and Nashua.
Encouraged, Anthony and Bohannan shipped him to Arkansas and gave
him two months off to get ready for the spring.

When a flu bug swept through Bohannan's barn in early February,
Pine Bluff almost became a victim. "He was coughing thirty or forty
times a day, and that was just when I was there," Bohannan said later.
"One day he ran a temperature that, if it was any higher, I'd have called
it sick. I thought for sure he was going to get sick. We would have stopped
and lost the spring." The colt never became ill, but Bohannan still was
training him cautiously for the Southwest.

Big Sur, a son of Alydar trained by D. Wayne Lukas, also was entered in the Southwest. Purchased as a yearling for $400,000, he had
failed to win in six straight races since winning the Sapling Stakes in
August, and had finished last in a field of ten in his last start. But he had
earned more than $150,000, and there was reason to expect him to im-
prove: he was under treatment for a blood disorder that had only recently been detected. The treatment? Two aspirin a day to "thin" the
blood.

Another entry that merited watching was In The Zone, winner of
the six-furlong Mountain Valley Stakes at Oaklawn. But Whiting and
Day were not concerned with the competition as much as their goal of
teaching E.T. to mind Day. "If we're going to have a horse in the future," Whiting said, "we can't let him dictate how the race is run."

Day nodded. He was working more with E.T. than he had with
any three-year-old he could remember. The horse was personable, intel-

ligent, fun to be around. Day enjoyed watching the close relationship between the colt and Whiting, whose nickname for E.T. was "Yard Dog." ("Because he acts like one," Whiting would say, feeding E.T. a carrot.) Day even found himself spending mornings at Whiting's barn when he was not scheduled for a workout; he would watch the colt gallop and discuss training and racing tactics with Whiting. He was becoming emotionally involved. He had even gone with Whiting to dig up clover for E.T. one evening. A friend of Day's wife had told her about seeing her Hall of Fame husband out in a field with a shovel, and she had laughed, scoffing. But it was true. Still, as fond as he was of the horse, Day wondered if Whiting's optimism was appropriate. Day did not see what Whiting saw. E.T. was not responding to Day's attempts to establish control. The colt was beating him.

YOU knew winter was over in Arkansas on the day the Southwest Stakes was run. The temperature soared to seventy-eight degrees beneath a clear blue sky. It was as if winter had dissolved directly into summer. Front-runners dominated the early races on a track rated fast. Speed on the rail was proving a decisive factor. This was bad news for Whiting and Day, who were determined to get E.T. behind horses and make him come from off the pace. Their tactics clearly were going to compromise the colt's chances.

Still, Whiting was confident enough to place a $500 win bet early in the afternoon. "We can still get it done," he told himself. His competitive fire was lit; he was pumped up, thinking he could beat Loblolly's best horse. In the paddock Day reiterated to Whiting his determination to show E.T. who was boss. He was adamant. Whiting nodded and swallowed hard, thinking of the big bet.

A crowd of thirty-five thousand fans made Pine Bluff the even money favorite. E.T. was the 2-to-1 second choice. Big Sur was 17-to-1. When the starting gate opened, Big Sur broke sharply from the first hole and took the lead by a head going into the first turn, followed by In The Zone and Pine Bluff. Day took E.T. down to the rail, two lengths behind the leaders. They raced that way through the first half-mile. E.T. was covered up, racing calmly and patiently behind horses, as if he had done so all his life. But then In The Zone's jockey, Robbie Davis, moved toward the outside, opening a slim hole between the two leaders—right in front of E.T.

E.T. did what he always did when he saw daylight. He accelerated.

Not this time, Day said. Feeling E.T. change gears, the jockey grabbed the bridle ferociously. This was not the patient Pat Day familiar to fans. This was a stern teacher determined to send a message. E.T.'s head shot up, as if a bird had landed on his nose. His charge for the lead stopped as suddenly as it had started. Watching through his binoculars, Whiting practically heard the screech of brakes.

"Whoa!" Whiting exclaimed. He later said, "Pat just slammed him. He put a headlock on him that would have made Hulk Hogan proud."

As In the Zone drifted back down and Pine Bluff began to make a strong run at Big Sur, E.T. and Day wrestled up the backstretch and into the second turn. E.T. fiercely tried to shake Day's grip and satisfy his urge to run, swinging his head from side to side in protest, but Day held on. The leaders opened ground on them. By the middle of the second turn, E.T. was four lengths back and plainly disgusted. He had plenty of daylight in front of him but could not run. Finally, he just turned the bit loose.

"It was more out of frustration than relaxation," Day said later. "It was like, 'Awwwww, OK, fine!' That kind of attitude."

Up in front, Pine Bluff had drawn within a head of Big Sur. The crowd cheered the big move by the favorite. Four lengths back, E.T. balked when Day finally asked him to run. "It was like, 'Well, I wanted to run and you wouldn't let me, so I'm not going to go now, take that!'" Day said later. "He was being very temperamental."

E.T. did pull himself together for a run to the wire. But there was not enough time to make up the room. No one was going to catch Big Sur anyway. The son of Alydar had repulsed Pine Bluff's bid and was pulling away.

"With a sixteenth to go, Big Sur is on his way to a major upset win!" track announcer Terry Wallace shouted. The margin at the wire was two-and-a-half lengths. Pine Bluff, fading, held off E.T. by a head for second.

Big Sur had won for the first time in seven months. "All we wanted was a good effort and we got a gigantic one," said Randy Bradshaw, who trained Lukas's Arkansas barn. Anthony and Bohannan were satisfied with second. They knew Pine Bluff was not at a peak. They preferred to win, of course, but they were seeking a larger trophy than the Southwest Stakes. This was a start.

Whiting had conflicting emotions. Losing was disappointing, but Day had intentionally not used the right tactics on the speed-biased track.

The race had set up perfectly for a front-running sprinter such as Big Sur. The loss was easily explainable. And Day had given E.T. a necessary lesson. Considering all that, finishing a neck behind Pine Bluff was no crime.

Of course, it also was possible that Day's lesson would not take. Whiting had trained numerous fast horses that never fulfilled their potential simply because they were too headstrong. E.T. had talent, but was he destined to underachieve?

8

"It's just God-given talent."

Five days after the Southwest Stakes, Pat Day recorded three victories in six races at Oaklawn Park on a Thursday afternoon, then took an evening flight to Miami. He was scheduled to ride a colt named Scream Machine in the Florida Derby that weekend.

Many of the top jockeys strayed similarly from their bases early in the year to ride in three-year-old stakes around the country, all angling for the first call on a horse that might develop into a Kentucky Derby contender. The more horses they rode, the better their chances. With thirty graded stakes and thirty other major races for three-year-olds scheduled between the first of the year and the first Saturday in May, there were plenty of options.

Day rarely left the Midwest, where he had ruled the jockeys' colony for a decade. The only trips he made every year were to Florida; he had tried California only twice, New York once. It was a somewhat restricted itinerary, but it had served him well. He had found Summer Squall as a two-year-old at Churchill Downs, Demons Begone and Rampage as three-year-olds at Oaklawn, Forty Niner in the Lafayette Stakes at Keeneland just weeks before the Derby, and Easy Goer as a two-year-old when he spent a summer in New York. From that quartet had come two Derby betting favorites, three second-place finishes and one fourth.

Of course, Day's search for a Derby mount was unpredictable. There were years when he was dissatisfied with his choices just weeks before the race. Then there were years when he was up to his silks in top contenders, such as 1990, when he had to choose between Summer Squall and Unbridled, the horses that wound up running first and second in the Derby.

As he flew to Miami for the Florida Derby, Day saw 1992 shaping up as a lean year. None of his two-year-old mounts from the previous year had developed. He was not on Pine Bluff, probably the best three-year-old at Oaklawn. Valenzuela was on Arazi. The best horses other than Arazi were in California. E.T., a colt that had proven nothing, was his best Derby hope at this point. Day could not recall feeling so bereft of choices with the race just seven weeks away.

Still, he was sure he would wind up on the back of a contender. He probably would get the call if a decent mount came open in the final weeks before the Derby. Trainers sought Day much as movie producers sought the best actors for their films. He was at the crest of a career encompassing more than five thousand wins and $100 million in earnings. Four times he had won the Eclipse Award as the nation's outstanding jockey. He had won the Preakness twice, the Belmont once, and six Breeders' Cup races. Four times he had led the nation in wins in a year. At thirty-eight years old and one hundred taut pounds, with creases branched across his face and leathery hands as soft as tufts of cotton, he was a modern racing icon, famous as a portrait of serenity amid the thunderous flailing of half-ton athletes.

His twin signatures were his patience and soft touch. In a typical race he saved ground along the rail and waited until the last moment to ask his horse to run, then came from off the pace to win. "He's very hard to get by at the eighth pole; he always saves some horse for the finish," Lynn Whiting said. Trainers marveled at his ability to get more out of their horses than other jockeys, yet rarely was he harsh with the whip.

"It's just God-given talent," Day said.

That talent had kept him at the top of his profession for a decade. If anything, he was improving as he neared his fortieth birthday. In 1991 he had won four hundred thirty races and his fourth Eclipse Award, set a North American record with sixty stakes wins, and been voted into the National Museum of Racing Hall of Fame in his first year on the ballot.

His career was complete—almost. One accomplishment still was lacking. He had not won the Kentucky Derby. It almost seemed impossible. Day was the winningest jockey in Churchill Downs history. He had ridden Derby winners Alysheba and Unbridled to victories in other big races. How could he not have won the Derby?

But it was true. Several unlucky mount decisions had conspired with the mighty whims of racing—and, said some racetrackers, overly conservative riding in a couple of cases—to prevent the jockey with everything from winning the one race he most wanted. Day's Derby record was as stark as the rest of his career was brilliant: nine starts, no wins.

In 1986, he was in contention at the top of the stretch aboard Rampage, a 9-to-1 shot, when Ferdinand and Bill Shoemaker beat him to a small hole. Day pulled hard to avoid a collision and swerved out toward the middle of the track, then rallied strongly to finish fourth, passing the three horses ahead of him within yards of the finish. "With some breaks from the quarter pole in, I could have won," Day said later. But Ferdinand did.

The next year, Day gave up the mount on Alysheba six weeks before the Derby, when the colt was lagging behind the other contenders, having recorded only one win in nine starts. Alysheba's trainer, Jack Van Berg, begged Day to keep the mount, to no avail. The colt then underwent surgery to free an entrapped epiglottis just days after Day gave up the mount and became a different horse. In the Derby, Day rode the favorite, Demons Begone, but the horse bled through the nose so profusely that Day had to pull up on the backstretch. Alysheba came from off the pace to win with Chris McCarron riding.

In 1988, Day elected not to take Forty Niner out with Winning Colors, the front-running filly, then got pinched off at the first turn and dropped far behind. Rallying late, he ran down Winning Colors but lost by a neck and was criticized by some in the racing media for a conservative ride. Forty Niner went on to win the Travers Stakes and Haskell Invitational. Winning Colors did not win again that year.

Day disputed the notion that his tactics had kept his horse from winning. "Forty Niner ran his butt off that day," he said later. "I don't think he had a full quarter-mile run in him, because I asked him right at the quarter pole and when I come to the eighth pole I said 'I'm gonna win' and at the sixteenth pole I said 'Hmmm, it's gonna be close' and as we came to the wire he was tiring and Winning Colors was very game."

The toughest loss of all came in 1989. Day's mount was Easy Goer, the heavy favorite, regarded by many as a possible Triple Crown winner. Day won five early races on Derby Day and held up six fingers to cheering fans as he mounted Easy Goer in the paddock. But Easy Goer ran a dull race and finished second to Sunday Silence. Again Day was criticized for waiting too long to make his move, and for failing to more aggressively coax the horse into running. "But Easy Goer didn't handle the racetrack," Day explained. "He never fired a lick. He came down there like he was in second gear and it was just because he had so much natural ability that he finished second."

The next year presented Day with his toughest decision. He won the Florida Derby on Unbridled, then the Jim Beam Stakes and Blue Grass Stakes on Summer Squall. He picked Summer Squall as his Derby mount. This time he moved earlier in the race and had the lead in the stretch, but ran out of horse and was caught and passed—by Unbridled. "I still think Summer Squall was the better of the two," Day said later. "He just didn't put it together in the stretch."

A ninth-place finish on Corporate Report in 1991 left him 0-for-9. His Derby failings had become an annual Derby talking point for fans and reporters. Was he hexed? Did he freeze in the big one? Was it just bad luck? Day steadfastly refused to admit he was troubled or haunted. Sure, he would say, he was frustrated; his loss on Easy Goer had galled him particularly. But as for the notion that he was unable to sleep at night because he had never won the Derby, he always shook his head, no. He exhibited no frustration, none of the angst that would make it a sexier story. He was honored just to compete, he said, and thrilled with finishing second.

"I know there's a Derby out there with my name on it," he said repeatedly, in what had become his Derby mantra. This explanation was difficult for many fans to fathom. The best athletes were not supposed to accept second place or to compromise on the concept of winning at all costs. But Day never wavered. He never offered even the slightest hint that he was being less than truthful, hiding some darker emotion behind his saccharine answers.

"It was very difficult for most people to understand," his wife, Sheila, said later. "I'm the one who got frustrated at times, frustrated for him. But I never had him tell me that he regretted his second-place finishes. He always does the best he can. That's the key to Pat. Everything he does he gives it one hundred percent, and that's why he can't be disappointed. If he's done his best, what more can you ask? Pat isn't the kind who believes in carrying around guilt or shame. In order for him to accept that he's mad or angry that he didn't win, he's got to feel ashamed or embarrassed that he ran second. Personally, I was devastated after Easy

Goer. Pat was no different. He accepted that he was to run second, that there was still one out there with his name on it. He had that confidence. He wasn't going to waste his time saying it's not good enough to run second."

The foundation for this conviction, and for all others he held, was an intense religious faith he had possessed since a dramatic awakening one night in a Miami hotel room in 1984. He became known almost as much for his born-again faith as for his riding.

"If I win, praise God; if I lose, praise God," he said. "I haven't had any disappointments since that night in Miami."

PATRICK Alan Day was the second of four children born to Mickey and Carol Day, in the small ranching community of Eagle, Colorado. The family lived on a small acreage with a milk cow, horses, and chickens. Mickey owned a body and fender repair shop and took the family to a Lutheran church on Sunday mornings. Pat Day and his older brother were responsible for milking the cow. Pat learned basic horsemanship from his father, mostly on a kindly pony named Blackie.

All four children competed in junior rodeos while in elementary school. "When I was nine, my goal was to become a champion professional bull rider," Day said. "In my first rodeo I tried to ride a six-hundred-pound steer. I'd like to say he bucked me off, but the truth is that I fell off and he stepped on me right between my shoulder and chest. It hurt unbelievably bad."

"Being the best at what he did, no matter what, was important to Pat from the time he was little," his mother, Carol, said. In high school he won almost one hundred matches as a varsity wrestler. Though he was not meant for the rodeo—"I was on the ground more than on the bull"— he was tough and competitive and stuck with it despite the bruises. After his graduation from high school, his parents tried to convince him to attend college or trade school, but he wanted the rodeo life. He took a job as the manager of a gas station his father had bought, earning enough money to enable him to compete in a weekend rodeo circuit.

"I had a love affair with the cowboy lifestyle," Day said later. "In my mind to be a cowboy was to drink coffee and drive all night to the rodeo, drink and chase women until the sun came up, then hit the road again. I loved the camaraderie between the cowboys, the carefree existence." But it was a dream more than a realistic proposition. "It cost $25

to enter a rodeo and you had to pay your expenses. I never came anywhere near making it back. I could never have made a living."

After a year he tired of the gas station and got a job on an oil rig in
Wyoming. When he tired of that, he moved to Las Vegas and shared an
apartment with some rodeo buddies. A friend suggested that, because of
his small size and feisty nature, he try riding thoroughbreds. "I had never
even been to the races," Day said later. "I had heard of the Kentucky
Derby but never seen it on TV."

He left Las Vegas for a job a friend arranged at a California horse
farm with a training program for jockeys. For a month he walked hots
and mucked stalls, then called his parents and told them he did not have
to come all the way to California to shovel horse manure. He left the
farm and returned to Las Vegas. "I found the farm very confining," Day
said later. "They told me it was going to take two years to get to the
track. It was the right way to go. But I couldn't see the light at the end
of the tunnel. I didn't know the thrill of what I was working to become."

Back in Las Vegas, he planned to make money pumping gas or
washing dishes until the rodeo season began. Unable to find work, he
took a job galloping horses and working the starting gate at a training
track. The man who hired him worked on the Arizona racing circuit
and took Day to Prescott Downs. Day won for the first time on a horse
named Forblunged in a seven-furlong claiming race worth $631 on July
29, 1973. Day was nineteen years old and quickly fell in love.

"Being a jockey just seemed to have everything I enjoyed," he explained. "I was kind of a vagabond, enjoyed being able to flit around,
not have any roots, be a free spirit. I was able to be around horses, ride,
compete, win, make money. I thought I had died and gone to heaven."
The lifestyle suited him, too. There was always a party. Drinking and
drugs were commonplace. "I had started drinking in high school and
just got more involved at the racetrack, where it was the thing to do.
Drugs were easily available. I got involved with them."

He was raw and cocky, but also a natural rider with soft hands and
a strong-willed style. Soon he was ready for a higher caliber of racing. A
jockey's agent referred him to an agent named Jim Read, a gentle racetracker with four decades of experience booking mounts. Read was in
New England.

"He called me and I told him to come on up to Rockingham Park
and I would get him started," Read said later. "He was very green, just a

wild kid. He didn't know much about riding. We spent many hours together going over the riding game. Every race he rode, we went over and over. He had a lot of faith in me. He knew I was watching him close."

One of the outfits for which Day rode was the Cornerstone Stable. Lynn Whiting was not overly impressed. "He wasn't a polished rider at all then. Just a kid trying to learn."

But he finished second in the riding standings, then accompanied Read to Chicago and won the riding title at Hawthorne Park, beating out a rider who had dominated the track for a decade. "He listened to me and studied everything over and over," Read said. Day quickly emerged as one of the top riders in Chicago.

He married the daughter of P.J. Bailey, a trainer and former New York rider, who told Day that anyone who could not make it in New York was just a "bum in the ballpark." Less than three years after his first win, Day decided to go to New York. Read warned that it was too soon, but Day did not listen and headed for the Big Apple with big ideas. Read refused to go.

The venture started well. Day toured the barns selling himself to trainers and rode 137 winners, earning almost $2 million in purses in 1976. He won the Jockey Club Gold Cup and rode in the Belmont. But his success did not last. He had become a heavy cocaine user. His marriage broke up. He fought in the jockeys' room with Angel Cordero and Jorge Velasquez. "I was out of control," Day later confessed.

"He got in with the wrong people," Read said. "He was running crazy, staying out all night, talking back to trainers, all kinds of stuff."

"His temper almost got the best of him. If he didn't win he blamed the horse or the trainer or anything but himself," Carol Day said.

The center of his life was cocaine. He snorted before every race. "It makes you think you're superman," he said later. "It got to where I couldn't ride without it. It gave me the feeling of superiority, like I couldn't do anything wrong. I would take hits all afternoon. You didn't want to come down, so you stayed up."

His feeling of superiority was strictly illusory. He won less, lost his mounts, and ultimately left New York in debt and in the process of getting divorced, his career in disarray. He flew to Miami to ride at Hialeah, but there was no spark. Finally, he stopped going to the track altogether.

"My life was in a shambles and I was on a self-destructive kick," he recalled. "There was a period of a month there when there would be two or three days at a time when I was not aware of the sun going up or coming down. Periods of which I had no recall. I'd drink myself into oblivion, keep walking and talking, but not remember a thing. The next day people would tell me what an ass I had made of myself. I spent the first three-quarters of my day apologizing to everyone I had embarrassed or belittled or treated badly or rudely. Then I was back off on the same trip."

A racetrack friend dragged him away—"got me out of the gutter"—and took him to New Orleans. Day begged Read to take back his book. They wound up back at Sportsman's Park in Chicago. "I had run up some bills and my inclination was to ride out the meet, take the money, go to Colorado, buy me a saddle horse and a packmule, and go to the mountains. I was going to be a hermit," Day said. "I had had it with racing. I thought the racetrack was responsible for my broken heart."

He started winning again, though, and began dating Sheila Johnson, who became his second wife. "I found a great deal of comfort in her company. She helped me realize the world hadn't crapped on me, that I had sort of made my own bed. I came to realize that my problem wasn't the racetrack, but me. I also realized I still enjoyed what I was doing."

For the next six years, Day finished first or second in the standings in every meeting in which he rode, mostly in the Midwest. But he won despite a continuing fondness for cocaine and alcohol. He had temper tantrums and picked fights with Sheila. He would say he was going out to buy a *Daily Racing Form* and not come back until after midnight, drunk or high. Sometimes he would just get high and drive all night. Once he became so angry after an argument that he jumped off the balcony of their second-story apartment.

"I lived in a roomful of mirrors," he said later. "All I could see was myself. My priority list was me, me, and me."

But he could ride. Whiting watched him dominate at the Fair Grounds over several winters and talked him into coming to Oaklawn in 1982. Almost immediately Day established himself as the top rider there.

"I wasn't using him at first," said Shug McGaughey, then training for Loblolly Stable. "But my barn was by the three-quarter pole, and I would stand there on the rail, and he had only been there a month or six weeks, and finally one day I said 'I got to get on this bandwagon.' He was just making fools out of the rest of us. He was giving clinics out there. The same type of stuff you see now. A lot of patience. A horse could win by a head and win easy."

In 1982 Day rode in the Kentucky Derby for the first time, finishing fifteenth on a longshot named Music Leader. That year he also finally appeared on the national racing radar, edging Angel Cordero to win the national riding title for most wins in a year. As the year wound down, he was riding in New Orleans, and Cordero was in New York. Each had 397 wins at the end of the last day. But Day had a trick up his sleeve: there was New Year's Eve racing at little Delta Downs, in Vinton, Louisiana. Jim Read secured two mounts and arranged for a private plane to fly Day to Delta Downs. Day won twice. He was the national champion.

"Of course," Day said later, "the only way to celebrate something that momentous was to get totally blitzed. My first stop was the liquor store. I got off the phone after calling my mom and dad and bought a couple of six-packs. My wife was at the Fair Grounds, and they were having a big party. I was excited, of course, and by the time I got there I was blitzed. We went nuts for two weeks. Drugs, drinking. The whole thing was a blur."

Then came a sobering turn: "When I came down out of the stupor, that feeling of success was gone. After having reached the top and embraced that fleeting feeling, which was like trying to embrace the wind, and now to be back facing reality, I was an empty, lost, and lonely man. I was disenchanted with everything life had to offer. It seemed to have no meaning. The climb to the top had meant a whole lot more than being there."

He began searching to fill the void he felt. Nothing changed on the surface—in 1983 he won the national riding title again, with fifty-four more wins than the year before—but this time it sparked no joy. "It was like, 'Ho hum, big deal,' " he said later.

He was more concerned with spiritual matters. "I realized I had this void I had been trying to fill up with a crazy kind of lifestyle, drugs, alcohol, fame and fortune, material items, and it was going nowhere. It was not satisfying and it was not enough. Throughout 1983 I was on a spiritual search. I would go out and look at the stars. I was asking questions. Who was I? What was I here for? I had been raised in a Christian home. I had all the head knowledge. I was kind of a closet Christian. I was not beyond prayer. I knew the story, but had not embraced what it meant to me."

On January 27, 1984, he flew to Miami to ride in the Seminole Handicap the next day at Hialeah. He checked in to his hotel, went to his room, and turned on the television for company while he hung up his clothes. He started watching Jimmy Swaggart, the evangelist.

"I didn't think what he was offering was what I wanted," Day explained. "I thought Christianity the way he was preaching it was for women and children and wimps. I thought I was a self-sufficient man who could take care of himself. I flipped through the channels and nothing got my attention, so I flipped it off, laid down and went immediately to sleep, which was very unusual for me. I had backed off most of the drugs at that point, but I was drinking heavily, and usually without several drinks as a sedative I couldn't go to sleep. This night I hadn't had any drinks, yet I was out when my head hit the pillow, and I slept so soundly that when I awoke I thought I'd been sleeping all night. I mean, I thought it must be time to get up. But I awoke to the distinct feeling that I was no longer by myself in that room. I sat up, looked around, couldn't see anything, had no comprehension of what was happening. I don't know if God prompted me to turn the TV back on, but I got up and turned it on, and the reality came over me as the picture came on that the presence in the room was Jesus. Jimmy Swaggart was still on. He had just completed delivering his message of salvation through Jesus and was having an alter call. And that alter call was for me. Jesus was there, giving me the opportunity to accept him into my life, into my heart, to receive the forgiveness of my sins. And it was so clear to me all of a sudden that that's what was missing in my life. I needed God.

"They say when a person dies his whole life passes before his eyes. Well, in a manner of speaking, mine did. I could see the times when I would walk right to the edge of destruction, I mean one more step and I was a goner, be it car accidents or drinking or drugs or whatever, I would wander right to the edge, and I could see it was God's hands that gently nudged me back away from the edge. Back into this world. Then I would stagger off somewhere else and God's hand would stop me again. The decision was mine: do I accept Christ in my life, give him the reign over my life and let him sit on the throne in my heart, or do I deny Christ and go my own way? I knew if I did go my own way, God was going to take his hands off me, no restrictions, no restraints, no interference. Man, I just fell on my face in that hotel room and wept and cried and begged Christ to come into my life. Which he did."

The next day he rode a horse named Eminency in the Seminole

Handicap, then flew to Colorado and met Sheila. "It was like they had switched guys on me," Sheila said later. "Before he left on the trip to Florida, we had partied, done cocaine and marijuana. The man that came back from that trip was completely different. Suddenly, all that other stuff he had done, going out late and all, just stopped. He was a completely different individual."

He stopped drinking and using drugs—stopped cold after years of use, without so much as a day of rehabilitation or counseling.

"On the flight back from Miami the stewardess asked if I wanted a drink, and the idea repulsed me," he said later. "Since then I've been in situations with cocaine right in front of me, and had no inclination. I'm obviously around people in social settings having drinks, but it's not like the alcoholic fighting not to take a drink. I have no desire. I don't find it appealing. I find it repulsive, sickening, and that has been true from that night on."

He was so moved that he thought about retiring from racing and entering the ministry. How could he remain in a sport based on gambling? "But after a time in prayer and searching the scriptures," he said, "the Lord revealed to me that he had saved me to work within the industry, not to leave it, but to take the talent he had blessed me with, take it and the opportunities and do the very best I possibly could to be a role model."

He became an outspoken born-again Christian. His religion became so integral to his character that it often came up in discussions with trainers and owners. Before the 1985 Preakness, D. Wayne Lukas, for whom Day was riding Tank's Prospect, cornered the jockey and spent a half-hour reviewing strategy. Day just shrugged at the end of their conversation. "If it's God will for us to win, it will happen," he said.

When Lukas told the horse's owner, Gene Klein, about the remark, Klein was furious. "Don't tell me we've got one of those!" he said. Klein was not as angry when Day and Tank's Prospect won the race.

The change in Day was viewed by many racetrackers with a skepticism similar to Klein's; they had a hard time forgetting the rowdy, nocturnal Day. But such skepticism waned with time. Day's faith never wavered. Those who knew him best knew the change was real.

"For all those years when he came home to visit his buddies from the rodeo and school, all they would do is party, party, party," Carol Day recalled. "After the change he would invite them out to the house. The change in him was obvious. He learned to control his temper. Just got it together."

His father died in 1986. "I think he passed away still not believing Pat had been so involved in drugs," Carol Day said later. "It was hard for me to accept, too. I was just grateful he got through it."

What was the impact of Day's personal change on his riding? Day insisted it was crucial, that being free of stress—"I give it all to Jesus"—and inspired by his spirituality made him ride better. Jim Read was not so sure. "He was a great rider before and a great rider after," Read said.

In any case, Day took the last steps to the pinnacle of his profession that year. He led the nation in wins again. He won his first Eclipse Award. He won the first Breeders' Cup Classic on a 31-to-1 shot named Wild Again. The latter was the seminal moment of his career. Day had almost lost the mount before the Breeders' Cup because Jim Read had been stricken with cancer and communication with the trainer lagged. But Day regained the mount shortly before the race. The owners of Wild Again were so confident that they put up a $360,000 late nomination fee. Wild Again was entered against Slew o' Gold, Desert Wine, Gate Dancer, and Precisionist. "He didn't have the talent of the others," Day said later. "He was a nice little horse that tried hard and occasionally threw in the towel at the start. But on that day he was terrific."

With sixty-five thousand fans roaring at Santa Anita and a national television audience watching on a landmark day for racing, Wild Again took the lead after a half-mile, was bumped repeatedly down the stretch, but hung on to win. Suddenly, Day was no longer just a regional star. "That was the race that catapulted my career and was the catalyst for what has come," he said.

When Read retired to fight and ultimately beat cancer, Day approached Fred Aime, the agent for his rival on the Midwest circuit, Randy Romero. Aime was friendly with Romero, but finally agreed to go with Day. "He was more talented," Aime said later. "It was the right choice."

Aime had been raised like Lynn Whiting: the son of an agent, he had grown up around the races and never really doubted that he would follow his father into the profession. He began booking mounts as a teenager in New England, where his jockeys rode for Lyle Whiting. By 1986 he already had more than fifteen years of experience.

Day and Aime proved a formidable team. In March 1986 Day rode a spectacular eighty-eight winners. In 1987 he won ten races valued at $500,000 or more. On one fairy-tale day in 1989, he rode eight winners in nine races at Arlington. In 1991 he rode Dance Smartly, the first filly to win the Canadian Triple Crown. He won Breeders' Cup races on Lady's Secret, Epitome, Theatrical, Unbridled, and Dance Smartly. He won the Preakness on Tank's Prospect and Summer Squall. He won the Belmont on Easy Goer.

He was not without his detractors, particularly after Easy Goer failed to win the Derby. His critics called him Pat "Wait All" Day and said he was just a big fish in a small pond in the Midwest. The criticism did not please him, but the debate over geography was moot. Yes, he would have had more competition in New York or California. But he was not a city boy. He preferred the smaller cities and slower pace of the Midwest. He and Sheila had adopted a daughter in 1987 and were particular about where she would be raised.

Whiting laughed at the criticism of Day. "A lot of easterners think a jockey isn't trying if he isn't beating the horse with the stick. They don't understand Pat. I've seen him win photo finishes without using the stick. He gets horses to run with his head, with his ability to communicate. He doesn't fight the horse. He relaxes the horse with his hands. He's won more races without the whip than anyone."

It was hard to fathom a jockey so skilled, consistent, and accomplished not winning the Kentucky Derby, but that required luck as much as skill. With its large fields and choking traffic problems, the Derby was an exercise in randomness: "the hardest race to predict," Lukas said. The best horses often lost, and jockeys with far less ability than Day had won.

Day had been blessed with a windfall of good fortune, racing and otherwise, on his ride to the top of his profession. He just needed a little more.

DAY and Aime always selected three or four three-year-olds to ride in the Derby prep season, hoping one would emerge as a contender. Aime, who usually decided where, which horses, and how often Day rode, deferred to Day on the year's biggest call. "A lot of it has to do with his opinion," Aime said. "My job is to get him on as many candidates as possible." The first candidate they tried in 1992 was Never Wavering, a gelding that had recorded two firsts and two seconds as a two-year-old. Day flew to Miami to ride him in the Fountain of Youth Stakes at Gulfstream on February 22, two weeks before the Southwest. Never Wavering took a two-length lead around the clubhouse turn, but faded and finished seventh.

The favorite in the race was Pistols and Roses, but the winner, by four-and-a-half lengths, was Dance Floor, a colt with which Day and Aime were familiar. Day had ridden Dance Floor in the Breeders' Cup Juvenile the previous fall, but had given up the mount after getting left in Arazi's dust. Day and Aime had not felt that Dance Floor, sired by a $15,000 stallion named Star de Naskra, had the breeding or talent to become a Derby-caliber horse. It appeared they might be wrong.

The colt was owned by the family of Hammer, the rap music star. Hammer's father, Lewis Burrell Sr., a racing fan for years, operated the family's racing operation, Oaktown Stables. A year earlier the Burrells had tried to buy a Derby contender, approaching the owners of Jackie Wackie and ultimate Derby winner Strike the Gold, but their half-million-dollar offers were turned down and they wound up buying a top filly named Lite Light. Now it appeared they had their own Derby contender, trained by D. Wayne Lukas and ridden by Chris Antley. "If our horse is OK, we'll be in Kentucky for the Derby," Lewis Burrell Sr. said after the Fountain of Youth.

Three weeks later, Day returned to Gulfstream to ride Scream Machine in the Florida Derby. Scream Machine had won only two of eight races as a two-year-old but seemed to be improving lately, finishing second in the Spectacular Bid Breeders' Cup Stakes and Preview Stakes. He was ranked tenth in the *Thoroughbred Times'* Derby poll. Day and Aime also gave Never Wavering a second chance in the Swale Stakes, a Grade II race run on the same day.

Two years earlier, Day had ridden Summer Squall and Unbridled to victories in the Florida Derby and Swale Stakes, making for a memorable day. This time, the day was a certifiable disaster. Never Wavering finished eighth. Day pulled up Scream Machine on the backstretch when the colt pulled a suspensory muscle.

Dance Floor was the favorite in the Florida Derby, but the winner was a 12-to-1 shot named Technology. Making only his fifth career start, Technology took the lead around the second turn and finished four-and-a-half lengths in front of Dance Floor, with Pistols and Roses third. Trained by Sonny Hine, Technology had been sold for $29,000 as a yearling and resold for $102,000 as a two-year-old; he had won two allowance races as a three-year-old. He was not nominated for the Triple Crown. The jockey, Jerry Bailey, had convinced Hine that the colt deserved to run in the Florida Derby.

The second-place finish disappointed the Burrell family. Hammer himself had come to Gulfstream for the race. Dressed in a red jacket, red pants, and red suspenders, with no shirt, Hammer cashed two checks worth $70,000 just to bet on the races, and later tipped a mutuel clerk $200 after she gave him $8,000 worth of tickets. He was trailed by television news film crews all afternoon before the race, and cries of "Hammer! Hammer!" were heard in the grandstand when Dance Floor appeared to nose in front at the top of the stretch.

But Technology spoiled the party. When Hine and Hammer ran across each other on the backside after the race, Hammer politely declined Hine's offer to join the celebration at Hine's barn. "Congratulations, but I've seen enough of your horse for one day," Hammer said.

Technology's owner, Scott Savin, said he would pay the $4,500 late nomination fee to enter the horse in the Triple Crown. "The check's as good as in the mail," Savin said. As Savin spoke, Pat Day was already on his way to the airport and a flight back to Arkansas, no closer to finding his Derby mount than he had been when he arrived.

9

"Bet him."

At eleven years old, the Jim Beam Stakes could not begin to match histories with such hallmarks of the Derby prep season as the Wood Memorial Stakes, Santa Anita Derby, and Blue Grass Stakes. But of the five dozen races constituting the season, the Beam was undeniably the rising star.

It had been a minor race with a different name, the Spiral Stakes, when Turfway Park was known as Latonia Race Course in the 1970s. After the Jim Beam Brands Company began sponsoring the race in 1981, the name was changed, the distance was lengthened to a mile-and-an-eighth—making it more suitable as a Derby prep—and the purse began growing. It started at $150,000, added $50,000 for the second running, then another $100,000 for the third. When J.T.'s Pet won in 1987, the year after Latonia was sold and renamed Turfway Park, the purse was a half-million dollars.

Not coincidentally, the race quickly increased in quality and prominence. Classic-caliber horses began shipping in every year. Broad Brush, Kingpost, Brian's Time, and At The Threshold were horses that ran in the Beam in the '80s and later hit the board in a Triple Crown race. The 1990 Beam winner, Summer Squall, ran second in the Kentucky Derby and won the Preakness. The next year's winner, Hansel, won the Preakness and Belmont.

Lynn Whiting had won the Beam twice in two tries, with At The Threshold in 1984 and J.T.'s Pet in 1987. He was an example of a trainer who had been swayed by the Beam's increasing allure. He had previously used the Rebel Stakes, run at Oaklawn around the same time, but the Beam's purse was five times larger and the race was longer. It was a hard package to turn down for a trainer of a Derby-caliber horse in need of graded stakes earnings.

Whiting planned to follow the same pre-Beam itinerary with E.T. that he had used with At The Threshold and J.T.'s Pet. E.T. would ship from Oaklawn to Churchill Downs a week before the Beam, train at Churchill for a week, and van the one hundred miles to Turfway on the morning of the race. The plan had worked twice before. Why not use it again?

Shortly after the Southwest Stakes, Whiting called Mike Hargrave, the stall superintendent at Churchill, to reserve a stall for a week before the Beam. "No problem, I'll put him in your barn," Hargrave said.

"If you would, just put him in one of the Derby barns," said Whiting, who wanted E.T. close to the grassy fields by Longfield Avenue.

Several days later, Hargrave was approached by Jennie Rees, the turf writer for the *Louisville Courier-Journal*. "Got anything shipping in for the Beam?" Rees asked.

"Lynnie's got one coming in," Hargrave said. Rees and Hargrave knew what that meant. Whiting never shipped unless he thought the horse could win.

THERE were three weeks between the Southwest and the Beam. E.T. trained steadily and without incident through the first two, working a half-mile in :48²/₅ on March 16. It was impossible to tell if the furor of the Southwest had taught him a lesson; only in a race could E.T. prove he had learned to obey. Whiting scheduled a final pre-Beam work for March 21 at Oaklawn, a week before the race. Whiting's custom was to work a horse five days before a race, but he wanted to ship E.T. to Kentucky as close as possible to a week before the Beam, and he wanted Day to work the colt. Scheduling the work for that Saturday was the only way to make all the pieces fit. Day was riding in the Louisiana Derby at the Fair Grounds later that afternoon, but he could work E.T. in the morning and still make it to New Orleans for the race.

The morning dawned cloudy and cool, smelling of rain. Day and E.T. were on the track early. E.T. warmed up, found his stride, and left the pony at the three-quarter pole. He covered the first half-mile in a steady :48²/₅. Whiting had told Day to work five-and-a-half furlongs and gallop out seven-eighths. As E.T. passed the quarter pole, he began to pick up the stragglers of a group that had left the starting gate in front of him. Suddenly, he had something to shoot for, a reason to run. He found a new gear, one Whiting had not seen. He picked off horse after horse as he came down the lane and hit the wire.

When Whiting checked the time, he was surprised. E.T. had worked six furlongs in 1:11⅗, the last quarter in :23⅕.

It was a bullet work, exceptionally fast: barely different from E.T.'s winning time in his allowance race in February. He had basically thrown an extra race into his schedule a week before the Beam. Whiting shook his head. This was living dangerously. Yet the time and the horse's strong, driving finish were nothing if not signs of a horse with major-league talent.

"It looks like we've got the real thing," Whiting said. Day admitted he was impressed.

"Stay with me, Blondie," Whiting said, smiling.

Day won the Louisiana Derby by disqualification on a colt named Line In The Sand, but the field was mediocre and Line In The Sand impressed neither Day nor Fred Aime as a Derby-caliber horse. Their search was still very much alive. Six weeks to post time.

ON Monday, E.T. flew from Hot Springs to Louisville on a jumbo cargo jet and moved into barn forty-three at Churchill. Bob Ray traveled with him. Whiting would follow later in the week.

Christine Martin had been angry at first when she heard Ray was making the trip with E.T. She had thought she was going. But she soon saw the logic. E.T. was going to eat four times a day, graze twice a day, and take an hour of boot therapy on his shins every morning. It was going to be a tough week. Christine reluctantly agreed that maybe Ray was the right choice.

"If I had known what kind of horse he would become I'd have probably put him in Bob Ray's hands [from the beginning]," Whiting said later. "When E.T. was keen and aggressive he might have been a little too much for [Christine]. He was a big, tough horse. A kind horse, but he wasn't going to take any abuse."

Whiting had hired Larry Dixon, a veteran jockey, to gallop E.T. during the week. Dixon had galloped E.T. the previous autumn and not been impressed. This time he raved when he came back to the barn on the first morning.

"He's a Cadillac," he told Bob Ray. The next morning he was even more enthusiastic. "This is one of the best horses I've ever been on."

That was encouraging. But there was bad news to balance out the equation: E.T. began leaving feed in the tub. That had never happened before.

Whiting was concerned. He trained by the feed tub, using a horse's appetite to gauge a training regimen. Horses were the opposite of humans: the more they exercised and more tired they got, the less they ate. A horse turning away food often was overworked or not one hundred percent healthy. "If a race is going to hit a horse hard, it usually shows up the next day at noon," Whiting said. E.T. had basically thrown in an extra race with that fast work at Oaklawn. Perhaps that, the stress of the shipping, or both, had upset him. He seemed fine otherwise. "Let's just proceed," Whiting told Ray.

BY running E.T. in the Beam, Whiting had avoided a rematch with Pine Bluff, however unintentionally. The Loblolly colt was running in the Rebel Stakes at Oaklawn on the same day. But the Beam loomed as a tougher challenge. An assortment of quality three-year-olds were entered.

The morning-line favorite at 3-to-1, off his performance in the Southwest, was Big Sur. "Ever since we put him on aspirin to thin his blood, he's been a different horse," D. Wayne Lukas told reporters.

The second choice at 7-to-2 was Treekster, a California-based colt that had sold for $85,000 at the same Ocala sale at which Al Jevremovic had bought E.T. for $25,000. Treekster had only four lifetime starts, but had broken his maiden by seven lengths at Santa Anita in January, and in his last start had finished a strong second to A.P. Indy in the San Rafael Stakes.

The third choice at 9-to-2 was a New York-based colt, Snappy Landing, which had run third to Arazi in the Breeders' Cup Juvenile and compiled a quarter-million dollars in earnings. Behind him at 6-to-1 were E.T. and another California-based colt, Vying Victor, winner of the Remington Park Derby in his last start.

The rest of the field included Waki Warrior, a 12-to-1 shot that had won the Preview Stakes at Gulfstream in wire-to-wire fashion in his last start; and Saint Ballado, a full brother to Devil's Bag that had two wins and two seconds in four races in Florida, and was listed at 15-to-1. Beam officials had hoped to lure Alydeed, a promising Canadian-based colt that had won two starts after early injuries, but the trainer opted for a shorter race in Florida.

"The California horses were getting all the hype," Turfway general manager Gary Wilfert said later. Wilfert, who had worked at Churchill and knew Whiting, gave E.T. little consideration until he spoke to Jennie Rees one morning.

"I've never seen Lynn so excited about a horse," she said. "[E.T.] may not look like much on paper, but Lynn really likes how he's performing."

Wilfert thought the best argument for considering E.T. was Day, who had won four of the ten Beams. "He knows this track better than anyone. I have never seen one rider dominate a track like him here."

Whiting certainly thought E.T. had a better chance than 6-to-1. Whiting was not impressed with the other horses in the race. Yes, some had better credentials than E.T., but none were standouts. The favorite had won the Southwest, Whiting felt, only because Pine Bluff was rusty, the track was biased, and Day had headlocked E.T. attempting to teach him to race. School would not be in session this time. Whiting thought E.T. stood an excellent chance of winning.

"What do you think?" Jennie Rees asked Whiting before the race.

"Bet him, Jennie," Whiting said. Rees decided she would. In the decade she had known Whiting, she had never heard him say such a thing.

WINTER was lingering in the Ohio Valley. A snow flurry dusted Turfway on Friday, and a cold rain fell through the night and into the morning of the race. The weather was so poor that Cal Partee was unable to fly up from Arkansas in a private plane. Cal Partee Jr., who had flown commercially the day before, represented the family. By the time E.T. arrived shortly after noon, the rain had given way to periods of sun, chilly breezes, and forty-degree temperatures. The track was initially listed as muddy, but upgraded to fast late in the afternoon.

E.T.'s odds were down to 9-to-2 by post time, demonstrating the influence Day held with bettors. But Big Sur still was the favorite when the starting gate opened with seventeen thousand fans in the stands and a slanting, late afternoon sun peering through a thin covering of clouds.

Every race, from the Kentucky Derby to the cheapest claiming race, assumes a certain character. It can be a runaway, a one-on-one confrontation, a four-way chess match; the possibilities are many. The eleventh Jim Beam Stakes, from the first step to the last, was a brawl.

It all started with Waki Warrior. The front-running colt tended to bear out, angling away from the rail and into traffic. He did so in the first fifty yards, bumping up against Saint Ballado, which bumped Big Sur. Leaving behind the chaos he had caused, Waki Warrior took the lead, followed by Treekster.

Breaking from the third hole, Day maneuvered E.T. to the rail in sixth place, with the twin purposes of saving ground and getting E.T. behind horses. The colt relaxed and moved along easily. It seemed the lesson of the Southwest had taken. "He was kind and cooperative early, took his instructions well," Day said.

Waki Warrior assumed a clear lead on the first turn. Patrick Valenzuela, riding Treekster, took second, slipping slickly past Big Sur and Saint Ballado into an opening on the rail. Moving out of the turn and up the backstretch, Waki Warrior opened a two-length lead on Treekster, with Big Sur third. Saint Ballado was another two lengths back.

After running sixth for a half-mile, Day began pressing toward the leaders as they approached the second turn, effectively running up against their heels. At the same time, Saint Ballado, with Julie Krone riding, made a move on the outside. In front, Treekster crept up on Waki Warrior as Big Sur began to drop back.

"They're all bunched up!" said track announcer Mike Battaglia as the horses moved into the second turn. Saint Ballado's move was strong. The colt passed Big Sur and Treekster and closed in on front-running Waki Warrior.

Day continued to wait on the rail, running behind Waki Warrior. He thought he was positioned well. He had ridden Waki Warrior as a two-year-old and knew about the colt's tendency to bear out. He had watched Waki's jockey, Larry Melancon, straining to control the colt all the way up the backstretch. In the last strides of the turn, Waki finally got the best of Melancon. Just as Saint Ballado was passing Treekster and closing in on him, Waki bore out sharply into the middle of the track. It was as if Melancon had signaled a right-hand turn.

"It was like Waki put his chin out and said, 'OK, I'm just going this time,'" Day said later. When Waki bore out, he swept the onrushing Saint Ballado with him. Krone was forced to bear out with Waki to avoid a collision. Her horse's charge was abruptly halted.

Suddenly, there was a huge hole on the rail. E.T. stepped into it.

"He basically inherited the lead," Whiting said. "The other horses went wide and there it was. He didn't have to do much."

Treekster's jockey, Patrick Valenzuela, who was inside Waki and had avoided being swept out, also had designs on that hole along the rail. Day was concerned about Valenzuela beating him there and establishing position, in which case Valenzuela could pin him against the rail. Day clucked his tongue in E.T.'s ear, asking for a sprint. E.T. responded, bursting past Treekster to take the lead entering the stretch. Beautiful, Day thought, as the lead quickly grew to a length.

"We're home!" Whiting announced in the grandstand, where he was watching through binoculars.

Then E.T. stopped running. Not literally. But almost. "Just as we came into the stretch, his head went straight up in the air, his ears went straight forward, and I thought he was going to flat stop," Day said later. "He went from aggressive, in the bridle, to nothing. He practically dug his toes into the dirt. I went, 'Whoa, what is this?'"

E.T. came down the stretch idling. As Day explained, "I changed holds. His ears never changed. I turned my stick up and went to hit him everywhere but on the bottom of his feet. I went to crucify him. I hit him on the shoulder, hit him on the rump, on the belly, hit him right-handed, left-handed. At no time did he give me even a little flicker of the ears. At no time did he say, 'OK, let's go.' He just stayed the same. There was no response whatsoever."

Whiting was stunned. Moments after proclaiming that the race was over, he considered the possibility of E.T. not even hitting the board. The horse was moving that slowly in the lead. Bizarre.

Yet E.T.'s natural speed was enough to keep him in the lead despite his idling. No other horses moved up to challenge him. Krone straightened out Saint Ballado, but it was too late there. The only viable contenders left were Treekster and Vying Victor, the latter having raced wide around the track from the eleventh hole and moved into contention when Waki Warrior bore out. But Treekster and Vying Victor exchanged bumps down the lane, and E.T. held his lead into the final furlong, and held it, and held it...

"Lil E. Tee takes the Beam!" Battaglia shouted as the colt passed under the wire a length in front of Vying Victor.

Cal Partee Jr. and the rest of the party exulted in their box. Whiting smiled and shook hands but also shook his head in dismay. "I was as disgusted as you can be with picking up a check for $300,000," Whiting said later. "I felt like I'd been beat up in an alley. I was disappointed that he didn't run away and hide from those horses. I thought he should have won by a lot. I thought he was a better horse than his race, a much better horse than his race. I was just totally confused. It wasn't the horse that I knew. He should have just galloped in. Pat should have been holding that saddle when the rest of them got to the wire. But he quit running and Pat couldn't get him back in the race. It happened the first time we ran him when Pat just put him to sleep. This time he did it on his own."

The winning time of 1:53²/₅ was the slowest since the Beam went to a mile-and-an-eighth in 1982. Hansel's winning time the year before had been almost seven seconds faster.

Predictably, after such a rough race, there were angry losers. "I hope the connections of Lil E. Tee split half of their purse with Larry Melancon," said Clint Goodrich, the trainer of Saint Ballado, referring to Waki Warrior's jockey. "I don't mind getting beat, that's part of the business. But I hate to get eliminated when I'm running a winning race."

Gary Wilfert sympathized with Goodrich. "I think Saint Ballado would have won," the Turfway general manager said later.

Vying Victor's trainer, Ian Jory, also sounded suspicious of the merits of E.T.'s victory. "I think maybe we had the best horse," Jory said. "[Vying Victor] had to go awfully wide. He had the worst of it, for sure."

Patrick Valenzuela lodged a foul against Vying Victor for three stretch bumps, but the foul was disallowed. The brawling Beam was official. E.T. paid $11 to win. The winning party gathered for the win picture with former president Gerald Ford, whose son, Steve, worked at Turfway.

Whiting had improved his Beam record to three wins in three attempts spanning eight years, a superb achievement. As he received the golden bowl that served as a trophy, he joked, "I thought they gave you the grandstand when you won three times." If you could not laugh on the day you won a half-million-dollar race, when could you laugh?

Still, that finish had upset him. Just when he thought he had conquered his No. 1 problem and taught E.T. to use patience early in a race, up cropped an old problem: the colt's tendency to loaf on the lead. Speaking to reporters, Whiting could not hide his displeasure: "We think a lot of him, but he's got to prove himself. He's got to learn to do the bidding of the rider."

Day also was pleased with his fifth Beam win, but not enthralled with E.T.'s performance. He could not recall reaching the wire in a big race on a horse so lackadaisical and unresponsive. Day's agent, Fred Aime, saw the race in a more positive light. The victory convinced Aime that Day should ride E.T. in the Derby.

"The Beam got me pretty high on the horse," Aime said later. "Vying Victor was pretty highly regarded, and no one was getting to E.T. at the wire. As long as he was running well, it was kind of an unspoken thing after the Beam that everyone knew Lynn wasn't going to have to shop around for a ride. The Beam is like the Blue Grass or Florida Derby. Once you win, the horse would have to disprove himself pretty badly for you not to go with him in the Derby."

Of course, Day and Aime had few alternatives.

AS E.T. was winning the Beam, Pine Bluff was easily winning the Rebel Stakes at Oaklawn. He took the lead early, held it down the backstretch, and closed impressively, winning by almost three lengths. His reputation as the best three-year-old in Arkansas was restored.

John Ed Anthony spoke to reporters afterward. He was asked about E.T. winning the Beam. "Our goal," Anthony said, "is not to win the Jim Beam."

CAL Partee was peeved the whole day of the Beam. He had intended to take a private plane up to Turfway and watch the race in person, as he had when J.T.'s Pet and At The Threshold won, but the people at the airport in nearby El Dorado, Arkansas, told him he could not fly because of an approaching storm. He would have to watch the Beam at home, on television. Then the storm never came. He could have flown, or so it seemed.

Partee drove over to Oaklawn to watch the early races, then went with his daughter and son-in-law to their lake house outside Hot Springs. ESPN would broadcast the Beam on delayed tape, after an America's Cup sailing race. Fittingly on a day when nothing had worked out, the "damn boat race" dragged on. Partee moaned as dinnertime approached. The Beam was over by now, and he was watching sailboats. The suspense was almost too much. "We were about to die," said Jane Burrow, Partee's daughter.

Partee's friend Bill Miller arrived at the lake house around sunset. Miller and his wife had been with Partee earlier that afternoon at Oaklawn and had stayed to watch the Rebel before coming out to cheer on E.T. with Partee. They were all going out to dinner after the race. While the Millers had been at Oaklawn, they heard the results of the Beam announced on the public address system.

Finally, the America's Cup race ended and the Beam came on. When

E.T. was running sixth early, Partee sighed. "Doesn't look good," he said.

"Don't worry, Cal," Bill Miller said. "I bet it works out."

When E.T. got caught behind the leaders entering the second turn, Partee again said, "Man, it doesn't look good."

Bill Miller said again, "He'll probably be OK."

When E.T. threw up his ears and almost came to a halt in the stretch, Partee shouted, "What in the world?"

Bill said again, "I bet it works out, Cal."

After the race, with shouts of joy ringing in the lake house, Miller laughed at his practical joke.

"You S.O.B., you knew all along," Partee said.

EVEN though Partee was eighty-two years old, had been widowed for eight years, and had undergone a heart bypass operation, back surgery, and two hip replacement operations in recent years, his love for the races had not dimmed. He still spent almost every weekend in Hot Springs during the Oaklawn meeting and thought nothing of driving to Shreveport for a weekend at Louisiana Downs. "No one loves racing more than Daddy," said Cal Partee Jr.

Every morning he awoke in the same house in Magnolia that he had owned since the 1950s, drove to his office at the Partee Flooring Mill, not far from the town square, and spent the early morning tending to his lumber, banking, and oil businesses. The walls of his office were cluttered with pictures of his favorite horses among the many he had owned. A large glass trophy case full of wares shone across from his desk. By ten o'clock he had turned to the love of his life. He read the *Daily Racing Form* and sales catalogs. He made phone calls to Whiting and discussed plans.

"He's a tremendous enthusiast," said his Arkansas rival, John Ed Anthony. "More than anything, he just loves it. He loves the races. He loves to bet. Racing certainly has been one of the reasons he has lived a long life."

That life began in 1910 in Stephens, Arkansas. His mother died when he was an infant, and he went to live with his grandparents. When they died, he moved back in with his father, a doctor who made house calls on a horse.

His entrepreneurial mind stirred early. "His father brought in one of the first oil wells in Arkansas," Jane Burrow said, "and he got those little bottles from his father's pharmacy, filled them with oil, and sold them."

While growing up he worked in a sawmill and later as an oil field roustabout. His talent for football earned him a scholarship to what became Henderson State University. But he suffered an injury and his father died six weeks after he matriculated, and he returned home and went to work hauling logs to his brother-in-law's mill. Eventually he started his own mill with a partner, sold it, and started another. Soon he bought out his partner and started two more mills. In 1938 he sold his mill in McNeil, a tiny town near Magnolia, for $60,000. Ten years later he owned the Partee Lumber Co. and Partee Flooring Company and invested in an oil well. When it came in and he sold his share, he was a millionaire.

He was always fond of racing and betting. In the early 1950s one of his best friends was Jack Carnes, chairman of the Arkansas racing commission. "Why don't you buy a horse yourself?" Carnes asked him one day.

Partee soon bought a horse from John [Trader] Clark, a stakes-placed colt named Winning Count. By the next spring he had a full stable.

"I loved having a horse," Partee said later. "I was young and full of piss and vinegar." His bright, polka-dotted silks ("they were easier to pick out") became a common sight at Oaklawn and Churchill Downs. Johnny McDowell, Otto Rasch, and J.J. Weipert were among his early trainers.

In the late 1950s he dabbled in the exportation of foreign horses such as Silver King II, a stakes winner in England that broke down before racing in the States, and Babu, a horse bought in Chile that won the Brooklyn Handicap in 1959. In the '60s Partee built a large broodmare band to breed to Silver King II, and his racing operation dwindled; in 1966 his stable won just six races, while horses he had bred won forty-seven.

But he preferred the racing side of the game and returned to it in the 1970s. He won five Oaklawn stakes and the Clark Handicap at Churchill with Sado, a tough colt named after a sheriff. In 1974 he stepped up to the national arena with J.R.'s Pet, a horse that fulfilled Partee's longstanding goal of winning the Arkansas Derby and also became Partee's first Kentucky Derby entry, running fourth.

"Over the years in Arkansas, the Partee name came to mean the epitome of racing," said Dr. Wilbur Giles, a Little Rock surgeon who became Partee's frequent racing and dinner companion after Partee's wife died. "Everyone identified him with that more than lumber. He was the top man in the game as far as people around here were concerned. If anyone was going to have a good horse, it was Cal Partee. Before I knew him, when I was just going to bet, I wouldn't bet against a Partee horse. They were going to win."

Partee's stable made money in the good years and lost money in the bad years, but his love for the game never wavered. He often brought his wife and two children to the track and made the day a family affair. "If we weren't into the races, we wouldn't have gotten much attention," Cal Jr. said. For Partee the races were a festive occasion. He never wore a necktie. The floor of his box was covered with parimutuel slips. Partee was a serious bettor who, so the story went, bet by the touch, fingering the thickness of the stack of bills instead of taking the time to count them. His success was such that other bettors followed him to the window and bet on the horses he had picked.

"I call him an aristocrat among owners," said Charles Cella, the owner and president of Oaklawn, "because anyone in this business knows it is a triumph of reality, and with all the heartbreaks Cal has had through the years, all these horses that almost worked out and didn't, he never offered an excuse. He never said the jockey should be be fired or the trainer was a bum or the track was too hard or soft. The next day it was like water over a duck. People in the East may not have heard of him, but contrary to what the Yankees think, racing does not stop at the Hudson River. And Cal Partee has been a lion in this game for years."

He ran his stable as he did his other businesses: without meddling. Many owners believe their money entitles them to a say in racing decisions, but Partee saw the devil in that from the beginning.

"If I pick a man to run [the stable], he's got to run it; if he can't, you get somebody else," Partee said. "The owner and trainer have to be together. So many owners push, push, push 'em, run, run, run 'em. I always said, 'If he's not ready, don't run him.' If you've got a $20,000 horse and you run him in stakes races and whatnot, you take away his courage and you've got a horse that can't win for $10,000."

He was wealthy but unpretentious, accomplished but humble, powerful but shy—a mixture that made him a popular figure in Midwest racing.

"You won't find anyone I know who would have an unkind word to say about Cal Partee," Dan Lasater said.

"He's a real guy. His word is his bond. A delightful guy," said Don Grisham, who covered Oaklawn for the *Daily Racing Form.*

"Even though he is extremely wealthy, he doesn't treat people that way," Dr. Giles said. "I have never seen him be anything but nice."

When he hired Whiting in 1978 he entered into his most successful period. In the previous decade his horses had earned an average of $150,000 annually; in the next decade that jumped to a $525,000 average. But then he began to scale back his outfit after his health declined. He sold off most of his mares and concentrated on buying two-year-olds that had shown promise on the track. The dwindling stable meant his hopes for a Kentucky Derby winner were pinned on fewer horses every year.

Whiting's wife, Nellie, always wrote a note to Partee after Christmas, thanking him for his presents to the family and expressing hope that the coming year would be the one in which they finally got that Derby winner. But as 1992 began, she decided she would just thank him for his presents this year and not mention the Derby. It just did not seem decent, after all the disappointments, to keep bringing up the Derby.

"I have to admit," Cal Partee Jr. said later, "I was beginning to think it was never going to happen. We all were."

ON the first Saturday in April, Bertrando and A.P. Indy, the horses widely regarded as the most serious Derby threats to Arazi, raced against each other in the Santa Anita Derby, the Grade I finish of the West Coast's Derby prep season. A.P. Indy had not lost a race in eight months. Bertrando had returned to the races in late February with a tough, front-running win in the San Felipe Stakes, raising his career record to five wins in six starts. A crowd of forty thousand made A.P. Indy the 4-to-5 favorite, just ahead of Bertrando at 11-to-10.

Bertrando broke sharply from the first hole and took the early lead, which he carried all the way up the backside and through the far turn, pressed by Hickman Creek and a bullish colt named Casual Lies, the 9-to-1 third choice. A.P. Indy cruised along in fourth place for six furlongs, racing wide and five lengths back, then dropped his head at the quarter pole and made another of his methodical charges to the wire. He caught Casual Lies, passed Bertrando at the sixteenth pole, and pulled away to win by a length and three quarters. Bertrando was second, Casual Lies third.

The trainers of all three horses said they were going on to Kentucky for the Derby. There was no doubt now that A.P. Indy would be the top American contender.

"When somebody spends a lot of money for a horse, you always hope that horse will be something special," trainer Neil Drysdale said. "And A.P. Indy is that something special."

Eddie Delahoussaye, the jockey, said the colt compared favorably to the two Derby winners he had ridden, Gato Del Sol and Sunny's Halo. "A.P. Indy is as good as those two and has a better pedigree," Delahoussaye said. "He does everything easy and can run all day. And he's smart. But I guess for that kind of money he ought to be able to talk."

Bertrando's trainer, Bruce Headley, was not displeased that the colt had run second in just his second race as a three-year-old. "He ran great," Headley said. "He just needed another race."

Bertrando developed a fever after the race, however. When it persisted, Headley had no choice but to abort his Derby plans. The illness was not serious, but the timing was poor. There was just not enough time to get Bertrando back in shape by the first Saturday in May. The bad luck that all horsemen feared had claimed a major victim a month before the Derby.

IN a normal year, the Derby prep season consisted of the usual races: the Beam, Blue Grass, Wood, Santa Anita Derby, etc. But 1992 was not a normal year, and there was an unlikely addition to the list of important preps: a small stake run on the turf outside Paris, France. The Prix-Omnium II, run at Saint-Cloud Racecourse, was the spot Francois Boutin chose for Arazi's heralded return to the races.

The colt had resumed training in February after Boutin declared him healed from ankle surgery. Boutin had elected to put him through a series of long workouts with stablemates instead of giving him a race or two to shake the rustiness. The Prix-Omnium II would be Arazi's only Derby prep. American trainers scoffed at the idea of running a horse in the Derby with only one short turf race as preparation. (The Prix-Omnium II was slightly less than a mile.) Not even the next Secretariat could overcome that disadvantage, they believed. The competition would be far more fit.

But Boutin was adamant. The colt was only 70 percent fit, he said, and more than one race was too much pressure. Boutin's firm stand symbolized much of the difference between racing in Europe and the United States. Europeans were easier on their horses. They raced on grass, which was easier on the legs, and rarely trained with a stopwatch. Americans stuck mostly to dirt racing, utilized workouts, and pushed horses to accomplish more. It made American horses more vulnerable to breakdowns—but also tougher.

Arazi was not just any horse, of course. He was special. A horde of reporters from two continents gathered at Saint-Cloud. Not only was the Kentucky Derby favorite returning to the races, but Steve Cauthen was debuting as his jockey. Sheikh Mohammed and Allen Paulson had an agreement: Paulson's "house" jockey, Patrick Valenzuela, would ride the colt in the States, and Cauthen, the famous American expatriate who rode for the sheikh, would ride him in Europe.

No matter who was on Arazi, the Prix did not shape up as much of a test. The colt was the lone stakes winner in the field. Three of the other seven starters were from Boutin's stable. Boutin was taking no chances: he wanted an honest pace.

On a mild, sunny afternoon, Arazi broke with a slow gallop and raced easily until Cauthen urged him to run with two furlongs left. The colt moved outside and pushed ahead, much as he had in the Juvenile, leaving stablemates Akiko and Carson Bay behind. Cauthen eased him up in the last hundred yards. The winning margin was five lengths.

"He went very smoothly in the end," Boutin said through an interpreter. "His action was very good. If he was just 60 or 70 percent today, he will be awesome come the day of the Derby."

Cauthen was impressed. "He has a chance to be the best horse I've ever ridden," said the jockey who won the Triple Crown on Affirmed. "Nothing will beat him in the Kentucky Derby. He was only 75 percent fit, and that was great. Everything about him is perfect."

Arazi's legend had grown to the point that a controversy already was brewing about what he would do *after* he won the Derby. His co-owners did not agree, or so went the barn gossip. Paulson wanted him to remain in the United States and try to win the Triple Crown. Sheikh Mohammed reportedly wanted him to compete in Europe's most prestigious race for three-year-olds, the Epsom Derby in early June. It was impossible to do both. American racetrackers shuddered at the thought of a high-profile Derby winner skipping the rest of the Triple Crown. Could it happen? Boutin had said at a luncheon in England in February that he was leaning toward Epsom. But Paulson desperately wanted a Triple Crown contender.

E.T. was vanned back to Churchill after the Beam and shipped to Arkansas the next day. High winds forced his plane to divert from Hot Springs to Little Rock. A van was sent from Hot Springs to collect him and drive him to Oaklawn. A trip that should have taken ninety minutes took four hours.

Back at Oaklawn, E.T. left more feed in the tub, two quarts a day between his four meals. Was he telling Whiting that the last ten days had been too taxing? Perhaps. Between that fast work at Oaklawn, two travel days, and the brawling Beam, life had indeed been pretty tough lately. It was a lot for a young horse to endure.

But then E.T. began to eat again, leaving fewer and fewer scraps, and then, finally, none. Whiting still trained him at a less demanding pace in the three weeks between the Beam and the Arkansas Derby. He worked a half-mile in :49 ten days after the Beam, then five furlongs in 1:01⅘ five days before the Arkansas Derby. The second work was somewhat troubling: once again Day had to harness the aggressive colt. Yes, they were still fighting that fight. Whiting sighed. As much as he was enthralled with E.T., there was always something.

DAY finished sixth on a colt named American Chance in the Lafayette Stakes on April 8, then eighth in the Blue Grass Stakes three days later on Line In The Sand. There was no longer a doubt: unlike in 1984, when Day rode Loblolly's Vanlandingham instead of At The Threshold in the Kentucky Derby, Day would ride Whiting's horse in the Derby.

JENNY Rees ran across Fred Aime one day at Keeneland.

"Is this gonna be your year to win the Derby?" Rees asked.

Aime smiled. "I'd rather be on Arazi," he said.

AS the Arkansas Derby approached, Cal Partee was so excited he could barely sleep. It was a toss-up as to whether he preferred to win the Kentucky Derby or Arkansas Derby. "I've heard lots of Arkansas people say they would rather win the Arkansas," Don Grisham said. "I remember when Partee won [in 1974] he said it was the ultimate."

It was hard for those not from Arkansas to understand. But in a small state without pro sports teams, racing was one of the few homegrown athletic institutions. For years Arkansas horsemen had been too small to compete on the national level, so they concentrated on beating each other. The passion of those wars was ingrained. And nothing could compare with winning in your backyard, in front of your friends and family.

"There are people from Arkansas who go to the Keeneland sales every year looking for horses not to win the Kentucky Derby, like you or I would, but for horses to win the Arkansas Derby," Charles Cella said. "It's the damnedest thing you ever saw. And it's real."

As the Arkansas Derby approached, Whiting felt pressure for one of the few times in the fourteen years he had worked for Partee. The pressure did not come from Partee, who would never put demands on Whiting. But Whiting knew Partee wanted to win. "Real bad," Partee said later. Not only because it was the Arkansas Derby, but also because the favorite, Pine Bluff, was a Loblolly horse.

Partee and John Ed Anthony were not best friends. They were cordial sportsmen who coexisted peacefully enough as the racing lions in their home state; Partee had written Anthony a supportive letter when Demons Begone bled in the Kentucky Derby in 1987. But they were longstanding competitors in the lumber and horse businesses. Both had lumber mills in southwest Arkansas. Both ran top-caliber horses. They were thirty years apart in age but shared a driving desire to succeed. "There's a horrible healthy spirit between them," one Oaklawn observer said. The tension was not hard to divine.

"We both like to win," Partee said. "We get along OK. We're not rivals or anything. But we go our separate ways."

Anthony said, "Cal is a friend. When we meet in the ring, he is always gracious when he loses and magnanimous when he wins. I try to be the same way. But we are competitors. We don't go to dinner together."

Whiting later said, "When they meet on the track, there's not much quarter given, particularly when it's in Arkansas. It isn't something that's discussed. But I'm sure there's a lot of feeling on both sides. They're not taking any prisoners."

The 1992 Arkansas Derby shaped up as particularly symbolic. With Loblolly's rise and Partee's health problems, Anthony was now the top man in Arkansas, the state's racing flag. "It's like Anthony is AT&T and

Partee is Sprint," said Arkansas turf writer Kim Brazzel. But Partee had been the flag before. Neither wanted to lose in such circumstances. Partee knew that losing would only confirm Anthony's position. Anthony, who had won the Arkansas Derby twice in eleven years, expected to win.

Partee wanted the race as passionately as he had wanted any in years. Whiting wanted to satisfy his boss. But E.T. was the one that would have to make it happen.

PINE Bluff, E.T., and four other horses, including Big Sur and Vying Victor, were entered in the Arkansas Derby. Pine Bluff was an even-money favorite on the morning line. He was regarded as the Midwest's top Kentucky Derby contender. He had trained sharply since winning the Rebel Stakes, finishing with an imposing half-mile in :46⅘ four days before the race—more than two seconds faster than E.T.'s work the day before.

"He is always capable of that," said Loblolly trainer Tom Bohannan. "I didn't train him real hard for the Southwest, and the Rebel was more or less maintaining his fitness. Now we're playing for all the marbles."

Anthony was confident. "Everybody always believes they're going to win beforehand, but I really didn't see that any of the other horses could beat him."

But Partee also was confident. E.T. was the second choice on the morning line at 9-to-5, and Partee was so optimistic he planned a Saturday night party for twenty-five friends at Coy's, his favorite Hot Springs restaurant. He could almost feel the Derby trophy in his hands.

"I'm more optimistic with this one than with J.R.'s Pet," he told a reporter two days before the race.

Big Sur and Vying Victor were at 6-to-1, then longshots Desert Force and Looks Like Money. The trainers of Big Sur and Vying Victor predicted big performances. Wayne Lukas explained that Big Sur had suffered from a cough before his tenth-place finish in the Beam and would shine again on the track where he had won the Southwest.

Whiting was skeptical. "Wayne has the horse on aspirin," he told reporters, smiling, "but pretty soon the horse is going to have Wayne on Excedrin."

Vying Victor had stepped on a nail since the Beam, disrupting his training, but he was fit again, according to trainer Ian Jory, who reiterated his opinion that his horse had been the best horse in the Beam despite finishing second.

"We just had a lousy trip in the Beam," Jory said. "I think we definitely started the better horse."

What about Whiting's state of mind? Well, it was funny. E.T.'s win in the Beam had turned the colt into a mainstream Derby contender, seemingly confirming the optimism Whiting had displayed all year. E.T. was now ranked eighth in the *Thoroughbred Times* Derby poll. Yet just as everyone else was discovering his horse, he was wondering if his optimism was so appropriate. Yes, E.T. was a certifiable talent, with four victories, two seconds, and a third in seven starts. But was he a Derby horse? His ambling finish in the Beam was evidence of his rawness. He had fought Day in his last workout before the Arkansas Derby. There were reasons to wonder if he would pull himself together in time to compete with the top horses in Kentucky.

Before the Arkansas Derby, Whiting was noticeably less enthusiastic than before the Beam. He was still confident, but not as sure. "We hope he's a Triple Crown horse," Whiting told reporters, "but if not, there are a lot of other nice races out there."

THE day of the Arkansas Derby dawned sunny, with a hot afternoon ahead. Whiting sent E.T. out at first light for a half-mile jog with Craig Pearl. Throughout the morning and afternoon a huge crowd gathered. Hot Springs is a resort town that loves a party, and the Derby is the biggest party of the year, a sprawling celebration with thousands of fans in the infield, traffic jams all over town, and women in fancy hats. By the time Christine Martin dressed E.T. and Bob Ray led him to the paddock, some sixty-seven thousand fans were stuffed into the old racetrack on Central Avenue.

Whiting and Day discussed tactics in the paddock. Whiting wanted E.T. behind horses for as long as possible. There were several losing scenarios that could play out if the colt took the lead too soon. E.T. might use up too much gas and have nothing left for the finish. Or he might think the race was over and stop running, as he had in the Beam.

The two speed horses, Big Sur and Desert Force, figured to go to the lead, with Pine Bluff close behind. In Whiting's ideal race, E.T. would lay fourth into the second turn, then make a move.

Day's main concern was giving E.T. a workout. The jockey was thinking of the Kentucky Derby as much as the race at hand. "The Southwest was school for him, and he didn't run in the Beam," Day said later.

"We needed to get this colt in shape for Kentucky. Get him some exercise."

Christine Martin and Bob Ray handed E.T. to the pony girl and rushed over to the grandstand apron to see the race, finding a spot near the finish line. Whiting, Partee, and their families assumed their place in Partee's box in the grandstand. Big Sur delayed the start, struggling with five handlers before going into the third hole in the starting gate. E.T. slipped into the fourth hole without a peep. Moments later, the gate opened and the crowd roared.

As expected, Desert Force quickly took the lead, followed by Big Sur. E.T. took third, with Pine Bluff inside him and close behind. When the pack emerged from the first turn and headed up the backstretch, Desert Force was a length and a half in front of a sandwich of three horses. Big Sur was the middle of the sandwich, with E.T. on the outside and Pine Bluff on the rail. But then Big Sur slipped back, and E.T., without any horses blocking him, pushed toward Desert Force. So did Pine Bluff. Suddenly, Day had the Loblolly colt and jockey Jerry Bailey pinned along the rail.

"I should have stayed there," Day said later. "I wanted to stay there. I had Pine Bluff right where I wanted him. I had him in jail. Jerry was pinned. I could have sat there all the way around to the eighth pole, until Pine Bluff flat-out died, and then said goodbye."

But once again E.T. was just too aggressive. Seeing the open space in front of him, he surged for the lead, pulling even with Desert Force and opening the "jail" door for Pine Bluff behind him. As soon as E.T. pushed ahead, Bailey swerved off the rail, moved outside E.T. and began a charge for the lead.

"Once again, E.T. just wouldn't listen to me," Day recalled. "I could have gone on and wrestled him again like the Southwest, but I didn't see where breaking his jaw again was going to help us. I felt like maybe if he went on by Desert Force he might relax a little and come out of it."

E.T. passed Desert Force on the turn as Pine Bluff approached from the outside, now charging dramatically. "Like a rocket!" shouted track announcer Terry Wallace.

Day took E.T. three wide, trying to force Pine Bluff into the middle of the track. The ploy worked, but Pine Bluff still pushed a nose in front of E.T. as they straightened out into the home stretch. His competitiveness stoked, E.T. responded with a surge. They were dead even at the eighth pole. The other four horses had fallen off. Only two horses were running now: Pine Bluff and E.T., Anthony and Partee, down the stretch together in the Arkansas Derby with a roaring crowd encouraging them on an idyllic spring afternoon in the Ozarks.

Stride for stride they ran, Pine Bluff outside E.T., still dead even at the three-sixteenths pole.

"It was one of the best races I ever saw," Charles Cella said later. "Head to head all the way down the stretch."

Pine Bluff pushed in front by a nose at the eighth pole. E.T. continued to dig in, pushing himself, running virtually even with the Loblolly colt. This was not the green colt that had strolled to the finish at the Beam.

As they passed the sixteenth pole, Pine Bluff was in front by a nostril. E.T. closed strong. The horses crossed under the wire so close to each other that Christine Martin and Bob Ray, from their vantage point on the apron, twenty yards up from the finish, thought E.T. had won. They raced excitedly through the crowd, down to the tunnel and onto the track. Only when they saw the tote board did they realize E.T. had lost.

Partee was devastated. His shoulders sagged. His friends in his box consoled him. "I came across Cal later and he was astounded that he had not won," Anthony said later. "That really surprised me."

Anthony was ecstatic, but also astounded. "I could not believe Pine Bluff had so much trouble putting [E.T.] away. Day did some sharp race riding in there, but Pine Bluff overcame it and I fully expected him to pull away with every step down the stretch. But E.T. was tenacious as hell and darn tough to bear."

Though disappointed at losing, Whiting was in many ways more pleased with this second-place finish than the Beam win. Finally, E.T. had put it all together. "The horse ran hard," Whiting told reporters. "He gave a good, honest effort."

Day was equally pleased. "I called on him and he finished strong," the jockey said. "He just got outfooted at the end. It was a good, stiff race to get into the horse, but it wasn't such a grueling all-out destructive drive that you'd think you'd have a washed-out horse in two weeks."

Whiting confirmed to reporters that he was taking E.T. to Churchill Downs for the Derby. Owners and trainers sometimes wrestled with the decision to take a horse to the Derby, the fame and spectacle of the race interfering with their good judgment. But this was not a case of "Derby Fever." This was an easy call. All along E.T. had been pointed for the

Derby with the understanding that he would not get pushed into it, that he would not run if his performances were not up to Derby standards. But they were.

"He deserves the chance," Whiting said.

Pine Bluff, with four graded-stakes wins, would be a Derby favorite. Maybe this was the horse that would get Anthony the Derby victory he wanted so badly. "All any of us wants is a good shot, and we've got one," Anthony said. "This may be the soundest, best-conditioned horse we've taken there."

Partee went ahead and hosted his Arkansas Derby party that night at Coy's, but it was a quieter affair than he had anticipated. He had a mild flu bug and left early. Whiting tried to cheer him up. "I still think this horse has a chance to win in Kentucky," he told Partee. "We'll take him there and give him the shot he deserves."

Partee tried to smile.

10

"We're gonna win it!"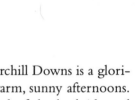

In the weeks leading up to the Derby, Churchill Downs is a glorious place. Clean, chilly mornings give way to warm, sunny afternoons. Derby horses fill the stakes barns at the east end of the backside and grace the track in the mornings. Trainers, jockeys, owners, grooms, veterinarians, track officials, and turf writers trade shop talk, opinions, brags, and bluffs. It is a convention of racing's best and brightest, the patina of dreams so strong you can almost feel it.

Arazi was not due to travel from France until six days before the Derby, but the American-based contenders arrived throughout April. Among the first on the grounds was Casual Lies, the brawny colt from Northern California that had finished third in the Santa Anita Derby. His was quite a longshot story. Purchased by owner/trainer Shelley Riley for $7,500 as a yearling at Keeneland's January sale of horses of all ages, he had earned $445,000, winning the El Camino Real Derby and Sausalito Stakes and finishing within striking distance of A.P. Indy in the Hollywood Futurity and Santa Anita Derby. Riley's sharp wit made her an instant favorite with the press.

Technology, the Florida Derby winner, arrived after reasserting his validity as a contender with a gritty win in the Tropical Park Derby. The colt appeared on such an upswing that jockey Jerry Bailey elected to ride him instead of Pine Bluff in the Derby.

Another Florida-based contender was Pistols and Roses, the gray colt that had finished second in the Fountain of Youth Stakes and third in the Florida Derby after dominating Hialeah over the winter. His trainer had entered him in the Blue Grass Stakes at Keeneland, giving him one more chance to prove he belonged in the Kentucky Derby. Racing on the lead, he won by a nose over longshot Conte di Savoya. The three horses that finished behind him, including Dance Floor, also came to Churchill. Hammer pledged his horse's entry in the Derby even after Dance Floor faded in the Blue Grass stretch and finished fourth, raising doubts about the horse's ability to cover the Derby distance.

"We're going to be there, we're going to bring some more friends, and we're going to win the race," Hammer said.

Devil His Due was the leading challenger from New York. A near-black colt trained by Hall of Famer Allen Jerkens, he had finished in a dead-heat with Lure in the Gotham Stakes and won the Wood Memorial, giving him four wins in six starts. Jerkens, who was nicknamed "Giant Killer" for having beaten Secretariat and Kelso five times, did not want to come to Kentucky at first; no horse had won the Gotham, Wood, and Kentucky Derby. But he quickly changed his mind. He would try to beat another giant, Arazi. Also on the grounds were such longshots as Sir Pinder, My Luck Runs North, Disposal, West by West, Snappy Landing, and Al Sabin. A.P. Indy arrived in the second week of April.

E.T. quietly joined the lineup the day after the Arkansas Derby, shipping up from Hot Springs with Pine Bluff and taking up residence in barn eighteen. The flight was his third in twenty-nine days, but the frequent flying seemed not to have had an effect. As soon as he stepped onto the grounds of the racetrack, thirteen days before the Derby, he flourished, blooming as palpably as the flowers springing up in planters across the backside. His appetite roared back. His hair coat glistened. He was aggressive but mindful of Day and Craig Pearl. He was playful with Christine Martin, but not mean. "He was just full of himself and feeling good," Martin said later.

Whiting was ecstatic. Things were falling into place at the perfect time. Whiting's confidence, which had ebbed before the Arkansas Derby, returned. "I think we've got a real shot," he told Partee on the phone. "The horse is just doing great."

Whiting hovered over E.T., often returning to the barn after dinner to make sure things were going smoothly. The threat of injury was everpresent.

"He paced," said Craig Pearl. "He always seemed to have something on his mind. Of course, we were so close."

FROM the moment Arazi boarded a chartered jet outside Paris, six days before the Derby, his every move was recorded, as if destined for the chronicles of racing history. On board with him were his stablemate and workout partner, Akiko, and two other European-based Derby entries, Thyer and Dr Devious. The latter had won four of six starts in Europe, and made news in March when Jenny Craig, the weight loss magnate, bought him for $2.5 million as a birthday present for her husband. Still, he was little more than a shadow on a plane with Arazi.

Ron McAnally, the Hall of Famer who trained Dr Devious, had suggested to his good friend Boutin that their horses train for the Derby at peaceful Keeneland instead of hectic Churchill. Keeneland agreed to the idea, offering its facilities for use. But McAnally let Boutin decide and the Frenchman chose Churchill, where Arazi had trained purposefully before the Juvenile.

Newspaper reporters from around the country and television crews from across the Midwest met Arazi's plane at Standiford Field in Louisville on a cloudy Sunday afternoon. Authorities, fearful for the horses' safety, brought the transport van close to the plane, giving the TV cameras just a fleeting look at Arazi as he disembarked. The horses were driven to a quarantine facility in a refurbished warehouse across the street from Churchill, where they would stable until the United States Department of Agriculture approved their entry into the country. Their owners hired a private jet to take the blood samples to the National Veterinary Services Laboratory, in Ames, Iowa. Clearance took half the usual time.

Arazi left quarantine early Tuesday. A long silver trailer carried him to the backside. When word spread through the barns that Arazi was coming, seventy-five reporters and photographers gathered at barn forty-five to watch the colt emerge from the van and settle into his stall. A burst of camera flashes punctuated the moment on a cool, gray morning.

An hour later Arazi left the barn for a light workout on the track; he was ridden by his French exercise rider, Raymond Lamornaca. As the colt walked through the backside toward the track, several hundred reporters and cameramen followed. Arazi balked momentarily at the gap, took a walk up the chute, turned around, and cantered a mile around the racing strip. Horsemen flocked to the rail to get their first look at the famous chestnut as a three-year-old. They were startled. Arazi was among the smaller horses on the track.

"It was immediately clear that he hadn't taken a step forward since he was a two-year-old," Fred Aime said later. "He hadn't grown or matured. He wasn't a big, flashy, strapping horse, like a champion should be. I don't recall any Derby winner ever looking like that. If you'd seen him galloping with an exercise boy you'd have thought he'd come from some small track. He just didn't look like a class horse at all. A lot of people were very confident, once they saw him, that he wasn't what he was cracked up to be."

Of course, Arazi had not been one of the larger horses in the Juvenile, either. What you saw was not necessarily what you got with him. After the colt returned to the barn and cooled out, Lamornaca and head groom Fabien Gerard spoke to reporters through an interpreter. "He's even better than he was in November," Lamornaca said. "He's stronger. The knees are not a factor."

The next morning Lamornaca again took Arazi out for a light workout. Again, hundreds of reporters trailed them to the track and fanned out along the fence to watch. Again, Arazi balked and whirled at the gap, apparently shaken by the commotion and traffic. He was accustomed to the serenity of Chantilly. Afterwards, Boutin, who had arrived the previous afternoon, spoke to reporters through an interpreter.

"The horse seems to have recovered all of his physical ability after the operation," he said. "But he has had only two months of conditioning, two or three workouts and one race as a three-year-old. That's unfortunate. But he had eight races as a two-year-old, and more workouts were not necessary because he already has a good base and knows his stuff."

On Thursday Boutin scheduled a five-furlong workout with Patrick Valenzuela riding. After the Juvenile, Valenzuela had said that Arazi would win the Derby, a prediction from which he had not backed down. Now, two days before the race, he slowly rode Arazi from the barn to the track, followed by another clattering phalanx of reporters. When they reached the track, the colt balked at the gap for the third straight morning, whirled again, and dumped Valenzuela. The jockey stood up and got back on the colt. Arazi proceeded onto the track for his workout. The sky was a brilliant blue. A chill lingered in the sunshine. A crowd gathered two- and three-deep along the fence from the mile chute past the clocking stand in the middle of the backstretch. "It was the biggest crowd I ever saw on the backside," said Julian "Buck" Wheat, Churchill's director of horseman's relations.

Arazi slowly cantered a mile and then moved into a gallop. He followed Akiko for three furlongs and quickened through the stretch as he neared the wire, drawing applause from the grandstand. Though somewhat confused about when the work had started, *Daily Racing Form* clockers timed the five furlongs in an unspectacular 1:03⅕, the last quarter in a pedestrian :24⅕.

Valenzuela still crowed back at the barn. "We could win running around the outside fence," he said. "The other horses are running for second. We can go around them, go through them. I just have to pick the right route and point him. I'm on a horse with an afterburner. A push-button horse. The best horse I've ever ridden."

Better than Sunday Silence, on which he had won the 1989 Derby?

"Arazi can do more," Valenzuela said. "This race is over."

Many in racing were hoping he was right. Arazi was the most publicized horse since Spectacular Bid. If he won the Derby with one of his rushes to the finish line, he would do wonders for his slumping sport. "We've needed a horse like this for a long time," Tom Meeker, the president of Churchill Downs, told a reporter.

But as Arazi's hype piled up, American horsemen ranged from politely skeptical to downright scornful of the favorite. "Even though the hordes were following him, I thought they were following him to a hanging," D. Wayne Lukas said. "It was like discovering some acting phenom that everyone claims is the next Clark Gable, and the guy can't act! He didn't look good, wasn't working well. Every day he was more reluctant, less eager to get into his morning. When you have to pop a horse and use prompters to get him started, he's trying to tell you something is wrong. His legions grew day by day as he went to and from the track, but he wasn't going in the right direction."

The colt's ribs began to show as the week wore on. "He literally shrank away before our eyes," Shelley Riley said later. "He got skinnier, the poor thing. He'd come from this enchanted forest in France where people aren't allowed in, so he basically went on trail rides every day, in the quiet, with birds chirping. To go from that to this mass of humanity and confusion, he just couldn't adjust."

By Friday the Americans could not contain themselves. They began coming out of the closet with their skepticism. "How are they going to get the saddle over his wings?" Allen Jerkens asked.

WHITING scheduled E.T.'s last pre-Derby workout for Tuesday, four days before the race, then postponed it a day so Day could attend an uncle's funeral. On Wednesday E.T. worked four furlongs in :48, wearing a shadow roll for the first time since breaking his maiden at Calder.

Whiting had disdained the roll that Mike Trivigno had used on the colt, believing E.T.'s high-headedness resulted from a breathing problem. But Cal Partee had noticed on a tape of the Arkansas Derby that E.T.'s head was higher than Pine Bluff's coming down the stretch, and Pine Bluff was wearing a shadow roll. Partee rarely interfered with Whiting's business, but this time he spoke up.

"I think a shadow roll would help," he told Whiting.

Whiting disagreed. He felt a shadow roll had little effect on a horse. But Partee paid the bills. "My feeling was, 'If he wants it, let's try it,'" Whiting said later.

On went the shadow roll, and off went E.T. on one of the fastest works of the forty recorded by Derby horses through Wednesday.

"The shadow roll helped," Day told Whiting after the work. "His head came down real nice, and his stride evened out."

Whiting shrugged. Whatever. E.T. was coming together so nicely right now that he probably could race with a metal mask. "Finally," Day said, "he's doing things the way we want."

But he was doing them in virtual isolation, with few among the hundreds of Derby reporters paying attention. Whiting, as a Churchill regular, was stabled on the "townie" end of the backside, away from the stakes barns that were the center of Derby activity. Few reporters found it worth the time or trouble to trek across the backside to investigate a longshot that had done little except win a slow Jim Beam Stakes with a green performance. The only reporters who checked on E.T. daily were Harry King of the Arkansas bureau of the Associated Press, Randy Moss of the *Dallas Morning News,* and Kim Brazzel, an Arkansas-based freelancer. "It was really quiet over there," Gary West, who ran Churchill's Derby media notes operation, said later. "The other trainers had big circles of reporters around them. Whiting had a little one."

Those who took the time to visit came away with an indelible impression. Whiting was extremely confident that E.T. would run well and maybe win. Day just shook his head in amazement. He had never seen Whiting so cocky.

"It was almost like a change of a person," Day said later. "Lynn is a quiet, reserved individual, but leading up to the Derby he was extremely vocal about his optimism. He was willing to tell almost anyone and everyone that he was going to win. He was extremely confident. He had never been like that before, ever. I got to where I liked to just go over to the barn in the mornings and hang out. It was fun to be around him and listen. His optimism was contagious. It was a kick."

This was not just blind optimism, Whiting felt. He had scouted the opposition, a habit owed to all those years on the paddock fence, and he had seen no horses that intimidated him. He thought Arazi was an emperor without clothes; one short turf race just was not enough preparation. Technology and Pistols and Roses were not clearly superior to E.T. Pine Bluff had beaten E.T. by only a neck and had bombed in his only Churchill race, the Juvenile. E.T. had a victory and a second in two races at Churchill. "I felt we could deal with Pine Bluff," Whiting said.

The only contender Whiting feared was A.P. Indy—and the California colt was not training sharply. "I thought he was running real lackluster," Whiting remarked. "I was not impressed at all. He just seemed dull to me, not doing well at all."

Others agreed. "A.P. Indy was of no concern to me as the race neared," Shelley Riley said. "We were in the same barn. He was limping around. He was sore. It seemed clear to me that something was not right."

Riley's colt, Casual Lies, was another longshot training well in obscurity. Having recovered from a bizarre abdominal disorder resulting from an allergic reaction to wood shavings in his stall, the colt worked five furlongs in an even minute on Tuesday. The time was three seconds faster than Arazi's over the same distance two days later.

As the week wore on, Whiting shook his head in amazement. He thought the evidence in support of E.T. was relatively strong, yet no one else did. Or, almost no one else did.

"The horses training the best right now," D. Wayne Lukas told reporters one morning, "are Pine Bluff, Lil E. Tee, and my horse, Dance Floor."

That did not mean Lukas expected E.T. to win. "I had serious doubts about Lil E. Tee's pedigree," Lukas said later, "and about his overall ability, too. If it wasn't for Pat Day staying with him, he would have been 30-to-1."

But E.T. could not have received less attention had his odds been 100-to-1. Arazi-mania was in full bloom. "It didn't matter what anyone else did," Lukas said later. "It was fashionable to be on the Arazi bandwagon, and consequently some good solid horses training steadily and doing everything right were overlooked."

Joe Hirsch, executive columnist of the *Daily Racing Form,* commented, "I saw Lil E. Tee all spring and he ran some damn good races, but my perception of him was that he was an ordinary horse. He was not a big figure in my mind before the race. Arazi was dominating everyone's mind. But we tend to form perceptions of horses before a race, and we often don't let the facts interfere with our perceptions. Those perceptions often are wrong."

After E.T.'s Wednesday workout, Steve Morguelan dropped by Whiting's barn to encourage his friend. "You take that son of a bitch over there on Saturday with confidence, Lynnie," Morguelan said. "I've been watching the other horses work, and I watched your horse, and I don't care what the odds are or what anyone is saying, you've got as much horse as anyone. You can beat those guys."

LYLE and Lurline drove up from Arkansas. Lyle came to the track Wednesday morning. The backside was a madhouse, with reporters and cameramen hovering around Arazi. Lyle shook his head. This was why he had never gone to the Derby. The commotion was bound to unnerve a horse.

That afternoon Whiting took E.T. down to the field by Longfield Avenue to graze. "Don't take him down there," Lyle said. "Keep him close to the barn."

"Why?" Whiting asked.

"Something might happen," Lyle said. "He might get loose."

Whiting shook his head. He knew his father was just nervous about all the activity. "We take him down there every day," Whiting said. "He's always good, he likes the grass. Nothing bothers him. C'mon, let's go."

Reluctantly, Lyle tagged along down to Longfield Avenue. Lyle paced back and forth, fretting while E.T. grazed.

"Lynnie," said Terry Dunlavy, Whiting's friend and fellow trainer, "you better get that horse back to the barn before something happens to Lyle."

Whiting cut short the graze. "Let's head on back," he said to Lyle. "I don't want you to have a heart attack."

Lyle was still agitated back at the barn. He was retired now, but his handicapping skills were still sharp. He had seen the other Derby contenders. He knew E.T. had a legitimate chance to win. He paced the barn floor with his son.

EARLY Thursday morning, several hours before the post position draw, a reporter asked Whiting for E.T.'s ideal spot.

"Eight would be great," said Whiting, whose plan was for E.T. to lay fourth or fifth early, off the lead but not too far back in the nineteen-horse field.

Soon the barns emptied and everyone headed over for the post draw. E.T. drew the tenth hole.

"Suits me fine," Whiting said.

Arazi was the next-to-last entry to draw a post, and it was a shocker: eighteen.

The crowd gasped at the news that Arazi would break from the auxiliary starting gate, but Boutin was philosophical. "I would rather be outside than inside," he said. "You can't do anything about it anyway."

THAT afternoon Dr. Alex Harthill gave E.T. a routine injection of a blood-building agent. The colt was on the track early the next morning, jogging five-eighths and galloping a mile and three-eighths. Craig Pearl reported that everything seemed fine. But an uneasiness enveloped the barn as E.T. cooled out. He was not himself. He seemed lifeless.

"This isn't right," Bob Ray said.

Concerned, Whiting took him down to Longfield Avenue. E.T. ducked his head toward the grass, but pulled up. Then he ducked again, pulled up, and walked away. Now Whiting knew something was wrong.

"If you don't want to graze you really must be sick," Whiting said, reaching to pat the colt's neck. E.T. ducked away sharply.

"What's wrong?" Whiting said. He reached again to pat the colt's neck. E.T. flinched, then became agitated as Whiting probed his neck. Whiting immediately pulled the portable phone out of his back pocket and dialed Harthill.

"Doc," Whiting said, "you better get down here real quick because you got a Derby trainer that's about to pop."

Whiting and E.T. headed back for the barn. Now Whiting was the one who was agitated. E.T. would have to scratch if this turned out to be a major problem. What could it be? Whiting raced through the possibilities. He had given the horse a dose of sodium iodine, as he had countless times before, to combat an infection. Maybe some iodine had escaped from a vein.

Harthill arrived and quickly came up with a diagnosis: E.T. had experienced a muscular reaction to the blood-building shot from the day before. The muscles in his neck were sore. Harthill gave E.T. a dose of Banamine. Lyle told his son to rub the area with an anti-inflammatory agent. Whiting instead grabbed a bottle of dimethyl sulphoxide and sloshed the solution on the sore area.

Lyle raged. "You messed up, Junior," he said. "We're dead in the water now. We're gonna have to scratch."

"I know what I'm doing," Whiting said.

Lyle got in the car and drove home. Whiting rubbed in more dimethyl sulphoxide, put laser pads on E.T.'s neck for twenty minutes, then anxiously led the colt to a plot of grass outside the barn.

E.T. ducked toward the ground...and started eating.

Sighing with relief, Whiting took E.T. back to Longfield to graze. The colt was back to his usual self after his boot therapy later at the barn. That afternoon he got his pre-race butazoladin shot. All was well.

Whiting drove home. Nellie met him at the door. "Are we scratching?" she said.

"What do you mean?" Whiting asked.

"Lyle came home and said the horse had a reaction, and you put something on him, and he was going to have to scratch," Nellie said.

Whiting smiled. "The horse is fine," he said.

ON Friday morning Arazi went for an easy gallop. Again he appeared fractious on the track. "It's a change here from his usual atmosphere," Boutin said after the horse was bathed and put away. "He's used to a very calm life. Out here, seeing all these horses makes him nervous. He doesn't like it."

LATER that morning a group of Derby jockeys visited Kosair Children's Hospital in downtown Louisville. Pat Day spoke with Todd Hawkins, an eight-year-old who had recently undergone a bone marrow transplant as treatment for leukemia. Day was so touched that he put on a red-and-green painter's cap with Kosair written on the front.

"Todd," Day said, "I'm going to wear this hat tomorrow." Todd looked up from his bed and smiled.

"As a matter of fact," Day said, "I'm going to wear this hat tomorrow in the winner's circle after the Kentucky Derby."

Almost eighty thousand fans came to Churchill that afternoon for the Kentucky Oaks, the big race for three-year-old fillies. Prospectors Delite and Pleasant Stage were heavy favorites, but an 11-to-1 outsider named Luv Me Luv Me Not scored a half-length victory.

"I was very confident going in," said the filly's trainer, Glenn Wismer, "and you hardly ever hear me say I'm going to do good in a race."

Not unlike a certain trainer with a horse entered in the Derby the next day.

More than $1 million was bet on the Derby on Oaks Day, a record for early Derby betting. Some $238,000 was bet on Arazi to win, almost as much as the win bets for the other eighteen horses combined. Arazi's odds dropped to 3-to-5.

E.T. was supported with surprising conviction, with more than $22,000 in win bets—more than every horse except Arazi, A.P. Indy, Technology, Pistols and Roses, and the mutuel field. E.T.'s odds dropped from 20-to-1 to 17-to-1. The moral? There were plenty of bettors who would always ride with Pat Day at Churchill, no matter the circumstances.

ON Friday night Cal Partee took everyone to Hasenour's, his favorite restaurant in Louisville. Partee's family, Dr. Wilbur Giles and his wife, and the Whitings were at the table. When the food arrived, Whiting turned to Partee. "You know, I had this dream," he said.

"Is that right?" Partee asked.

"Yes," Whiting said. "It was a hell of a dream. You ate a mushroom and Lil E. Tee won the Derby."

Partee laughed. His aversion to mushrooms was a longstanding joke among his family and friends. Three decades earlier, a Kentucky breeder and horseman named Ira Drymon had suffered a fatal heart attack while playing golf. Partee had heard that Drymon ate a bad mushroom before dying. Partee said he had not eaten a mushroom since Drymon's demise.

When he heard about Whiting's dream, however, Partee hunched up his shoulders and pointed to a plate of mushrooms on the table. "Pass those damn things down here," he roared.

AS midnight on Derby Eve approached, the backside at Churchill was quiet except for barn forty-two, stall one, where Harthill was battling another emergency—one that, unlike E.T.'s earlier that day, was not concluding happily. Early that morning A.P. Indy had felt pain in his left front foot. Three-quartering his shoe had allowed him to gallop as usual, but the pain returned that afternoon. Harthill took x-rays that isolated the problem: a bruise on the inside of the hoof.

The good news was that there was no fracture. The bad news was that the second choice in the Kentucky Derby was lame twenty-four hours before post time. Through the afternoon and into the night the colt was treated with hot tubbing, ice packs and poultice. "We need a miracle," Harthill said.

A poultice applied at midnight was left on all night. There was improvement by dawn, but not enough to prevent trainer Neil Drysdale from making the shocking announcement he had known on Friday was inevitable: A.P. Indy would have to scratch.

"Timing is everything," Drysdale told reporters. "If it had happened a few days ago, then it would have given us some time to work on it. We just ran out of time. It's very disappointing. He looked fabulous."

WHITING'S custom was to have his horses gallop on the morning of a race, just to let them stretch out their legs and take the edge off. E.T. went out shortly after dawn. After he cooled out, Bob Ray took him down to Longfield.

"You can be a hero today," Ray said as they stood in the field and E.T. grazed. "This is your chance."

Gary Wilfert, the general manager of Turfway Park, dropped by barn eighteen. He had heard that E.T. was training well and wished Whiting good luck. "I'm rooting for you," Wilfert said.

Everyone at Turfway wanted the Beam winner to win the Derby. It would serve as the ultimate validation of the Beam's arrival as a major Derby prep race. Summer Squall had won the Preakness, Hansel the Preakness and Belmont, but even those successes would not compare to a Derby win.

"If your horse wins, Lynn, I'll get up on the roof of your barn and dance," Wilfert said. Whiting nodded, as serious as ever.

Around noon Whiting let his grooms and assistants go home to rest for a couple of hours, before the Derby madness began in earnest.

"Better brush your teeth and comb your hair before you come back," Whiting told Bob Ray. "You're gonna get your picture taken today."

THE weather in Louisville was warm and overcast, muggy, with rain

predicted for late in the afternoon, around post time. Through the morning and afternoon a great crowd poked through the clogged streets around
the track and gathered inside. As always, there were two Derbies: one
for the rich and famous, in the Turf Club, Skye Terrace, and other posh
addresses in the grandstand; and one for the hearty partiers in the infield. Elegant hats and bare chests, in concert.

The lure of Arazi brought out the stars. Ivana Trump was there
with her boyfriend, Riccardo Mazzucchelli, an Italian industrialist. Mark
Harmon was there, as were fellow actors William Shatner, LeVar Bur-
ton, Jim Belushi, Hal Holbrook, and Dixie Carter. Prince Albert of
Monaco was there. So was Kathleen Sullivan, the newswoman; Ron
Brown, chairman of the Democratic National Party; and Sheikh Fahad
al-Sabah, of the ruling family of Kuwait. Hammer was there, of course,
along with an entourage gearing up to cheer for Dance Floor.

The international press corps, which normally numbered around
ten, was increased tenfold by journalists from Spain, Venezuela, Germany, Russia, England, Japan, and, of course, France. "Arazi is a ce-
lebrity everywhere in the world," said Jorge Escovar, a Venezuelan
commentator.

The early races raised hope that this was indeed a day for history. A
six-year-old filly won a six-furlong allowance in 1:09^2/s, just four-fifths
of a second off the track record. The winners of three stakes races also
approached track records. It seemed possible that Secretariat's Derby record
of 1:59^2/s might fall if Arazi matched his hype.

Nowhere was the power of Arazi's legend more evident than on
the tote board. By post time he attracted $1.96 million in bets, includ-
ing $1.46 million in win bets, some 43 percent of the pool.

There still were naysayers, of course. "I had a number of 'bet you a
beer' or 'baseball cap' bets that he would not finish on the board," John
Ed Anthony said later. "I just didn't see how a horse could run one race
at seven-eighths of a mile and come to the Derby and win going a mile
and a quarter."

The Partee camp set up shop in box three-eighteen, Partee's usual
box at Churchill. Soon, Wilbur Giles went to the betting window and
wheeled a $100 exacta bet with E.T. on top. The doctor came back and
showed his tickets to Partee, who, as a bettor of some legend, was not to
be outdone.

"If you can do it, I can," he huffed. He went to the window and
put down the same bet—an exacta wheel with E.T.—only for twice as

much money. Later, he went back and put down more on E.T. to win. He had, after all, eaten those mushrooms.

After debating all week, Whiting finally made his bet: a $300 exacta box with E.T., Pine Bluff, and Arazi. He was highly skeptical of Arazi's chances and could not believe he was including the French horse in his bet, but if it turned out that Arazi was indeed the next Secretariat, Whiting would forever look foolish if he did not have the horse in his bet on Derby Day.

Whiting sought out Mike Hargrave, the stall superintendent at Churchill, whose job on Derby Day was managing the winner's circle.

The connections of each Derby horse received twenty passes to the winner's circle, for use in case they won. Whiting wanted more.

"I have a lot of people here," he said. "My daughters, my parents, my mother-in-law. I'm going to need to get those people in."

Hargrave was not carrying extra passes. "It's not a problem, Lynn," he said, "but check back with me." Several hours later Whiting came back: "Got those passes yet, Mike?"

Hargrave did not. He pointed to a door leading to a passageway underneath the grandstand and across the track to the winner's circle. "Listen, I'll be standing there," he said. "If you win, Lynn, I'll make sure everyone gets in."

Whiting said that would be fine. Hargrave smiled as Whiting walked away. Lynn must really be confident, Hargrave thought, to come back twice asking for those passes. Hargrave found his wife and told her the story. Knowing Whiting, she went to the window and bet on E.T.

AN ESPN crew taped an interview with Allen Paulson.

"Have you ever owned a horse like this?" the reporter asked.

"No one has ever owned a horse like this," Paulson said.

AS the afternoon wore on and post time neared, Whiting went back to the barn. The backside was a sprawling party, almost as rowdy as the infield. People sat on blankets by the rail, drank mint juleps and beer, and cheered on their bets. Music boomed from radios. Amid the revelry, barn eighteen was as quiet and serious as a symphony hall. Whiting paced silently as Christine Martin slowly dressed E.T.

Whiting told Christine not to bandage the front legs. That was a change in the routine. E.T. had worn bandages all year because the track at Oaklawn was composed of a coarse grain of sand, and Whiting felt horses tended to run down on it. Bandages provided extra protection. Of course, the presence of bandages on a horse's legs often led to speculation about soundness, and while Whiting had heard no whispers about E.T., he felt it was time to settle the issue. Besides, no horse had won the Derby wearing front leg bandages. Whiting was not about to tackle that superstition.

Jennie Rees stopped by on a final tour of the barns. She was one of two writers out of forty who had picked E.T. in a newspaper poll. "What do you think?" she asked Whiting.

"Jennie," Whiting said, "bet him."

E.T. was the last Derby horse to leave the backside. Craig Pearl, Bob Ray and Christine Martin led him onto the track and around the outside rail, heading clockwise for the paddock, located behind the grandstand. The other horses walked in front of him. From deep in the great, noisy crowd came scattered exhortations.

"You can do it, E.T.!" Christine Martin heard. "You're the one, Tee!"

At the paddock Day came down from the jockeys' room dressed in Partee's silks, raised his hand in acknowledgment of the cheers, and shook hands with Whiting. For an hour that morning they had discussed tactics and possible scenarios. It was an unusual Derby in that it lacked an obvious front-runner; predicting which horses would set the early pace, and where the contenders would lay, was even more difficult than usual. Whiting and Day agreed that E.T. should stay off the pace no matter which horse was setting it, yet not fall so far behind that he could not make up the ground later.

"You're just going to have to see what happens and use your instincts," Whiting said at the end of the conversation.

At the sound of the call for the post parade, Whiting patted Day on the back, wished the jockey good luck, and headed for Partee's box. His job was over. Getting the horse to the Derby had been a daunting proposition. There had been numerous doubtful moments along the way, but the post parade was beginning and E.T. was in it. There was nothing more a trainer could do. Day and E.T. were in charge now.

Christine Martin led E.T. into the alleyway and gave the horse to the pony girl. When E.T. stepped onto the track, the seventh horse in line, the crowd was already into a teary, beery version of "My Old Kentucky Home."

Whiting made his way through the stands toward Partee's box. E.T.'s odds had barely moved all day from 17-to-1. It was shocking to see a Day mount leave the starting gate with such little support at Churchill. Whiting had expected the odds to drop to 12-to-1, but E.T. just did not have the kind of record to drive down his odds. Whiting's low profile did not help. E.T. probably would be 8-to-1 if Lukas trained him, Whiting thought.

Yet there was a part of Whiting that agreed with the bettors' skepticism. As confident as he had been all week—all spring, really—he was overcome with doubt in the anxious final moments as the horses were loaded into the starting gate one by one, contender by contender, Technology, Pistols and Roses, Pine Bluff, Arazi. The task suddenly seemed so enormous.

"My feelings," Whiting said later, "were that, as much as I thought we could win, it was sort of an impossible dream and we couldn't really do it. Something would happen, he'd be bothered, pinched, forced wide, and he'd run second or third, and we'd say, 'If only we'd had a little bit of luck.' How can you say, here's a little country boy from Great Falls, Montana, and he's going to saddle the Kentucky Derby winner? You can't just win this race. I bet on him, and I thought he could win, but I didn't expect it. Look at the Phippses, Shug McGaughey, some of the most outstanding trainers and owners in the country, and they haven't been able to get the job done. How was I going to get it done with this little country horse by At The Threshold?"

AT precisely 5:32 P.M., twelve horses bred in Kentucky, three bred in Florida, and one each bred in New Jersey, Pennsylvania, and Ireland were locked into the starting gate at Churchill Downs. They were the finalists out of the original pool of more than forty-eight thousand foals delivered three years earlier, the chosen few that had made it to the Kentucky Derby on the guiding hand of talent, health, success—and a few cases of Derby Fever.

To call it an unlikely group would be a gross understatement. Only four of the horses were by Keeneland-caliber sires: Pine Bluff (by Danzig), Al Sabin (by Alydar), Thyer (by Nijinsky II), and Arazi (by Blushing Groom). Four others were by stallions with somewhat reasonable records of producing stakes winners, though not Derby-caliber horses: Conte di Savoya (by Sovereign Dancer), Dance Floor (by Star de Naskra), Sir Pinder (by Baldski), and Devil His Due (by Devil's Bag). The other ten starters were by stallions that were average at best, producing less than three stakes winners per crop.

Technology, the second choice, was by Time for a Change, producer of only seven stakes winners in three crops totaling one hundred ten horses. Dr Devious was by an Irish stallion named Ahonoora that had produced only twenty-one stakes winners in a decade in the breeding shed. Casual Lies was by Lear Fan, producer of five stakes winners in three years at stud. Disposal was by a Derby winner, Sunny's Halo, that had produced only nine stakes winners in six crops totaling two hundred forty-one horses. Two horses in the mutuel field, My Luck Runs North and West By West, were by new stallions that had never produced a stakes winner.

But none of the stallions that had sired Derby horses in 1992 had a poorer record of producing top horses than At The Threshold. In six years at stud, At The Threshold had sired 142 foals. E.T. was the first and only graded stakes winner, and only the fourth to win a stakes race of any caliber.

All but twenty-eight of At The Threshold's foals had made it to the races, and eighty-two, a healthy 57 percent, had won at least one race. At The Threshold was passing his soundness and desire on to his progeny—but none of his class.

If pedigrees were an accurate predictor, and they often were, E.T. had no chance when the gate opened and the eighteen starters in the 1992 Kentucky Derby emerged, competing for a place in racing history.

THE trouble Whiting had feared came early. The race was less than ten seconds old. The huge pack was hurtling down the front stretch, the horses seeking racing room and positioning as they passed in front of the grandstand for the first time. Snappy Landing, a member of the mutuel field, had taken the lead from the third hole, followed by Dance Floor, which had dropped down from the auxiliary gate. E.T. was hung up in the middle, sandwiched between and slightly behind Thyer and West by West. Suddenly, Thyer's jockey, Christy Roche, veered out sharply, directly into E.T.'s path.

"I don't know if Christy's horse got hit in the face with dirt and got to climbing or whether Christy elected to go outside to get some racing room," Day said later, "but he came directly out in front of me, and for several strides my horse's neck and shoulders were right up on his rear end."

Briefly fearful of a collision, Day had no choice but to ease up E.T. for a couple of strides to allow Thyer to move a safe distance ahead. By the time E.T. resumed running, as he passed beneath the wire and moved into the first turn, he was behind ten horses. So much for planning. Instead of running fourth or fifth, E.T. was closer to the laggards in the back of the pack. He had a lot of ground to make up if he was going to be a factor at the end.

"Aww, there we go," Whiting said disappointedly as he watched through the binoculars.

"What? What?" cried everyone else in the box.

"He got pinched back pretty good," Whiting said. "That's probably enough to get us beat right there."

Yet it was not a disaster. Day found racing room wide of the rail. E.T. relaxed and raced easily through the turn and into the backstretch.

"Getting pinched back may have been the best thing that happened to him," Whiting said later. "Daylight has proved to be his undoing in a lot of cases. But he got covered up back there and got relaxed and settled."

At the front of the pack, Dance Floor moved ahead of Snappy Landing on the turn and opened up a lead of a length heading up the backstretch. Pine Bluff was in third, running confidently and easily. The leaders moved up the backstretch at a slow pace. The first quarter split of :23⅘ was the slowest in the Derby in eight years. The half mile split of :47⅘ was the slowest since 1969, and just a fifth slower than E.T.'s workout time earlier in the week. There was no early speed, no horse pushing the others to run faster. The race was setting up for a fast finisher.

Suddenly, the fastest of them all, supposedly, began rallying from the back of the pack. Arazi was making his move. The famous favorite had fallen far behind early, running dead last under the wire on the front stretch, then seventeenth through the turn and into the backstretch. From the beginning Patrick Valenzuela had felt the need to apply the brakes; Arazi was just too fresh and anxious to go, the jockey felt, having raced so little in advance of the Derby. But then the colt relaxed, switched leads, and accelerated with a burst at the half-mile mark when Valenzuela moved him outside. Racing four wide, he began to put away horses in a dazzling rush.

Goodbye Dr Devious. Goodbye My Luck Runs North. Goodbye Ecstatic Ride. Goodbye Thyer. Goodbye West by West. Goodbye Disposal.

His momentum heightening with each stride, Arazi was at work on a replay of the Breeders' Cup Juvenile as he shot up the backstretch. "And Arazi is moving up in the middle of the racetrack. . . . Arazi is flying!" called Dave Johnson on the ABC broadcast.

Next up, running inside him near the end of the backstretch, was E.T.

"After we went around the first turn, I'd eased out and started creeping up on the horses down the backside," Day explained. "In his other races E.T. would take hold of me and just blast away from me down the backside. This time he was creeping very kindly. I was just catching the field at the half-mile pole, and I was in no hurry to make any big move. Just watching the horses in front of me, sitting toward the outside, not in the midst of all the traffic. And then out of nowhere comes Arazi. He had passed me at the same spot in the Breeders' Cup, when I was on Dance Floor. I remembered the sensation. You can feel the horse coming. Well, when I felt it coming again, I started to go ahead and ask E.T. to run a little because I didn't want a horse to come and trap me behind these horses in front of me. And just as E.T. started to pick it up a little bit, Arazi went by me like a shot. Pffffft, gone. I said, 'Well, there he goes again. I guess I'm running for second money.'"

As Whiting said later, "E.T. was creeping up on his horses. Nellie said to me, 'Where is he?' I said, 'Oh, about seventh or eighth.' And then Arazi just blew by him. Wham. It took your breath away. My wife goes, 'Ohhhhh.' It looked like the Juvenile all over again."

Goodbye Lil E. Tee. Goodbye Conte di Savoya. Goodbye Technology. Goodbye Pistols and Roses.

Up in front, Dance Floor was a length ahead of Pine Bluff as they angled into the second turn. Snappy Landing stalled out and began a fast fade. Casual Lies, the 30-to-1 shot, ridden by Gary Stevens, crept into third. In the grandstand John Ed Anthony felt a tingle. Dance Floor can not last in a race of this distance, he thought. The race was setting up perfectly for Pine Bluff. And Arazi.

"Arazi is gaining ground with every stride!" Dave Johnson called. Arazi passed two more horses as he entered the turn. Goodbye Al Sabin. Goodbye Snappy Landing. This was the moment the sport had hoped for: a brilliant confirmation of the arrival of a superstar.

"Going into the turn," Patrick Valenzuela said later, "I didn't think there was any way we'd get beat."

A half-dozen lengths back, amid the obscurity of the horses destined for the middle and back of the pack, E.T. began chasing the leaders. After being passed by Arazi, Day had taken the colt outside, into Arazi's footsteps, and asked for a run. E.T. moved past Pistols and Roses, Technology, and Al Sabin. Technology, the second choice, was finished. E.T. was in fifth place.

Dance Floor was still leading by a half-length in the middle of the turn when Pine Bluff began to lose ground along the rail. Casual Lies moved past the struggling Loblolly colt into second place and was immediately challenged by the onrushing Arazi. The moment was electric. Arazi had passed thirteen horses in a half-mile. He had run a race virtually identical to his Juvenile. It was the rare horse indeed that could make such a bold move. But there was a problem: the Derby was almost two furlongs longer than the Juvenile.

Pat Day was among the first to notice that Arazi was starting to slow down. "He had opened up about four lengths on me pretty quick after passing me," Day said later. "But I kept my eyes on him, and when we went into the turn he wasn't pulling away. In fact, I started closing ground."

Whiting looked up at the television monitor above Partee's box. The field had separated into two packs: four leaders and thirteen followers, separated by a four-length barrier. One horse was caught in the middle. One horse from the second pack was making a bid to join the first. Whiting squinted at the monitor. Who was it? Whiting saw a shadow roll bobbing furiously. Then he saw the huge polka dots on Partee's silks.

"Look out!" Whiting shouted. "Here he comes!"

At precisely that moment, slightly less than a mile into the Derby, all comparisons to the Juvenile suddenly ceased. Arazi engaged Casual Lies in the final strides of the turn. It was no contest.

"I had said before the race that there was no way that eight-hundred-pound horse was going to get by my thirteen-hundred-pound horse at the top of the stretch, if it came to that," Shelley Riley said later. "Arazi was going so fast, but my horse said, 'Not today, little guy.'"

The two horses ran head-to-head for several strides, but Casual Lies pushed in front as they straightened out into the home stretch. Arazi began to weave. He had exhausted himself with his half-mile sprint. Suddenly, stunningly, the king was dead.

Day brought the charging E.T. up to Arazi's heels. The hardscrabble longshot son of At The Threshold, turned down for auction, sold three times, finally met the silver-spoon favorite worth millions. It was no contest. Day paused for several strides, then swept E.T. around Valenzuela and the tiring chestnut.

Goodbye Arazi.

Running six wide, in the middle of the racetrack, E.T. bore down on the two horses in front of him, Dance Floor and Casual Lies. There was pandemonium among those in Partee's box. They knew it was hard for any horse to outrun E.T. once the colt started rolling. And he was rolling.

"We're gonna win it!" Partee shouted. "We're gonna win it!"

Dance Floor was still in the lead on the inside, a 33-to-1 shot putting forth a magnificent effort. In Hammer's box, the rapper and his entourage were jumping and screaming. "Go! Go! Go!" they chanted.

Dance Floor's jockey, Chris Antley, veered off the rail to try to cut off the onrushing Casual Lies. It did not matter. Dance Floor was spent. Casual Lies pushed past him into the lead as they approached the eighth pole. E.T. moved up on them from the outside.

In the grandstand, Shelley Riley was about to faint. Her $7,500 colt was in the lead in the home stretch of the Kentucky Derby. "When he made the lead I screamed," she said, "but I thought, 'Oh, no, too soon.' I started looking for the come-from-behind horse. And, sure enough, I saw him coming like a rocket."

As Gary Stevens said later, "My horse's ears went up when he made the lead. Lil E.Tee came up on him so fast on the outside that it surprised him. He rebroke with me, but by then Lil E.Tee had too much momentum."

Thundering down the middle of the track, E.T. drew even with Casual Lies near the sixteenth pole, then poked ahead. It was clear which horse had more energy left. And no others were coming.

"Do you believe this?" Whiting shouted. "Do you believe this?"

Day beat a hard tattoo on E.T.'s flank, whipping the colt again and again, almost in a frenzy. "I felt very confident at that point," he said. "I was laying the whip to him probably more than what was necessary. He was running good. I probably would have gotten the same response if I'd put the whip down and hand-rode him to the wire. But I was wanting to win the Derby."

Just past the sixteenth pole, E.T. was ahead by a half-length. In the mounting hysteria of Partee's box, Whiting knew the race was over. "Do you believe this?" he shouted again. "Do you believe this son of a bitch is going to win?"

Day put the whip to E.T. eighteen times in the stretch. "And to be honest, I wasn't getting a lot of response," Day explained. "It wasn't like I hit him and he just exploded. He'd gotten his momentum up and was running. When I come under the wire, I felt like he hadn't given me a hundred and ten percent. I felt that even though he was starting to draw away from the field, you can sense when a horse is really digging, and he wasn't. He'd done it until he come up on Casual Lies. And as he started by [Casual Lies], his head came up and he relaxed. He didn't let down like he did in the Beam, but he didn't just keep at his task and draw on like I felt like he was capable of doing. But it was more than enough."

More than enough, indeed. E.T. crossed under the wire a length in front of Casual Lies, four in front of Dance Floor, and nine in front of Arazi. Day stood up, looked to the sky, raised his right fist, and shook it.

"Hallelujah!" he shouted. "Thank you, Jesus!"

In box 318, Partee's son and daughter hugged him. Wilbur Giles grabbed the old man by both shoulders.

"Cal!" he shouted in the din, "you just won the Kentucky Derby!"

11

"Lil E. Tee Ate Here."

Larry Littman was in the living room of his house in Palm Beach. He and his wife, Roslyn, had dinner reservations with another couple. They were about to leave for the restaurant.

"Wait a minute," Littman said, "I want to see the Derby." Of course. Even though he had sold E.T. for $2,000, how many times would a Littman-bred run in the Kentucky Derby?

When Arazi passed E.T., Littman said, "Well, that's it." Time for dinner. But then E.T. rallied around the turn, ran down Arazi, and headed for the wire. Littman leapt to his feet.

"Goddam, Roz!" he shouted. "He's going to win the race!"

Jumping and hugging, they cheered E.T. home. Littman's hands started shaking when the horse crossed the finish line. He had enjoyed telling friends about the Derby horse he had bred and sold for peanuts. It made for a good story. But he had never seriously thought E.T. might win. Arazi was supposedly the next Secretariat. Several other horses had better credentials. How could an obscure New Jersey breeder cross At The Threshold and Eileen's Moment and win the Kentucky Derby?

But there it was, on the television in Littman's den. The phone rang shortly after the race. A reporter was calling from the Churchill Downs press box.

"How did you get my number?" Littman asked.

"Well, your name is in the media guide," the reporter said.

"I'll be damned," Littman said.

"So," the reporter said, "congratulations. Tell me the story."

Littman laughed. Who was going to believe this? He gave the reporter the short version. That he had bred the horse primarily because

172

the stallion was cheap and convenient to the mare. That the horse had been sickly, awkward, disdained by bloodstock agents.

"This is total luck," Littman said. "I take no credit." He hung up. The phone rang again. Another reporter. Littman repeated the story. The phone rang again soon after he hung up. Littman looked at Roz and their friends, shrugged, and picked up the receiver. Another reporter. Another time through the story.

When he hung up, he turned to Roz. "C'mon," he said, "let's go." As he closed the door, he could hear the phone ringing again.

BILL Solomon had spent the day as he spent every day, tending to business at Pin Oak Lane Farm. Late in the afternoon he came in, washed up, and sat down to watch the Derby with his teenage son, Christopher. He had developed a rooting interest three weeks earlier, when a reporter from a horse magazine had called him about E.T.

"You know," the reporter said, "a horse foaled at your farm is in the running for the Kentucky Derby."

"That's got to be a mistake," Solomon said.

"No," the reporter said, "the horse's name is Lil E. Tee. He won the Jim Beam." Solomon checked his files. Sure enough, there it was: a dark bay foal by a mare named Eileen's Moment, delivered on March 29, 1989.

Solomon would not have been surprised if a standardbred foaled at his farm had become a championship contender. Park Avenue Joe, a standardbred foaled, raised, and sold as a yearling by Pin Oak Lane, had won the Hambletonian, the Kentucky Derby of trotting, three years earlier. Several other standardbreds produced by the farm had won major races. But it was beyond Solomon's wildest dreams to have one of the relatively few thoroughbreds foaled at the farm become a Kentucky Derby contender.

"Is he going to win?" Christopher asked during the post parade.

"Probably not," Solomon said. "Arazi probably will win."

"Does he have any chance?" Christopher asked.

"Well," Solomon said, "if Arazi doesn't win, he's probably got as much chance as anyone else." They watched the start of the race without giving much thought to E.T. winning. But as the horses turned for home, they were on their feet.

"He's gonna win! He's gonna win!" Christopher shouted.

At 5:34 P.M., Pin Oak Lane Farm joined Calumet Farm, Claiborne

Farm, Darby Dan Farm, and the other glorious names on the roll call of racing history as farms where Derby winners had been foaled.

Television stations in Harrisburg and Lancaster sent out crews to file reports on the eleven o'clock news. A horse bred in Pennsylvania had won the Kentucky Derby for the first time. Solomon had to laugh at the headline in the local paper the next day: "York Horse Wins Derby," for a horse that had spent all of seven days in Pennsylvania.

The next week, a sign appeared in the front window of the New Freedom Farm and Garden Store, where Solomon bought his feed: "Lil E. Tee Ate Here."

AL Jevremovic was in Louisville on Derby Day, strictly by coincidence. He had bought a small hotel across town from Churchill Downs and was taking over in time to benefit from the lucrative Derby weekend.

Since selling E.T. seven months earlier, Jevremovic had followed the horse closely. Out of loyalty he had put down a $200 future-book bet at 150-to-1 in January, knowing it was little more than a prayer. (He later sold off parts of the bet to friends, retaining three-fifths.) On Oaks Day he went to Churchill and made his Derby bet, wheeling a $10 exacta with E.T. on top. But he was so annoyed by the big crowd that he stayed home and watched the Derby on a big-screen television in the bar of his new hotel.

When he saw E.T. wearing a shadow roll in the post parade, he cursed himself for not going to the trouble of fighting the crowd. He had been waiting for Whiting to do this. E.T. had not worn a shadow roll since the day he broke his maiden so magically at Calder. Jevremovic was convinced that a shadow roll made E.T. a super horse.

"Now you're talking, Lynn," Jevremovic said.

As E.T. came down the stretch, Jevremovic, normally stoic during a race, jumped up and shouted, "That's my horse!" All his life, he had owned bums: Finger Lakes horses, Penn National horses. Suddenly, he had touched history.

"It was worth having all those bums," he said later, "to have one like this."

His exacta and future-book bets were worth $24,800—almost precisely the amount he had paid to buy the horse of his lifetime at a nonselect sale in Ocala, Florida.

"WHEN the horse crossed the finish line, chills went down my back,"

Mike Trivigno said. "I had that bittersweet, happy-sad kind of feeling. Knowing the horse had been in your barn. You only get one in a lifetime, maybe. That was mine. But I knew the routine with Al all along, that he was always going to sell. The only thing you can do is start looking for another one. I'll tell you one thing, though. It sure makes you look different at some young horse that runs kinda funny."

CHUCK Wieneke sat up straight when he saw E.T. wearing a shadow roll in the post parade. "We're gonna win today," he said.

Joan, his wife, gave him a disdainful look. Sure, Chuck.

"He is," Wieneke said. "Look at that shadow roll."

He had tried to follow E.T.'s progress since selling the horse to Jevremovic. It was not easy. He was busy. But he had seen the Southwest Stakes and known that Whiting was trying to teach the colt to rate. He had seen the Arkansas Derby and recognized that the colt was coming together.

When he saw the shadow roll, he wished he had gone into Ocala and put down a bet at OBS, where they simulcast the Derby. "I wish I could have gotten into town," he said.

He stood and watched the Derby in his living room at Green Key Farm. After it was over, when everyone in the house finally stopped shouting, the enormity of his accomplishment hit him. He had pinhooked a Derby winner.

E.T. was unwanted when Wieneke saw him at Indian Hill Farm in December 1991. If Wieneke had just let him pass, as he let hundreds of other misfits pass, another horse would be the toast of racing right now. What he was watching on television had all begun with him.

"Is this unbelievable?" he said to Joan.

MARY Deppa drove from Lil Stable to Philadelphia Park on Derby Day. The race was being simulcast, and one of Littman's horses was running in a live race.

Littman's horse was Topretariat, the Topsider colt that had been one of the stars of the foal crop that included E.T. Topretariat had finished in the money in six of nine maiden and allowance races for Lil Stable, winning two. Forty-five minutes before the Derby, he ran seventh in a $15,000 allowance race. There were eight thousand fans in the stands.

Mary could not hear the announcer's call during the simulcast of the Derby. She could barely see the screen. But she knew what was happening. She screamed E.T.'s name. She cheered him down the stretch. When he crossed the finish line, she started shaking. A colt she had named, cursed, and nursed through colic surgery had just won the Kentucky Derby.

She ran out to her car, got on the phone, and called Littman in Florida. The line was busy. She tried again a few minutes later. Still busy. Again, a few minutes later: busy, busy, busy.

Finally, she drove back to the farm, trying to fathom the absurdity of a little girl from Kenner, Louisiana, raising a Kentucky Derby winner. Finally, she reached Littman that evening.

"Do you believe that?" she shouted.

MIKE Paramore went into Ocala to put down a bet on E.T. at OBS. He took along his oldest son, Austin. Paramore bet $20 to win. Austin bet $2. They drove home to watch the race.

E.T.'s success since Paramore and Wieneke sold him had become something of a joke in Paramore's house. After the Beam, Paramore had told his wife, Leslie, "This horse might be in the running for the Kentucky Derby."

"If he wins the Kentucky Derby, I'm divorcing you," Leslie said.

As E.T. came down the stretch, Paramore jumped up and down on the couch in his den, shouting, "He's gonna win it, he's gonna win it!"

Austin Paramore was a winner at the window.

THE McGreevy brothers got together in Atlanta to watch the Derby. They often used the race as an excuse to hold a family reunion. They watched with a mixture of shock and amusement as a horse that their brother Bill had almost bought at a nonselect sale outran Arazi and the others to the wire.

Unreal. That was the perfect description.

Unreal Zeal was the sire of the filly Bill had bought for $21,000 at OBS after he fell a thousand dollars short as the underbidder on E.T. The filly's name was Unquote. She had suffered from heart palpitations, fought stifle problems, started late, and accomplished little. On Derby Day she ran second in a maiden claiming race as a 23-to-1 shot at Delaware Park. Her rider dropped his whip at the top of the stretch.

Soon after the Derby, Bill called his brothers from his car phone.

He had not been able to make it to Atlanta. He was driving on a highway in Illinois.

"Where are you?" one of the brothers asked, hearing the sound of the wind blowing into the receiver.

"Oh, that," Bill said. "Well, I'm standing here on the ledge of the thirty-sixth floor, and I was just calling to let you know: I'm going to jump."

BARRY Irwin and Jeff Siegel, who managed the Clover Racing Stable and Team Valor syndicates, watched the Derby on television in California. As soon as the horses hit the wire, Irwin called the vet that had looked at the x-rays of E.T.'s shins and advised them not to buy the colt. "Did you see the race?" Irwin said.

"Yeah," the vet said.

"Do you remember who that horse was?" Irwin asked.

"You know," the vet said, "I was just saying to my wife that the name of that horse sure was familiar."

Irwin laughed. "Yeah," he said, "do you remember those x-rays I showed you?"

"IT was like jumping into a swimming pool of freezing water, that much of a shock to the system," Pat Day said, describing the moment he crossed the finish line. "I thought I had an idea of what it would feel like to win the Derby, but the feeling that came over me was indescribable. I was just so thankful that God sought that day and that time with those people to allow me to experience that. It was just tremendous. The first thing out of my mouth was, 'Thank you, Jesus, hallelujah, thank you.' And I kept saying it. I couldn't stop. Then I rode back, and the picture taking and all that up on the podium, that was basically a blur. The Lord let me experience this high and stay at that altitude for ten, fifteen, twenty minutes. The applause, riding back to the crowd, people asking for autographs, the ride up in the elevator to the press box—I can remember it, but it was almost like a dream."

In the winner's circle, Day wore the cap of Todd Hawkins, the boy he had visited at Kosair Children's Hospital the day before.

WHILE the crowd cheered the leaders coming down the stretch, John Ed Anthony watched Pine Bluff, grimly hoping for a final run, yet more aware with each stride that it was not going to happen. Finally, Anthony gave up and checked out the leaders as they headed for the wire. He saw Partee's silks.

"Look!" he shouted to his wife, "Cal's going to win."

BOB Ray, Craig Pearl, and Christine Martin watched the race on a small television in the track supervisor's office underneath the grandstand. They had gone there in desperation moments before post time, when, after handing E.T. over to Day and the pony girl, they realized they had nowhere to watch the race. The office already was crammed full of people when they got there, but they found room standing on a couch.

"Omigod, he's gonna win!" Craig Pearl shouted as E.T. passed Arazi and began running down Casual Lies.

"C'mon, Tee!" Christine Martin screamed. Bob Ray got so excited that he punched out one of ceiling boards while jumping up and down.

When E.T. crossed under the wire, the three burst out of the office onto the breezeway, laughing and crying. "We did it, we did it!" they said over and over, as if it would all turn into a dream if they stopped saying it.

They headed toward the finish line and met Day and E.T. coming back. Pearl grabbed the horse as Day jumped off.

"You did it, Tee!" Pearl said. "You're amazing!"

FRED Aime stayed home for the Derby. Since 1989, when Aime had spent $800 for a box and gone home disappointed after Day finished second on Easy Goer, he had said he would never again put himself through such torture.

When E.T. came in, Aime got up and poured a glass of champagne. He toasted his late father, Bud, who had also been a jockey's agent and won the 1961 Derby with Johnny Sellers riding Carry Back.

Like father, like son.

SUDDENLY, barn forty-five was the quietest place on the backside. For a week it had been the center of the racing world, Arazi's Derby home. Hundreds of reporters and horsemen had hung around all week, watching the colt prepare for his anticipated coronation. Who could believe this ending? Who could believe eighth place?

A light rain began to fall in the gathering dusk. Boutin arrived, pulled off his tie, and exhaled. His wife, Lucy, stood inside the shedrow, softly crying in her broad Derby hat. "I was the only one afraid to bring him over here," Boutin said through an interpreter.

For months he had expressed optimism about Arazi's Derby prospects, dismissing the notion that the knee surgery and lack of hard preparation would affect the horse. Now, after the race, after eighth place was a reality and criticism loomed, his story was different. He tried to deflect the blame.

"We were always rushing to get the horse ready from the moment he had surgery," Boutin said. "He was without training for two months. That put us back. But my owners wanted this. And now here it is."

In the jockey's room, Patrick Valenzuela faced a circle of reporters wanting to know about his prediction that Arazi could win racing around the outside fence. He blamed Boutin's one-race prep schedule.

"The horse could have used another race," the jockey said. "He was too fresh. I think he could have used a little more seasoning. The whole idea was to get him relaxed early, but he was so pepped and ready to run that I was having to hold him back. Maybe he lost some energy there. I still thought we were going to win turning for home. But he didn't fire."

Arazi's eighth-place finish was the worst ever for a Derby favorite. Considering that and the millions of dollars wagered on him, he qualified as the biggest flop in Derby history.

THE Partee clan, Whiting and his family, and Wilbur Giles and his wife were crammed into Partee's box in section 318.

"It's a good thing the cameras weren't on us," said Jane Burrow, Partee's daughter. "I'd have been embarrassed. We lost our cool. My brother was screaming the worst. Lynn was watching through the binoculars and giving us the blow-by-blow account. When [E.T.] hit the top of the stretch Lynn started going, 'We're gonna win it! We're gonna win it!' I was standing there beside Daddy. Tears started coming down his face. He cried all the way to the winner's circle. He cried in the winner's circle."

What was he crying about?

"Just the joy," she said. "I don't know, you can't explain it. It's just a moment when cry is what you want to do. You're thankful. You're excited. You're missing those that weren't there. We were all thinking of my mother."

Partee later said, "You're about halfway crazy. I've won a lot of good races, but there's no comparison [to the Derby]. There's just something about it. When Arazi passed him, it didn't look good, but I knew E.T. hadn't run yet. At the eighth pole I thought he had it. At the sixteenth pole, we done began to hug each other. It's a hell of a feeling, an awful good feeling. You can't put it in words, but I'd sure like to try it again."

Dr. David Allen, a Louisville physician assigned to Partee as a week-long host, led the party from the box, down a back staircase, and across the track to the winner's circle. As promised, Mike Hargrave was at the door to let everyone through. A policeman briefly prevented those without passes from entering the winner's circle area, but a security supervisor intervened and allowed them to go through.

Partee, Whiting, and Day were interviewed by ABC's Jim McKay after the winner's circle picture was taken. A national television audience watched the tears rolling down the old man's cheeks. Later, at a racetrack-sponsored party in the Kentucky Derby Museum, Partee waved off a chance to speak. Speeches were not his thing.

"Boss, you gotta get up there and say something," he said to Charles Cella, the owner of Oaklawn.

Cella took the microphone. "This couldn't happen to a man who has done more for the game," he said. "Cal Partee is a Gibraltar of racing."

It took two mutuel clerks ten minutes to round up enough money to pay off Partee's winning bets.

LYLE Whiting watched the race on television, in a grandstand bar where the horsemen hung out. There was too much commotion in the owners' boxes, too many people, too many cameras. Partee's box was just too crowded. As small as he was, Lyle was not sure how much of the race he would be able to see.

"I'm a nervous watcher anyway," he said later. When E.T. shot past Arazi, Lyle knew the race was over. "C'mon," he said softly, "c'mon, baby."

When E.T. crossed the finish line, Lyle was momentarily numb. He felt someone pound him on the back. Two old friends, jockeys' agents he had known for years, picked him up by the arms. "C'mon," they said, "you gotta get somewhere, Lyle."

Lyle said later, "They practically carried me across the track to the infield and the winner's circle." Sixty years after he had come home from the Buffalo County Fair with a mare to ride in relay races on the Nebraska plains, his son stood at the pinnacle of racing. There were no tears, no emotions run amuck. Just the quiet pride of the ultimate horseman.

"Ninety percent of what I learned I learned from my dad," his son told reporters in the winner's circle. "This is like he won, too."

AFTER meeting with reporters in the press box and accompanying Partee to the party in the Kentucky Derby Museum, Whiting finally made it back to barn eighteen around seven o'clock. The place was a rollicking sea of reporters, friends, and well-wishers. Outside, the light rain turned into a downpour. Water rolled off the roof and formed puddles in the grass. Inside, the phone rang constantly. E.T. stood in his stall, calm and relaxed.

At eight o'clock, Partee's son-in-law called from Hasenour's. "We've got a table here and we'd love you to join us," he told Whiting.

"I've got my whole family," Whiting said.

"That would be great."

When Whiting entered the front door of the restaurant twenty minutes later, the diners gave him a standing ovation. Ron McAnally came over and shook his hand. Whiting signed autographs before he ate his appetizer. He was a star.

"This is unbelievable," he thought. "Like a fairy land."

After dinner he drove home and crawled into bed at eleven o'clock. His alarm sounded at five the next morning. The trainer of the Derby winner got up and went to work before dawn.

The barn was still buzzing with activity the next morning. Trainers, exercise riders, jockeys' agents—all forms of backside creatures— came by to offer congratulations. Reporters circled, asking about E.T.'s health and Whiting's plans for going to Baltimore for the Preakness.

Whiting dedicated the victory to the people who work the backside. "This is really for them," he said. "This shows that with a little hard work and luck, anyone can get it done."

12

"He made history."

E.T. was shipped to Baltimore for the Preakness and installed in the traditional home of the new Derby winner, stall forty of the stakes barn at Pimlico. Christine Martin accompanied Whiting and E.T.

In the two weeks between the Derby and Preakness, turf writers around the country uncovered the text of E.T.'s improbable story. Larry Littman, Mary Deppa, Bill Solomon, Chuck Wieneke, Al Jevremovic, and the others experienced their Warholian fifteen minutes of fame.

"How could this big horse have been so awkward and weak as a yearling?" a reporter asked Whiting one morning.

As surprised as anyone about what the reporters had uncovered, Whiting just shook his head. "All I can say is that the horse must have taken a Charles Atlas course," he said.

THE night before the Preakness, Partee, Whiting, and the gang ate at a popular Baltimore crab house. Partee ordered mushrooms, now his good luck charm since he had eaten them before the Derby. The restaurant did not serve mushrooms.

E.T. was never the same.

The colt made only four more starts after the Derby, retiring in July of his four-year-old year after suffering the last in a series of physical setbacks that prevented him from having an opportunity to prove his mettle as a prominent Derby winner.

His problems began in the Preakness. Doubtful Pimlico bettors made him the 4-to-1 second choice behind Pine Bluff, his odds the highest for a Derby winner in the Preakness in thirty-nine years. But the bettors were prescient. E.T. was within striking distance at the head of the stretch, as he had been in the Derby, but he failed to fire and finished fifth—the first time in his career he had finished out of the money. Pine Bluff won.

"Coming out of the gate he got hit hard two times, and going under the wire the first time he dropped the bit," Day said. "That's never happened before. Then he got back into the bridle on his own up the backstretch and got to within three-quarters of Pine Bluff. He seemed to be in good position. I was going to ease him out and try to run them down in the stretch, but he never responded. He was tiring."

Dr. Harthill examined the colt after Whiting noticed him breathing harder than usual following the race. Hartill discovered that E.T. had bled internally. A more thorough exam three days later uncovered a lung infection.

Knocked out of the Belmont, sidelined for three weeks, and treated with antibiotics, E.T. resumed training in early June. Whiting considered running him in the Arlington Classic or Ohio Derby. But his left ankle was tender one day after a half-mile workout. X-rays revealed the presence of bone chips in both front ankles. Arthroscopic surgery to remove the chips ended E.T.'s year.

"It's a bummer, but this is the real world, not 'Black Stallion,'" Whiting said. "We were just lucky he got [to the Derby] and stayed in one piece. Thank God for the good things that happened. Fate didn't have to be this kind."

Healed by the fall, E.T. began jogging in mid-October and galloping in late November. He resumed training at the Fair Grounds during Whiting's annual winter trek to New Orleans. One hundred pounds heavier and more muscular, he was an imposing sight with his combination of size and speed. His legs were in superb condition. "He's as good as I could hope for," Whiting said.

His comeback was supposed to start at the Fair Grounds, but he came down with a cough and worked six furlongs slowly one morning, and Whiting decided to wait. The comeback began the next month in a six-furlong allowance race at Oaklawn on February 20, in which E.T. took on, among others, a six-year-old stakes-winning gelding named Darrell Darrell that had set a track record at Remington Park the previous year. The results were stunning. Trapped behind and between horses until mid-stretch, E.T. burst through a small hole on the inside and streaked past Darrell Darrell to win by a length. His time of 1:08$^{2/5}$ was just three-fifths of a second off the track record.

Impressive? "Lord, yes," Day said. "He's bigger and stronger now than he was as a three-year-old. He's filled out and all grown up."

As Partee said later, "They didn't think he could sprint, but he would have broken the track record that day if he hadn't gotten hung up."

E.T. was back. Whiting plotted a campaign of handicap races, mostly those on the American Championship of Racing Series, building to the Breeders' Cup Classic. The handicap field had been softened by A.P. Indy's retirement, so the opportunity for a successful, lucrative season loomed.

After winning the Razorback Handicap, E.T. trained up to the Oaklawn Handicap, a Grade I race worth $750,000. Despite having run only one race around two turns in eleven months, he was highweighted along with Best Pal at 123 pounds. Best Pal was a five-year-old gelding that had won the race the year before. "We got beat up in the weights," Whiting said later.

E.T. went off as the even-money favorite, tracked a speed horse named Conveyor into the second turn, and took a three-length lead heading for home. Best Pal was nowhere in sight; the race appeared over. But from far back, charging down the middle of the lane, came an English horse named Jovial, the third choice at 4-to-1. Carrying six fewer pounds, Jovial caught E.T. in the last furlong and won by two lengths.

"E.T. put away his horses and the race was over, for all intents and purposes," Whiting said. "I was already on my way to the bank. I had to bring the money back." It was the thirteenth race of E.T.'s career. And the last.

His training tailed off once Whiting moved back to Churchill. He worked seven furlongs in 1:28, the last quarter in a slow :27 and change. Something was wrong. After another slow workout, Harthill was called in for an exam. Sure enough, E.T. had a lung infection, again.

Whiting had to scotch his plans to run E.T. in the Pimlico Special against Strike the Gold, the 1991 Kentucky Derby winner. May, June, and July were washouts. E.T. resumed training in mid-July, now pointed toward the Breeders' Cup. Whiting was considering running him in the Sprint instead of the Classic, based on his winning performance in the six-furlong allowance race at Oaklawn in February. "He could have won the Sprint," Whiting said later. "To have a Kentucky Derby winner take the Sprint, that would have been historic."

Then one morning in late July, E.T. went out for a routine gallop at Churchill and ran headlong into the end of his career. He suffered a hairline fracture in his right front ankle, the crack extending a quarter-inch on the sesamoid bone. Harthill said the injury would heal in six months, but Whiting found it difficult to envision E.T. returning in top form. The next step, though difficult to accept, was easy to make.

"Retiring him just looked like the thing to do," Whiting said later. "Mr. Partee and I talked about it. I suggested it. We weren't going to find out if he could handle training and racing until the following May, which meant we would have been sacrificing a season of him in the breeding shed. And we didn't want to see him come back to the races as anything less than what he had been. People like us, we don't get hold of horses like this too often. He was just too good of a horse for us. If he wasn't going to be a horse of Grade I caliber, I didn't really want to race him."

Word leaked out to the press on July 28, 1993: the Derby winner from nowhere was being retired.

Maybe if that crab house had served mushrooms . . .

E.T. was an accomplished, consistent racehorse. He finished in the money in twelve of thirteen starts, with seven victories and earnings of $1,437,506. He won two Grade II races as well as the Kentucky Derby. "This is a horse that fired every time, always ran," Whiting said.

Yet unless he becomes a star at stud he will not be regarded as a classic or even a memorable Derby winner. The knocks against him:

• His winning time was slow. Recorded at 2:04 on race day, it was revised to 2:03 several weeks later after Churchill Downs determined that a timing mechanism had malfunctioned.

• He failed to win another Grade I race before retiring, becoming only the fourth Derby winner since Secretariat to fail to do so. Winning Colors, Gato Del Sol and Cannonade were the others.

• Although he beat six horses in the Derby that went on to win Grade I races (Strike the Gold also beat six in 1991, Unbridled just two in 1990), the two horses that proved to be the best of his class, A.P. Indy and Bertrando, did not run in the Derby.

Those factors and his commoner's pedigree will conspire to keep his victory as dim as a Kentucky Derby victory gets. "He's going to get buried in history," said Jeff Siegel. "He's going to be a Derby winner people forget about. He won't be remembered as a top-class winner."

But as much as E.T. failed to leave a classic champion's mark, he succeeded in leaving the alluring legacy of a longshot. One of the long-est to win the Derby.

The race's history is earmarked in many places with surprising win-ners, of course. There are many that lacked a classic pedigree, or over-came injury, illness, and other compromising circumstances. Literally the longest shot was Donerail, at 91-to-1 in 1911. But Spend a Buck and Carry Back were inexpensively bred, as was Dust Commander (1970), sired by a $1,500 stallion named Bold Commander out of a $900 mare. Proud Clarion (1967) was a 30-to-1 shot still running in condition races a month before the Derby. Count Turf (1951) was a mutuel field entry that ran so poorly during the prep season that his trainer refused to ac-company him to Louisville. Exterminator (1918) was bought before the Derby as a workout companion for a heralded stablemate that broke down. Bold Venture (1936) won at 20-to-1 with an apprentice rider. Gallahadion (1940) had won only one stakes race before the Derby, and never won another. The great Native Dancer suffered his only loss in twenty-two career starts in the 1953 Derby, finishing second to a 25-to-1 shot named Dark Star. Buchanan (1884), Sir Barton (1919), and Brokers Tip (1933) broke their maidens with Derby victories. Gato Del Sol (1982) won at 21-to-1 coming out of the nineteenth hole. Regret (1915), Genuine Risk (1980), and Winning Colors (1988) were fillies.

Determining E.T.'s merits as a surprise among those longshots is a subjective endeavor. How can one weigh the different factors? Is a filly or a maiden a less likely winner? Is a cheaply bred winner any less likely than a blueblood showing no brilliance before the race? Is an injury or a cheap pedigree more difficult to overcome? Who can say?

That E.T. was among the longest shots is undeniable, though. Con-sider this body of evidence:

• At 17.80-to-1, E.T. was the tenth-longest shot to win since Churchill began selling $2 Derby mutuels in 1911. Those ahead of him were (in order) Donerail, Gallahadion, Proud Clarion, Exterminator, Dark Star, Gato Del Sol, Bold Venture, Zev, and Ferdinand. (Canonero II, Count Turf, and Flying Ebony won from the mutuel field, so their odds probably would have been long enough to crack the top ten had they been separate betting entities.)

• Few Derby winners have had such an undistinguished pedigree. "E.T., Canonero, Gato Del Sol, Carry Back, Spend a Buck, and Dust Commander are the ones that would make the David Letterman Top Ten list of unlikely Derby winners according to pedigree," breeding analyst

Jack Werk said. "You can't really differentiate between them. But certainly, if you took Lil E. Tee as a newborn foal and looked at his pedigree, there's never been a longer shot that came in. He was an absolute miracle. A needle in a haystack. His pedigree is the epitome of nothing out of nothing."

• Only E.T., Gato Del Sol, and Canonero II are on Werk's Letterman Top Ten list as well as the list of high-odds winners. (Dust Commander, a winner at 15-1, belongs in their company.)

• There is no record of another winner overcoming colic surgery or any such major operation. "The type of colic that Lil E. Tee had and the surgery he needed were very, very serious," said Dr. Nat White, a colic expert at the Marion duPont Scott Equine Medical Center in Leesburg, Virginia. "We have a good success rate with it now, but it is not an easy thing to overcome. I can't think of another horse that has come back to win a major race."

LESSONS: E.T.'s "real-life fairy tale," as ABC's Jim McKay called it, offered many.

"Was he a bolt of lightning horse? In a way," D. Wayne Lukas said. "He wasn't exactly what I would call a roulette horse, where you spin the wheel and it stops on black and you win strictly by luck. He had good connections, a good rider, a good trainer; he was running on a track where he was comfortable. But there are thousands of horses like him. Every year there are hundreds of Lil E. Tees. On a given day, in the right spot, with a Pat Day and Lynn Whiting in their favor, and with the gods smiling on them, they can get there. That's what makes the stinking race so great."

You can get there. No matter how sickly a horse is, how average its pedigree, how lousy it looks in the field as a yearling, how many smart bloodstock agents and veterinarians turn up their noses—no matter what happens or what anyone says, the horse still can get there. The impossible is not impossible.

"The moral to the story, in my opinion," said Dr. Bill Solomon, owner of Pin Oak Lane Farm, "is that there are only two ways to win the Kentucky Derby. One is to buy in numbers as many of the best bred horses you can get your hands on. That takes money. The other way, and this isn't the first time it has happened, is to continue to participate at some level you can afford, hang in and keep playing the game, and if you do it long enough there is a chance that lightning will strike."

If it can strike with a Pennsylvania-bred sold for $3,000, a working-man's horse turned down as a two-year-old by the Ocala Breeders' Sales Company, it can strike with any horse from anywhere at any time.

"To me it reinforces the point that good horses come from everywhere," John Ed Anthony said, "which is an element of this game that particularly frustrates the people who try to figure it out, who try to win the Kentucky Derby or breed good horses. Because if breeding the best to the best doesn't get you the best, then how do you get the best? There are always horses raised in the backyard, in one-horse stables or whatever, that come along and win great races, including the Derby. When a Lil E. Tee wins, it frustrates and frightens the blueblood breeders and pedigree analysts because if good horses aren't where you get good horses, then what is the value of good horses? Of course, the ration of good horses leans heavily toward good families, but still..."

"To whom does he have to prove himself?" Joe Hirsch said. "He doesn't have to do anything. He won the Kentucky Derby. He doesn't have to do a thing. It's the greatest race in the country, and he won it. Sure, it's nice to do well in the Preakness and Belmont and later on, but it's not necessary. It's like being elected president and also the head of some big company. The other is nice, but you'll take the bigger one any day. He won the race to win. His name will last forever. He made history. Everything else is secondary."

History is written in indelible ink, not erasable pencil.

"When people who know what they're doing get their hands on a horse that can run, good things tend to happen," said Mark McDermott, executive secretary of the Pennsylvania Horse Breeders Association. "There are a lot of people who don't know what they're doing and a lot of horses that can't run, but there also are a lot of people at smaller tracks, without high-profile reputations, who are every bit as good at this game as the well-known people. Lil E. Tee benefited from that. From the very beginning, from Bill Solomon right through to Lynn Whiting, he was around smart people who knew what they were doing. There is no substitute for that."

At countless intersections in his life, E.T. could have swerved in the wrong direction and headed for the obscurity for which he was intended. One frown from the racing gods would have been enough. Remember racing's first commandment: thou shalt be lucky, or else.

"Lil E. Tee's success is the kind of thing that keeps the racing business going, really," said Steve Morguelan. "If everyone thought they had to be an Ogden Phipps or an Allen Paulson to be a success in this business, there wouldn't be many people in it. It's a tough game if you don't have a lot of money, but when things like this happen it gets people to thinking they have a chance. When those horses get into the gate, they don't know if they were $2,000 yearlings or $2 million yearlings. They're all equal. As trainers, we like to have well-bred horses, the best we possibly can. But I own horses myself and I can't afford hotshots. So, when you see something like this happen, you feel like you really do have a chance. That someday you might be the one getting lucky instead of someone else."

JIM Plemmons was looking for an anchor for Old Frankfort Stud, the new stud farm he was opening on Old Frankfort Pike in the bluegrass country west of Lexington. He needed a star, a stallion that not only would put the place on the map but also generate a steady stream of business.

Plemmons, a developer and horseman from Seattle, Washington, had bred, trained, and raced horses for two decades. He had owned several other farms along the way in Kentucky and Washington, built a training center in Kentucky and a sales pavilion in Seattle, and owned still another training center in Kentucky. But it had always been his dream to own a stud farm near Lexington, at the center of the breeding industry, and he had always promised himself he would do it with a Derby winner.

He bought a three-hundred-acre farm, sold 40 percent, and broke ground on an office/barn complex in the spring of 1993. His dream was becoming a reality. He just needed a stallion to give his venture a chance to succeed in a depressed racing economy.

He read about E.T. in the *Daily Racing Form*. The story said the colt was being retired and Cal Partee wanted to sell a majority interest. Plemmons figured the price would be reasonable for a Derby winner, considering E.T.'s lack of stature. He studied E.T.'s pedigree and found there was some depth to it. The colt's fifth dam, Native Gal, also was the fourth dam of Affirmed, and was descended from Correction, a full sister to Domino, the legendary speed sire. Despite E.T.'s reputation as a cheaply bred Derby winner, his tail-female line was of high quality.

Plemmons called Whiting and asked if he could come see the colt in the barn at Churchill Downs. The process moved forward rapidly from there. Partee set a non-negotiable price and Plemmons met it, buying a three-quarter interest for $600,000. Partee retained one quarter. Whiting received two breeding shares.

"I hated to sell him," Partee said, "but at my age I got no business with a stud. I kept an interest. That way I had a piece but didn't have to fool with him."

Whiting said later, "Mr. Partee wanted to take the money and use it toward [buying] other prospective [young] horses. At eighty-four years old, you don't want to plan too many moves down the road."

The deal was contingent on a semen evaluation, which came back positive. "He showed incredible life to his semen," Plemmons said later. The sale of E.T. was announced at a press conference at the Fasig-Tipton complex on Newtown Pike in Lexington on September 14. Whiting, Partee, Pat Day, and Plemmons spoke. E.T. posed for pictures. There was a champagne toast.

After E.T. was led away to be loaded into Plemmons's van, Partee abruptly turned and headed for the door. Plemmons' wife ran to her husband. "Mr. Partee is upset," she said. "He's leaving. He told me to come get you."

Plemmons walked Partee out to the car. The old man was hobbling along tearfully. "I'm sorry about this," Partee said. "I didn't realize how much it would upset me to see him sold."

Plemmons nodded sympathetically. "The horse is going to be treated right, Mr. Partee, you can be sure of that," Plemmons said. Partee looked away, then back at the younger man. Their eyes locked.

"Son," Partee said, "just get me another one."

Epilogue

Larry Littman cut all but a few strands of his connection to racing in 1994. He shut down his farm in New Jersey and pared his broodmare band to two. He retained ownership of Lil Fappi, his stallion.

"Some people would say that anyone who gets into the business and breeds a Kentucky Derby winner is a success, and it's certainly something they can never take away from me," he said. "I did it. I accomplished it. No matter how I accomplished it, I did it. Out of the millions of horses that have been foaled over the years, mine was one of the hundred or so to win the Derby. It's an unbelievable thing, unheard of, that a small breeder from New Jersey who breeds mostly Jersey-breds could breed a Derby winner. But success to me is measured financially, and therefore I consider myself the least successful breeder you know. I did some things right, bred some nice horses, enjoyed myself immensely, but I lost money. And judging my career as a failure has nothing to do with the fact that I sold a Derby winner for $2,000, because I would have done the same thing year after year given the same set of circumstances. Anyone who understands racing knows that."

Of the seventeen horses that composed Littman's foal crop of 1989, a crop produced by more than $350,000 in stud fees, fifteen made it to the races and eleven were winners. But aside from E.T., the others produced only a combined $406,959 in earnings through their four-year-old seasons. The only other stakes winner was Don't Touch Lil, a filly by Caveat that won the Tanaka Family Farm Handicap at Bay Meadows.

Lil Danzig, the Danzig Connection colt that had initially impressed bloodstock agents as the best of the crop, raced four times for Littman as a three-year-old at Santa Anita, earning $100. He was sold privately, raced once at Golden Gate, and sold again. After running seventh in a $10,000 claiming race at Longacres, he suffered an injury and was retired.

Topretariat, the Topsider colt bred for an $85,000 fee, out of a Secretariat mare, won five of thirty-five starts in claiming and allowance races and earned more than $60,000 through his four-year-old year. He was claimed off Littman for $15,000 at Philadelphia Park in July 1992.

Allemaz, the colt sired by Alleged for an $80,000 fee, was bought privately from Littman and renamed Deuces Are Wild. He finished out of the money in two claiming races at Del Mar as a three-year-old, then resurfaced as a four-year-old running in claiming races at Portland Meadows, in Portland, Oregon. As a four-year-old he won four of nineteen races and more than $15,000.

Camawaki, the filly sired by Miswaki for a $40,000 fee, was claimed off Littman for $5,000 at Philadelphia Park in July of 1992. He won five of twenty-five starts and $39,000 through his four-year-old year.

"If I made a mistake with that crop, it's that I overbred it," Littman said. "The stallions I used were too good for the mares I had." Only four of the seventeen horses were sold at public auctions, for a total of $35,000—ten percent of the amount Littman spent on stud fees.

A.P. Indy recovered from his injury, won the Belmont Stakes (in which he defeated Pine Bluff), and finished the year by winning the Breeders' Cup Classic. He was named Horse of the Year for 1992 and retired to stud at Lane's End Farm in Kentucky. His stud fee was $50,000.

The Belmont was Pine Bluff's final race. Six weeks later, he tore a distal sesamoidal ligament in his left foreleg during a gallop and was retired to stud.

Bertrando returned to the races and won the Pacific Classic, Woodward Stakes, and San Fernando Stakes. He had won more than $3 million by the end of his four-year-old year.

Six horses that E.T. defeated in the Derby later won Grade I races. Pine Bluff won the Preakness. Dr Devious returned to England and won the Epsom Derby. Technology won the Haskell Invitational. Devil His Due won three Grade I races—the Pimlico Special, Gulfstream Park Handicap, and Suburban Handicap—as a four-year-old. West by West won the Jockey Club Gold Cup as a four-year-old. Pistols and Roses won the Donn Handicap as a five-year-old.

MARY Deppa went to work at a farm in Middleburg, Virginia.

CHUCK Wieneke and Mike Paramore had a falling out over a bill. Paramore continued to pinhook horses in partnership, but with a different trainer. Wieneke kept on doing what he was doing.

"The only difference now," Wieneke said, "is that any time I get a horse looking good, the owner asks, 'You think he could be another Lil E. Tee?'"

ENCOURAGED by Wieneke's success, Al Jevremovic tried his hand at pinhooking, buying yearlings and selling them as two-year-olds. One day at a sale in Kentucky he ran into Lynn Whiting. "You should buy my horse," Jevremovic said. "Things worked out pretty well last time."

Whiting smiled. He did not buy the horse.

CHRISTINE Martin quit her job in Whiting's barn eight months after the Derby and returned to Nebraska. Bob Ray got married and quit as Whiting's assistant trainer. Craig Pearl continued to work for Whiting.

TWO months after the Derby, Gary Wilfert, the general manager of Turfway Park, made good on the promise he had made to Whiting on the morning of the Derby, when he said he would dance on the roof of Whiting's barn if E.T. won.

A stand was erected on the roof of barn eighteen. Wilfert, who weighs close to three hundred pounds, wore an extra-large version of Partee's silks. A stereo blared the Paula Abdul song "Videology." Wilfert boogied. The roof did not buckle.

BRENT Fernung and a partner, Ned Jelligan, bought Eileen's Moment privately from Littman early in 1992. The price was $25,000. When E.T. won the Derby four months later, the value of the mare and her progeny increased tenfold.

Littman sold E.T.'s half-sister, a filly sired by Great Impulse, for $95,000 at the Saratoga selected yearling sale in August 1992. Fernung and Jelligan sold Eileen's Moment for $280,000 at the Keeneland breeding stock sale in November of 1992.

At The Threshold moved from Sylvan Crest Stud in Ocala to Airdrie Stud in Kentucky for two years, then to Grayrock Farm in Hot Springs, Arkansas. Two years after E.T.'s Derby victory, his stud fee was $1,500.

PARTEE and Whiting set out to repeat their success. In the fall of 1992, they considered buying a gelding named Prairie Bayou, one of a strong crop of two-year-olds owned by the Loblolly Stable.

"We'll take $600,000 for him," John Ed Anthony told Whiting. "You do know he's a gelding, don't you?"

The sale was off. Partee preferred not to buy geldings. If he did, he might have bought Ima Big Leaguer instead of E.T. Prairie Bayou finished second in the Derby as the betting favorite, then won the Preakness. He shattered a leg in the Belmont and was destroyed.

"Amazing," Whiting said later. "We almost could have had the Derby favorite in the year after E.T."

In the fall of 1993, they spent $200,000 for a two-year-old colt named Trialist. But the colt stepped on a nail in New Orleans, missed training time, and was not ready for the 1994 Triple Crown season. Trialist's setbacks and problems only reaffirmed how difficult it was to get a horse to the Derby, much less win it.

"We're gonna keep looking for another one, I know that," Partee said.

Winning the Derby had little effect on Whiting's stable. He had an easier time attracting high-profile clients, most prominently country singer Reba McEntire, but he continued to limit the size of his stable, attack his job purposefully, and enjoy steady success. Fifty percent of his starters hit the board in 1993.

"The only thing winning the Derby did," he said, "was make us more conscious of the fact that you can get there. It reinforced to us that that type of horse is out there."

ARAZI returned to the races six weeks after the Derby, finishing fifth in the St. James Palace Stakes at Ascot, in England. After a third-place finish in the Prix du Prince d'Orange at Longchamp, he won the Prix du Rond Point in September against mediocre competition. In the fall he returned to the United States for the Breeders' Cup at Gulfstream. Bettors made him the 3-to-2 favorite in the Mile, but he finished eleventh. It was his last race. Paulson sold his half-interest to Sheikh Mohammed and Arazi was retired to stud in England. His stud fee was $30,000.

What happened to him in the Derby?

"He made his move after a half-mile," said Ron McAnally, Boutin's friend, "and had nothing left for the stretch. The horse had real greatness, but he had no chance racing that way. It was unfortunate."

European racing is based on covering up. Trainers teach their horses to race behind others, then move only when wheeled outside for racing room in the final furlongs, at which point they accelerate and pick up other horses. When Valenzuela moved Arazi outside on the backstretch, Arazi instinctively took off. He raced precisely as Boutin had trained him.

"If Steve Cauthen rode him, things might have turned out differently," Joe Hirsch said later. "Steve had ridden in Europe for years and understood how to ride a horse trained there. The horse would have had a hell of a shot, because he wouldn't have been ridden anywhere near the way he was ridden. He had a very curious ride. [Valenzuela] moved much too soon. He made a run up the backstretch the likes of which I haven't seen in thirty-eight years of covering the Derby. It was astonishing. Had that come at the end, the horse certainly would have been in it.

"As it turned out, the story is like a Greek tragedy and one of those operas all rolled into one. So many mistakes were made. God knows, there were plenty of them. Going back to the previous year, he should never have come back to the United States for the Breeders' Cup. He had a hell of a campaign in France, won the Grand Criterium, that was enough. But once he did come and run so brilliantly in the Juvenile, he should never have had the operation. Many top veterinary men who saw the [x-rays] told me [the bone chips] were only spurs. Nature takes care of that. There should not have been an operation, but (Paulson) was so intent on winning the Derby and doing everything that he thought would speed him toward his goal.

"Then they tried to come back and win the Derby off one prep race. He should have had two preps, one in the U.S. and one in Europe. That was a mistake in judgment, but of course time was against Boutin. The surgery and the Derby were too close together. So, a lot of mistakes were made, most of them the fault of the owner. He meant well, and God knows he's been wonderful for racing, spent hundreds of millions of dollars. I like him very much. But he made a lot of mistakes and put too much pressure on the trainer. Still, Boutin is a master horseman and he did a super job. After all that, the horse still was ready to run in the Derby and could well have won the race had he been ridden properly. It's one of the great tragedies in the history of the Kentucky Derby."

Francois Boutin died of cancer in 1995.

E.T. took up residence in a double stall in the bright, new barn at Old Frankfort Stud. His rise from an obscure birth at Pin Oak Lane Farm was complete. He was a star, living in what amounted to a plush penthouse suite. Once a sign announcing his presence went up along Old Frankfort Road, a steady stream of visitors dropped in for a look. Four hundred people signed up for a visit while attending a horse fair in Lexington.

"He's a hero," Jim Plemmons said, "On an average weekend we'll have ten to thirty visitors in to see him. People love to see the lowly commoner who became a king. They love to be part of the rags to riches story."

As he embarked on his stud career, E.T. again faced long odds. Surprisingly few Derby winners have become top sires. "It's astonishing when you look at it, but many have been busts at stud," Jack Werk said.

Still, Plemmons recruited seventy-five mares for E.T.'s first book in 1994. The interest was so high that Plemmons had to begin turning down applications. E.T.'s stud fee was $7,500. The first book included five mares owned by John Franks, one of the top owners in the country.

"We were hoping for fifty mares and got a whole lot more," Plemmons said. "But you just can't get to a Derby winner with that kind of speed for that kind of money. The outpouring of feeling from around the country was amazing. Not really people from Kentucky. People from Canada, California, Mississippi, Texas, and elsewhere, people who love the game and love the idea of breeding to a Kentucky Derby winner for $7,500."

Plemmons's pedigree analyst, Les Brinsfield, developed a software package measuring the compatibility of stallions and mares. Relying heavily on it, Plemmons sought to breed E.T. to mares with ancestry including female Buckpasser, Tom Fool, and Northern Dancer blood. The horse's fertility was exceptional. He needed an average of 1.1 covers, or breeding sessions, to impregnate a mare in his first year. A 1.5 or 1.6 average is considered superior, and 2.0 or higher is not unusual.

"It's a blessing, and a direct reflection on Lynn's ability as a caretaker," Plemmons said. "He didn't give the horse steroids or compromise his body in any way."

There was a scare in April when E.T. was kicked along the shaft of the penis while dismounting a mare named Bubuli, and he had to miss two months. But he recovered in time to impregnate fifty mares in his first year at stud.

His progeny began to "hit the ground" early in 1995. The first was a filly, out of a mare named Sound Alarm, foaled on January 31. Then came a colt, out of a multiple-stakes-producing mare named Flag De Lune, foaled on February 18. Bubuli delivered a filly on March 5. By April a consensus was forming. The majority of E.T.'s foals bore a striking resemblance to their father.

"He's throwing himself, basically," said Plemmons, who, to prove the point to the public, took out an ad in the *Blood-Horse* magazine showing pictures of four of the foals. "My stall manager said, 'Once you've seen one Lil E. Tee, you've seen them all.' They have short cannon bones, low hocks, very strong rear ends. They're very athletic looking. Of course, that doesn't mean they're going to run like their father did. But most good sires with the ability to dominate mares physically have a far higher percentage of success at the races. So we're hopeful."

If E.T. could succeed as a stallion, it would do much to answer the questions about his credibility as a Derby winner.

"Whether he'll be a great sire, only time will tell," Plemmons said. "But with his natural speed and conformation, we fully expect him to be a good sire. Maybe some people don't believe it. But then, people have underestimated this horse since the first day of his life."

INDEX